Moldovan Diary

Two years in the Peace Corps

SAMUEL J. SCHEURICH

ISBN-10:1497409365
ISBN-13:9781497409361

"We have to be continually jumping off cliffs and developing our wings on the way down"

Kurt Vonnegut

DIARY ENTRIES

ACKNOWLEDGMENTS

As Sam's mother, I would like to thank the public libraries for promoting literacy, furnishing my son with many choices to read over the years, thus helping his creativity in penning this journal while in Moldova. And author Barbara Hinske for suggesting Createspace as a self publishing tool and my daughter, Michelle, for helping with the finishing touches on publishing Sam's journal. Finally, I want to thank my husband for just being there.
Patricia Scheurich
Editor
2014

2008

San Francisco

2008-05-03 to 2008-06-03

Willie, Charlie and I visited Michelle and Nate in San Francisco to celebrate birthdays, and to see Michelle and her fiancé before my departure. We ate and drank our way through the city - Michelle would have it no other way - and took the ferry out to see Alcatraz, among other activities. It was a great time, thanks Michelle and Nate.

First day in Philly

2008-06-06 to 2008-06-08

Today is the first full day in Philadelphia and, after taking a run through Love park and city hall, I have decided that this is one of the best cities in the US - Michelle, San Fran is in close second. only complaint I have is that it is very hot and humid, like popsicles in the armpits, sweaty, sunglasses falling off the nose hot. Today is registration and check-in - I don`t know what this entails exactly. What I do know is that we will be taking a bus to JFK tomorrow for our 9 p.m. flight to Frankfurt, then onto Moldova. Some of the photos I added are from Philly - a solo walking tour - and some are from the night before I left for PA.

Chisinau

Wednesday and Thursday (11/12)   We arrived in Chisinau on an unmarked, all white plane I believe to be a Boeing 727. The flight was actually much more comfortable than the air travel the day before, from JFK in New York to Frankfurt. This was primarily – in my case specifically – due to two issues. First (most of us shared my ill will towards this problem) was that the plane didn't actually get off the ground until 12:30ish NY time which added up to three hours inside a large, flightless bird. We did eventually take off and got to Frankfurt in time to make our connector. My second issue was that I was in the middle, of the middle of the plane. From left to right, the seating arrangement is three (left), four (middle) and three (right). I was in the sixth seat, which was fantastic. One hang-up in the German airport was Moldova's EU status, which is non-existent. For this reason, we all had to go through security off the plane and then back through it again to get into the right terminal for Eastern European flights. The difference between the carriers was striking. The Air Moldova plane had obviously been repainted etc. and when compared to our Lufthansa 747, it looked very antiquated. There was no team of German flight attendants marching with purpose to prepare our plane before the flight, but, considering the latter flight was on time and our Lufthansa was very untimely….

So as I began, arriving in Chisinau was exciting. From the aero plane all one sees are stepped fields (you know, like flat then little plateaus), rivers and small towns. It is very green. The weather outside was more humid than I am used to – Phoenix doesn't give the rest of the world a chance in that category – but on the warm side of pleasant (85 F?). We got off of the plane on a stairway deal and onto a bus, which promptly drove us about 100 meters to the terminal. (By the way, for you face bookers, you might want to check out a group called either 'Peace Corps Moldova' or 'Peace Corps Moldova M23'. The M23 stands for Moldova's 23rd group of volunteers – I am one of them – and there should be some photos from different people on there, along with the ones I add on this website.) At the terminal we were greeted by the country director and some other admin., along with a group of our mentors, all of whom are in the group of volunteers before us.

We basically grouped up at this point and boarded a sweet bus – it had curtains - to the capital. Our mentors gave us tough plastic-weave type bags as of us had seen online, but now we were there. So, next was a school house where we went through some logistics (money and a general run through of schedules and safety) and ate pizza – provided by the Peace Corps staff via ?Eddie's? Pizza, which was interesting, but good. When all was said and done, I was 800 lei the richer (80 Bones) and we all boarded two Mercedes Eurovans and left for the hotel Zaria. The rooms here (where I am now sitting typing at 6:00 a.m. on Thursday the 12th) are hilariously different, but fortunately bearable. Mike is the volunteer I've been hoteling with the past few days, and we were both relieved, as we both wrote stories in our heads as to how bad they could have been. After unpacking what little we had (we were only allowed a bag with three days worth of clothing), some of us met current volunteers downstairs and walked to a bar where there were many more volunteers who are in country drinking

and talking. The PC's that had been in country for the past year came off as a raucous group of battle-hardened, Romanian slinging, beer/vodka drinking pros. (I'm exaggerating a tiny bit, but really I'm telling the truth. It was funny to feel like a green-horn type around a bunch of seasoned volunteers.) The PC person's were helpful and Zio, Leni, Jon and I sat with a girl who has been in country and grilled her for information, which was very helpful. After three very Budweiser-ish beers, poured from a three liter decanter filled at the bar, – which costs about 100 lei – we walked back to the hotel, where I slept. Or tried to sleep; you see, dogs bark back and forth in some sort of painfully loud doggie language that I cannot understand. Oh, and at 5:00 a.m. the roosters start making whatever noise roosters make. I guess I don't have to say Chisinau is a three rooster town? Cock-a-doodle-doo!   After another day of gifts which are commonly used here. Driving into Chisinau was crazy, mostly because the view of the city is one that most talks, medical interviews, seminars and language lessons, a group of us, including some past volunteers ate dinner at a Syrian restaurant. It was amazing time. We found a Russian beer that was ranked on a numbering scale from 0 to 9, zero being the least alcoholic. Because of the slow service – a trait that I am told is common in Moldova – we enjoyed a couple of these beers, which were a whopping 20 lei each or, two US dollars. When the food did arrive it was a mixture of beef and chicken kabobs, salads, hummus, rice, tabouleh, pita bread and what I believe to be a beef dish made with a thick tomato sauce. Dinner was awesome. On the walk home, I attempted my new phone, but after sending a couple texts and talking to the twins, it had used up the entire credit (45 lei) that my phone came with. I am assuming international calls are very steep? On a side note, it turns out that one of the two PC's picked to speak Russian does not want to learn the language as their primary, so there is a chance that I may be able to make it my primary language. I would love the opportunity but the only downfall is that because there are only two speakers of the language, they are somewhat separated from the rest of the group (They live in the main hub village, but see the rest of the group on Tuesday and Thursday's. The alternative is my current situation, where all of the English teachers (TEFL's) live in Costati (ko-shtats), split into groups of two on opposite ends of the town.). On the whole, Russian would be my pick I think, as it actually has a practical application after the Peace Corps and the Cyrillic alphabet is terrifyingly cool.

Ilovani

2008-06-13 to 2008-06-15

The last day in Chisinau was similar to the day prior. We went through more language lessons – this time Russian – and seminars. We were even given a speech on how to listen to speeches, we were rapt with attention as you can imagine. At the end of the day, I headed to the Peace Corps office to go online and post some photos – the first time I used my thumb drive. I met with some fellow PC's afterwards at a patio-type restaurant named after Renoir (it was called 'Renoir'). Judy, Leni and I got a Carlsberg beer and some pistachios and headed back to the hotel Zarea. When we arrived, a group was already forming up to go to dinner, so we ran up stairs to change and joined them. On a side note, I have to add how terrifying the elevators are in the hotel. We were all on floor eleven, so the ride wasn't short. Add to that the size, which was barely large enough to hold three people, and you were faced with a claustrophobic's nightmare.

So, back to dinner. A few decided to split off from the bulk of the dinner group and went to a nearby Moldovan restaurant and bar whose name I can't recall. Dinner was fun and we split a couple Bazooka's between us.

On the following day, my Russian teacher took Emily – the other Russian trainee – and myself shopping in town. I was going to buy a guitar, but it was cheaply made and overpriced. Michael Scheurich is going to take care of shipping that little baby, along with starburst, skittles, and the big postcards Charlie and I bought in San Francisco, Da? We also purchased gifts of flowers and chocolates for our families before heading back to the hotel, where we waited for Eurovans to pick us up. After boarding, we headed to the high school and me our host families.

My family consists of Luba (mama), Visili (dada), Veektor (brot), and a sister who is studying in Detroit, Michigan. The family has a cat and dog as well named Visili and Donna – and yes dad and cat share a name but, I have no sympathy as I too shared a name with a certain canine. On the 14th Veektor and I walked around the area and spoke broken English. I ventured out by myself later and took photos of the area, which should be posted. I should mention that lunch was potatoes and fish, boiled in some sort of broth. The potato's were great and made with dill. Dinner was much different; I get the idea that this culture treats the last meal of the day as a lighter snack than a big American feast. It basically consisted of a plate of Ricotta type farmers cheese, bread, sliced tomatoes and cucumbers and tea. It was good but there was lots of cheese on the plate. I am told almost hourly that Luba is worried about me because I don't eat enough. There is however, only so much cheese I can eat in one sitting.

After dinner Veektor and I walked to the internet café, but had to wait to use computers, so we bought beers at a market and drank them on the bench of a bus stop. We then went back to the café and used the Internet to Email all the peeps. It is very cheap, about 1 lei per 10 minutes of 6 or so lei for an hour's use. That's like 60 cents. On the way home we stopped off at a bar type establishment and had a beer with peanuts on a patio. After our delicious Chisinau beer, we headed back to the house, where I read and fell asleep.

I woke up late and ate a breakfast of tea and cheese blintz's (last night's cheese) and cookies. Today we went to the 'classroom' – a woman's house – where the other Russian and I will start our classes on Monday. At the house we had a long and fun lunch of tea, rose pastries, pyroogy (spelling? They were fried and filled with cheese dill and green onion. I think there are lots of fried cheese filled foods in this country.), fresh cherries and chocolate hazelnut candies. Meals have been treated much differently than I'm used to. You don't really load up a plate with food, it is just set out and you eat everything one at a time. It is probably because they save everything, and what is left on the plate is fed to the cat or dog. The food that is untouched is saved for breakfast leaving almost no waste. The meal was fun and now I'm back at the house waiting for the food to settle before I go out on a run. By the way, if a Moldovan mom ever asks you to eat and eat and eat, just say ya suit, which means I'm full. Even if you do though, she'll just laugh and ask if you're hungry…

Half of Week One (June 16 - 18)

It's been a couple days. Let me attempt to recapture and explain Monday, Tuesday and Wednesday.

Monday was the first day of class. Russian has proven to be just as overwhelming as expected – when asked which of the six languages we spoke was the most difficult, our teacher said Russian was the hardest; English the easiest (go figure). I was a day late as you know coming into Russian lessons, so I had a flimsy yet optimistic grasp on the alphabet – a grasp that was pulled apart quickly. Never-the-less, it was a fun day and I was promised that in two years I will be an advanced Russian speaker. By the way Russian language spelled phonetically is pronounced "Roosky Yazika."

After class, I went home for lunch (leftover pasta with a butter/cream/cheese chicken sauce, topped with a piece of braised chicken thigh – bone-in – with shredded carrots and tomatoes and cucumbers). After lunch I ended up going back to the Internet cafe to write Emails, forgetting my thumb drive, making blog posts impossible. I ended up getting home around eight or so and getting in bed to read. I was asleep by ten, with the sun still glowing in the lower reaches of the sky. Sunrise here is at five and sunset is past ten. I woke up on Tuesday at 5:30 and lay around until 6, when I made myself go run. I took a similar route (I'll try to include a picture of the road I ran down, although it is taken in the wrong direction; use your imagination.) and ran about four miles. It was early enough that I dodged many of the looks of concern – "What is that boy doing? Is he drunk? Why is he running in those little shorts?" – because it was so early in the day. It is beautiful out here in the early hours as the sun comes up over the endless fields, and an ideal temperature for running.

Breakfast of breakfast roll, coffee and hard cheese (ciur) was eaten after a shower (I shower: ya douche). I walked to class after breakfast, where we studied for an hour and a half. My host mom packed me a lunch for the day, because three or four days a week we meet with the other English teachers for technical training. Michelle may love the lunch she packed: two boiled eggs, a sandwich consisting of butter and cheese, a cucumber, a whole tomato. It was actually good, and I ended up coming home to eat, where I mixed the egg with shredded carrot salad, a great combination. A peace corps Euro van picked us up and we drove to Costeti, where the technical session was held. It was fun seeing everyone else and talking about our respective host families, outhouses, bowel issues, etc.

I came home and was asked to go drink a beer (piva) with Victor. We went to a local outdoor bar and had a starri melnuk, which translates in to old lighthouse operator. I thought that was hilarious, maybe the piva laughing? Night time held the usual reading followed by sleep.

I managed to wake again to a breakfast of roll and coffee and cheese. Class was stressful, mind boggling and exhausting. We learned words to describe the family, which was made difficult as words change depending on whether you are male or female and if the family member in question is a blood relation or in-law. Woof. After class (we are just about up to present) I came home to find Visilli in the kitchen. He made us a huge lunch of fried potatoes (kartoshka), beef stew from the night before, bread, cucumber tomato mayonnaise salad, mortadella, cheese, carrot salad and compote (fresh and homemade cherry drink). I also had my first taste of house wine, which is supposed to be downed in one gulp. It tastes like no other wine. House wine is not sweet at all; try to imagine two-buck-chuck with absolutely no flavor. I was excited anyway, as I had heard a lot about this popular drink which, in my case, turned out to be rather elusive.

Oh, on a side note, every Russian word I write out is phonetic, because I don't have Cyrillic on my key board. Secondly, today is Mama Luba's 50th birthday, so I will write later on what the night holds.

до встречи!

End of First Week in Iolveni

June 19

Luba's birthday dinner, which took place today, was the
first big Moldovan dinner I have been to. I had heard about
tables groaning under the weight of food, but had yet to see
this spectacle. From where I left off last will be the
beginning. After my interview with the program directors,
which went well, I walked to the market to buy a bottle of
wine – La Vincha Cabernet – for Luba; the bottle was a
whopping 25 lei. From there I made my way to the Internet
café to check up on Email. It was a humorous experience
because the owner's daughter and her three friends (I
assume they were friends) took an interest in the pictures
on my face book profile - at one point taking the mouse
from me, much to my dismay. After posting one of many
blogs which I'm sure will come back to embarrass and
haunt me, I made my way home where Visilli, Luba and
two in-laws were waiting. Eventually dinner rolled around
and the food was set out on a collapsible table in the living
room. Here we go: egg batter dumplings stuffed with an
eggy ground meat mixture, shredded carrots, cheese and
herbs wrapped in puff pastry, potatoes in stock and butter
and dill, tomatoes and cucumber, bread, smoked fish in oil,
compote and fruit nectar, cognac, my bottle of wine, cheese
and of course, Cholula (I guess they're into Mexican food?)
Dinner was like no other in the way it was consumed. Once
again we all had small, bare plates and took what we
wanted to eat *and* finish. The dumplings were amazing and

I will learn how to cook them. We will be eating them at Michelle's wedding. The oddest part though, was besides the cognac and wine there was really nothing to drink until Luba brought the juices into the room. Instead, small glasses were filled with cognac and every ten minutes or so, a toast was made and the glasses were drained. There was no beverage to sip on in between toasts. After the (small) cognac bottle was finished between the six of us, the wine was opened and it was consumed in the same aggressive manner. The wine itself was vastly different from American/Californian/French/Italian wine. It was much like the house wine I described in the last entry, dry and...odd. A rule of thumb seems to be that at dinner, alcohol consumption would seem to be high, but it is not. No one goes through glass after glass. The method is: drain glass, eat, drain glass, eat and so forth. After trying to decipher the family's conversational Russian and giving up, I thought about how odd it came off to me to drain your glass at every pour, but it is done in moderation, like at family dinner in the states. I think we all relate a "shot" with getting drunk and it is not the case here. Regardless, dinner was fun even though I didn't really understand anything. I will be sending some wine home soon, but I'd like to try to find some that would be more palatable to everyone, I don't think you guys would like the wine I've had so far, but who knows.

June 20

Okay, it has been a few days since the last time I wrote anything, so if things are out of order it is because I am disoriented. Ahh. Yes, so on Friday, we had language class and then a team building activity at a summer camp-type spot in the woods. I was told it was for Peace Corps to go out and relax, etc. I jokingly referred to it as "Camp David." It was fun, even though my official position on team building is not positive. I won't go into what we did, I think you can imagine what 40 people do in the woods with bricks, 2 by 4's, blindfold and ropes. After we were done boosting our moral and bolstering our cohesion we were allowed to eat barbecued chicken and pork. It was actually very good but I've noticed that no matter where I am, if food is being made from scratch, it will always include bread, cheese, cucumbers, and tomatoes. I can only assume it is seasonal and right now these two veggies are in season. Among other plants in season are those that produce raspberries, strawberries, cherries and red currants and they are fantastic. Tomorrow, I was – see how I'm jumping ahead here – picking cherries for a compote with Victor and Luba and she was feeding me raspberries, amazing.

So after the team build, I went home and walked to get a beer with Emily, the other Russian speaker. I went home and ran into Victor, who was on his way to the Internet café, so I followed him and after responding to Dad's Emails, we went to go drink another beer and discuss our respective lack of knowledge in English and Russian. Slight mental lubrication makes linguistics discussions run more smoothly, in my opinion.

June 21

I set my alarm on Saturday morning in the hopes that I would be going for a monster/epic run, but the moderate amount of beer I had consumed the night before made staying in bed a much more appealing option (I had class at nine, give me a break). After my short hour and a half language class, my counterpart and I were taken to Costeti for a cross cultural session; which was a woman reciting the history of the region to the English teachers. She only spoke Romanian though, so the language teachers took turns translating for us — who knows what got lost in, well, translation.

I was home by one thirty to eat lunch. After lunch, I played a video game on the computer for a while and went with Victor to a friend's house near Chisinau. We barbequed sausages in his "back-yard." Apparently his family owns a country house. After we were done drinking wine and eating, we walked to his personal apartment and sat around until nine or so. On this occasion I, naturally, forgot my camera — we just so happened to walk through an abandoned Soviet factory. Victor said that it was the furniture factory which supplied chairs, tables and beds, etc. to the entire Soviet Union. Apparently it was the 2nd largest factory in all of the Union. It was impressive and sinister in its Sovietness (if you know what I mean). There were train tracks running through everything, loading docks, gigantic rusty power poles and transformers, fenced off warehouses and tall unkempt grass everywhere. I felt like I was a character in one of Willie's video games. Again, I forgot the camera, but when and if I go back there was an amazing view of rusty power line towers running down in a line as far as the eye could see. On the walk we also crossed a small river on an old rusty bridge. According to Victor the river at one time, around 200 years ago, was miles wide and accommodated large steam ships.

I was in bed reading "Fierce Invalids Home from Hot Climates" by 10:30 (mom I "borrowed" this book from the

Phoenix Public Library system, sorry) and asleep soon after.

June 22

I woke up this morning and went for a run. On the way to the team building activity the other day, I notice a large lake or wide river section, I'm not sure which, and I made a mental note to run to it. It took about 30 minutes round-trip, and while this isn't terribly long for me, the hills here are killer. The last quarter mile up to my house is horribly pockmarked and relatively steep. For breakfast, I realized why peanut butter is amazing and, while I though beer was proof that there is a God and he loves us, it turns out that peanut butter is proof of this (I may have mentioned this earlier). After a week and a half of delicious, but different food, it is great to have a cup of coffee, bread and peanut butter. We are now up to the present! I may have a skipped a day in there, I'm not sure....

Anyway, sorry for the lack of photos, they are difficult to upload and I don't really carry the camera around all the time. I'll try to do so. In response to Dad's third world question, I can only say I don't know. When I get to my post, maybe quality will drop down to his standards? I do regret not being able to show you the Soviet factory, I am sorry, use your imagination. Nate, try to hold off on the Russian comments until I know what they mean, you show-boater.

Mom, on the dumplings I wrote about earlier. I saw my house Mom make them and here is how I **think** they are made – you should try even if they come out badly (they involve lots of oil...).

Take ground pork and make small patties with them

Make a wash with egg, flour, butter (it's called masla in Russian, it might be lard…ha-ha), salt and pepper

In a cast iron skillet or deep sauce pan, heat about a half cup of olive oil

Wash the patties and fry them on a medium heat

I'm pretty sure this is it, they are really good and don't require too many spices. Just kinda salt and pepper them to taste. After Luba makes them, she puts them in a pot. They are never too greasy either; I think that the egg acts like a little biological oil barrier.

Another good food was a lot like dolmades, and wasn't greasy at all, which was nice. They were steamed or boiled grape leaves stuffed with rice and ground meat. Seven of those babies were lunch yesterday. Ciao.

Start of Week 2

June 22

On Sunday the family had a BBQ in celebration of what I believe to be the anniversary of Russia's entrance into the Second World War – if it isn't reason enough to celebrate wine and meat, war seems good enough. We started cooking the meat at noon, and were eating by about one p.m. The faire (did I spell that right?) was pork Kabob with onion; I think the marinade was white wine, bay leaf, garlic and onion. The meat was really good, and it was set out with all the usual: cheeses, cabbage salad, placenta (probably misspelled, puff pastry filled with potato/cheese or cabbage/cheese), dumpling, bread, wine. So, this was the first time we ate. When Victor came to me and asked if I was ready for the second round of grilling, I was amazed, I had assumed the first go was it for the day. I took a homework break while all the men were in the backyard grilling and drinking wine again (I think they bought 9 or 10 liters from the factory for the day. It is low in alcohol though I think, 8 or 9%.). The second setting was eaten outdoors, definitely not as formal. The focus seemed to be on the wine at this point, with food brought out everyone once and a while.

After dinner I went out for a bit with Victor, to a friend's apartment. Why he chose a Sunday to show me the sights I don't know, but we stayed out too late and class was a rough 5 hour slog the next day.

June 23

As I said, class wasn't fun today. After class, I ate some lunch and played computer in bed. I managed to make it out for a run right as the heat peaked. I think it got up to 28 C, which is like 90ish F, I believe. After the run, I went to the internet café and chatted with Ness. I noticed that all the kids here play video games at the café constantly, and they all seem to be playing some bootlegged World of Warcraft. Not to come off as rude, but I doubt the children can afford to play a game that runs them $15 an hour. I wrote up some note cards after the surfing session and drank a beer at the little joint next door. I have so many note cards, now I just need to start studying them....

Monday was boring, sorry – although I did make my first sandwich, out of salami, tomato and cheese for dinner.

June 24

Class was ok today, we had a review by the teacher and I seem to be doing alright. We have just started verbs and they are as confusing as verbs in any foreign language, only in Cyrillic – which is just fantastic. I ate my second Moldovan sandwich for lunch today, which was good, because I love sandwiches.

We had hub site today in Costeti, where we had technical training. Today was basically an intro to lesson plans and long-term lesson plans. We split off into groups and on July 1, we will 'teach' everyone in the group in a mock class room setting, putting into practice the plans we write. This is going to be good for a lot of us, because we don't have teaching experience. I didn't get back to Ialoveni until around 5:30 or 6, at which time I ate Salami and Cheese (Surprise!) and some yellow beans (Fasol). I tried to go do some callisthenic workout stuff on a dip/pull-up bar deal near my house, but it was kind of embarrassing because as soon as I arrived, four kids decided to sit right next to me, and alternate doing pull ups. I should probably also mention the old women herding goats around me. Anyway,

I came home and did some push-ups. I think I may just stick to running.

Let's see:

Ted, I don't really know how to download photos at a lower size, but my camera does take photos at 12.1 mega pixels, so the files are pretty big.

I was hoping a Scheurich could call Ness and explain how you are calling me; she has tried a few times and can't figure it out.

Tell Willie to get a job, but tell Charlie to quit his, it sounds horrible. I think he is making less than me. (HAHA)

26th – 30th

I've been slacking off on the blog, sorry to all of my loyal readers; I hope you stay loyal (I assume you were loyal to begin with?). I'll try to piece the week together, but as my brothers have pointed out, I have a memory like a spaghetti strainer – or maybe a hard drive with no interface (there is no way to retrieve and organize the information…).

26

This was a Thursday. I skipped Wednesday on purpose, because nothing interesting happened. On Thursday though, woof, what a day. We had a technical/cross-cultural/alcohol and substance abuse/tetanus shot in the arm day. The marathon took place at the school in my town and began with me showing up late, as God intended. A needle was promptly plunged into my shoulder and the 2nd shot in a series of 3 was given for that rusty, lock-jaw inducing disorder no-one I know has ever actually gotten.

After the medical staff was through with us, we had an hour or so of Tech. session, where we learned about online Peace Corps stuff and other Wiki-type sites for volunteers. The upper echelon of Peace Corps put on an hour and a half about the downfalls of alcohol, with an informative skit about confrontation and abuse of drink. A cultural session about certain language and cultural issues was next, which I can't really talk about (don't ask don't tell; wait, that might be a different branch of the government).

Everyone broke for lunch and I ate my SALAMI, CHEESE AND CUCUMBER sandwich, with a bag of pizza flavored (flavor*less*) puffed-rice-rings and a coke.

We had TEFL stuff for the rest of the day, and were split off into groups, where we will begin to teach abridged lesson plans to each other, for practice's sake.

27

Friday was a language day and unless I am forgetting something, our five hour class was the only thing we did. I'm lying. We had a panel of volunteers that have been in country for a year or more answer our questions about life in PC etc. It was a fun time and either startled or put us at ease. There was a Russian speaker in the group and he had a very firm grasp on the language, which is something I too hope to have after two years.

After everything during the day, I came home and ate Borsht. Victor and I went out later for a beer.

28

Today was the trip down south, where we visited a couple cities in the autonomous region of Gagauza, which is where I will be living during my time as a teacher. The capitol of this Russian speaking area is Comrat, which was our first stop (I will add a history of the region at the end of the blog). In Comrat, we sat in a conference room at city hall and heard a brief about the people and problems from a higher-up in the government and then went to a museum.

We then went on to two other towns whose names I cannot remember or, cannot spell (one was dearalunga, I believe and it will be a site location for either myself of Emily). In these two towns, we first stopped at a water factor – I think it was a factory or store – and ate lunch. The town put on a small performance for us, with traditional song and dance by Moldovan children. The food was plentiful and good, although I miscalculated and filled up on chicken noodle soup, Platcenta (Плацинды) (this is how it is spelled I think okay. I understand what Placenta is, but remember, in Romanian, a 'C' has a ch sound. Its plachenta, but in Russian I think it is pronounced plah ts een dui, so stop telling me that I'm eating embryo food.), bread and cucumber and tomato salad. After this course came a plate full of potatoes and Schnitzel; there was dill on the potato of course. After the lunch and dancing, we went to the horse farm which was really cool. At the end of the tour, 30 or so horses ranging from very young to old, big to small, came running up to the well, where they sated their equine thirst. The trough was fed by a well nearby, which was really unreal to see, coming from the land of hoses and running water. As my luck would have it though, the trusty Canon crapped out on me right as the picture taking was getting good. I added what I could from the farm. Sorry!

29

Today was the trip into Chisinau, which was fun, but pointless. All of the volunteers split off into groups and went on scavenger hunts around the city. Luckily, the scavengerial agenda wasn't adhered to – by my group at least – and within fifteen minutes we were drinking Chisinau brand beer at a McDonalds. After the libation, we spent the rest of the day wandering around an art piazza, some girls went to a Mango store (clothes), we headed to the Peace Corps office (where I picked up 'The Crack in Space' by Phillip K. Dick) and ate lunch at the "Rock hard café." Pizza wasn't bad nor was the Budvar I had – apparently it is the original Czechoslovakian Budweiser, which was stolen by the similarly named American beer manufacturer.

We also walked through the central market area which was as just as bustling and crowded as I had hoped. To get home, we took a bus, which was also crowed, filled with stagnate air and people; I think I had a little heat stroke….No, just joking. I got home though and ate and slept and woke to…

30

...the alarm clock. After waking I ate, sat through a frustrating Russian class and then went to Chisinau again to get my debit card, which will hold the income Peace Corps gives me for the remainder of service. I ran into a hitch though, because in attempting to check my account balance, I entered the wrong pin number one too many times, making a call to the main office necessary – luckily English was a requirement for phone answerers. The worst part of the ordeal was that about ten minutes into my first call to the bank, the minutes on my phone ran out and I had to go spend another 100 lei on a new card.

The English teachers are presenting their lesson plans to each other's small groups tomorrow, so I'd best be getting back to work.

FYI, Russian for Peace Corps is Корос Мира – Corpus Meera

Here is the alphabet:

A – a in car

Б – b in boy

В – v in very

Г – g in go

Д – d in do

Е – ye in yes

Ё – yo in York

Ж – s in measure

З – z in zero

И – I in machine

Й – I in voice

К – c in clean

Л – l in lift

М – m in make

Н – n in no

О – o in nor

П – p in please

Р – r in rich

С – s in say

Т – t in to

У -- oo in booty

Ф – f in fat

Х – h in house (but strongly aspirated)

Ц – ts in cats

Ч – ch in check

Ш – sh in shoe

Щ – shch in fresh

Э – a in ate

Ю – u in use

Я -- ya in yard (but shorter)

Blah!

Oh, please let me know if there is anything you would like me to hunt down and send to you packaged and pixilated in my blog. I take random photos, but I'm sure there are things you would rather see. Let me know! Пока!

First three days of July

July 1

We had Russian class today from 8 to 10 today and then hopped onto a bus to Costeti, where we met with the TEFL's and Health teachers. For the first hour – 11 to 12 – we were given talk about Moldavian history, focusing on politics. It was very interesting and the speaker (state department? I don't remember) was great. After the talk, we had lunch for an hour (two boiled eggs, a piece of bread, small piece of cheese and a coke) and split into our small groups for practice teaching. Everyone did well with their lessons; I did the best, of course. The lesson I chose was on food – surprise – and I brought in the lap top to help out. For the lesson, I made a slide show on different foods by taking photos of everything in our fridge and labeling them. This was my vocabulary introduction. Other than that, I basically used activities in the book.

After practice class we grouped back together for grammar and vocabulary teaching sessions (how-to's) and were done at around five. On my walk home I grabbed a beer – an Effes today, which is a Belgium style, or recipe brewed and bottled in Moldova; it's pretty good – and did my homework. The rest of the night was boring. I ate dinner, soup and rice, and read some Tom Robbins. I was pretty pumped for rice, but I think she boiled it in oil. I think I'll try washing it in a bowl to get the grease out.

Despite all the grease though I think I've lost a little weight. I found an old scale in the kitchen and it says I way 67 kg, and if a kilo is 2.2 lbs, I weigh 147 lbs. I can't really see how this is possible but, who knows; I guess the масла is lubricating my digestive tract.

July 2

Another whopping 5 hour Russian class today; this language is difficult and I half wish I had stuck with Romanian – if I'm not going to learn the language, I might as well be with friends during pre-service training. I am, of course, being overly dramatic, but I do wish I had a crew with me in my town.

After class today I ate rice (I tried to wash the oil out) and some soup and cheese and Fruitella, the equivalent of American Starburst — which were different but good; very European-ish. We had to go to Costeti today for "handicraft" exposure (I think 'exposure' is the right term). For the other Russian speaker and I, the activity turned out to be an ordeal, as we boarded a bus, went to the village looked at needle point hangings in a woman's house for twenty minutes and went home. The trip took one and a half hours though; do the math. The trip also reminded me that the other teachers, whom I'm friends with, live in their own village and can complain and drink beer together after school every day. I just get the beer part. Another aspect of the town I noticed (We had been dropped off at their school previously and picked back up after. I had the chance to walk around today) is that it is *much* smaller and, as Dad would put it, more "Peace Corps." My village is like Vegas, Paris, London compared to Costeti; an observation leaving me wishing I lived in such a community (I'd like to follow that statement with another, admitting that I will probably regret ever wishing I lived where there is no toilet inside and no washing machine). But yes, I didn't realize how good I had it until today. My town is a Raion center, as I said, and it is fairly bustling and noisy, what with the road and cars — let's give the friendly and prolific dog (собака) population some credit as well. We have more than one bar — any place that sells beer is a bar in my book — and even a few restaurants (almost on par with Monaco, I believe they are building a track so dad, we can forget about the Gran Prix and watch it here).

Okay, I think I've digitized/pixilated most of my complaints (I really am having a fun and amazing time and I see my friends, don't worry (oh and my iPod and sunglasses have yet to be stolen.) The biggest news yet is that after the handi-craft session, I got to eat my first homemade mamaliga, which has been a goal of mine since the dawn of Sam (Сэм) + Moldova (Молдавия, I assume you are reading up on your Russian alphabet...) When I got home I asked Luba: "Luba, we cook mamaliga?" Mamaliga is actually cornmeal mush, cooked in different ways by different people; just as grits is cooked differently in different parts of our country – for example, I heard from Ness that those hillbillies in Florida cook it in cream! My house mom cooked it in water (no oil thank F%@#ing God) and served it with grated Brinza (soft, salty sheep cheese) and Smetana (sour cream). It was delicious and would be good for breakfast. The compote (fruit juice made from the garden) was changed up and contained our apricots and some apples from the store.

Speaking of meals, breakfast has been my favorite because I brought peanut butter. I'm telling you, bread and peanut butter and coffee is the best combination in Moldova. I've also been feeling a little plugged, so I bought some Danon yogurt with fiber and muesli. Good stuff. I recommend the yogurt Willie (you know it buddy). I'm running really low on good old Starbucks though, because the only machine my family has is a percolator – which takes five scoops for a couple cups of coffee (sorry mom and dad for wasting so much coffee, it is like gold to me now). I've used some local stuff, but it isn't good. The corporation that Michelle dreads so much makes a mean cup of coffee and Michelle,

I don't know what I would do without them, sorry. I need to get my hands on a French press or something similar.

I think that's all I've got for this round-of-rant. If you have questions, post them, I try to answer *and* again, if you want me to take pictures of certain things (foods, stores, people are some objects that come to mind) please let me know. Also and this isn't addressed to anyone in particular, but if PC Washington reads this little blog, they may not want to hear certain comments about certain person's bellies/appearance. I don't think it is a big deal but you never know. In any event, I think my disclaimer is to the point; I've established my ignorant stupidity to a level that should sate the desires of any government agencies agenda. Oh and dad, nothing can ever compare to the Norocs at my Bon Voyage party but, now you can say 'Meer' to cheers instead, it is Russian for peace baby.

July 3

Today we had a blessedly short language class from 8:30 to 9:15 and then a hub-site day in Ialoveni (my town). On Thursdays we would normally have no language, because of the vaccination sessions in the morning, but on this particular morning, only one volunteer needed to get injected with this particular vaccine (It was for measles/rubella/ mumps; their parents must not love them enough to have had it performed. Thanks Mom, I'm luckier than that guy.) Before lunch and after language, we had a **3** hour safety session on everything you can possible imagine. We then had lunch (two eggs, bread and a tomato supplemented with ice cream, sprite and Lay's sour cream and dill chips bought at the local shop.) and moved on to gender diversity. The TEFL's then split off and we learned some things about being teachers, the specifics of which I will spare you all.

There are some new and exciting activities coming my way soon. First I'll start with the weekend: as you may know, Friday is the Fourth of July, a popular American holiday and the American consulate or embassy or something throws a party for us Yanks somewhere in Chisinau – I bet you love all the specifics I have to offer. It should be a lot of fun as most of us PST-stage volunteers and currently serving volunteers attend. It is 150 lei to get in and there are libations and American food (I'm curious to see what they can come up with in the food department) available to all. It is also the end of week three, so I can stay in other villages – meaning if the party continues after the party, I may end up sleeping in Costeti. This is a definite possibility because in attendance at the Independence Day party will be Moldovan Nationals (of all government levels I believe) American embassy types and, most importantly, for impressions sake, the PC country director Jeff Kelley-Clarke (I think there is an E in Kelley, sorry if I misspelled your name Jeff); we will all be on our best behavior.

My second bit of news is that week four is next week, meaning, we all go on permanent site visits the weekend after the fourth. On Friday the 11th we will meet our school directors and partner teachers (we're all going to be team teaching). On Saturday we travel to our sites and meet our potential host families-there are three or four possible homes for every volunteer. I personally think that this is a very important weekend as the families we choose (we have to let the directors know by the following Tuesday) are going to be our host families for the duration of our stay in Moldova(pick the family with the Ferrari and hot-tub, right?)

I'm sure trepidation and excitement, with a pinch of anticipation and providence-driven acceptance will surround us all as we walk into the relative unknown.

That is all for today from this daring *yet* sagacious blogger. Hope all is well in the U.S. On a side note to the Scheurich family: (Dolars and Techners are welcome too, as are Strattons, Gavans, Craigs, Dewans, etc.) please post any random happenings that happen randomly, but don't warrant the use of expensive phone time. Its fun to hear news from home – I heard Willie and Charlie were dating a set of twins, one blonde and one brunette, is this true? (Way to go guys! Do you like, switch it up sometimes?)

4th of JULES

4th

I'll try to wrap up these days in a page or two, I don't think you need vivid details of everything I do; don't worry there are still two more years of my blogs to come.

Friday was the Fourth of July and I made my house mom Kraft Mac and cheese. She absolutely loved it and had seconds. The dish she made for the night though, was kidneys, lungs and heart with onions and cabbage; she didn't hesitate to pile them on top of her plate of mac 'n cheese...ha-ha. I went out for a little with my house brother and drank a beer in honor of the good old U.S.A.

5th (Party day baby)

We had language class today and then it was off to
Chisinau to the big ID4 party. There was some really good
wine to be had, pseudo American food (they took the ham
part of hamburger very literally). It was an embassy party
by the way and they also had Chisinau beer on tap for
everyone and by 6 p.m. there were a large handful of
volunteers swimming in the pool – the party was at a health
club – but I refrained for decencies sake (Good god man!
What do you take me for?!). I also have absolutely
AWESOME videos of me and others dancing to a
Moldovan band covering CCR, the Beatles etc. You
probably wouldn't guess it, but a Moldovan accent adds a
lot to 'Born on the Bayou."

I was allowed to go to my friends' neighboring village that
night around 9 p.m. and we hit the bar/café until close. It
was a fun day and I was even a little impressed with my
Russian that night at Patrick's (the volunteer whose house I
stayed) dinner table.

6th

The sixth was a headache. Or I should say it was going to
be a headache until I said the word shashleek, which means
BBQ in Russian. I didn't ask to have one, I just said the
word, but Pat's family decided that we were going to drink
house wine and BBQ all day. I'll refer to this day from now
on as 'Red Sunday, Bloody Red Sunday'. Needless to say, I
got home later than I wanted, called you know who earlier
than she needed to hear from me and had to wake up early
to do my homework. It was a very fun day indeed and I

had a great time with Pat's family though, and I think it was worth the trouble to be able to hang with fellow volunteers and enjoy the beautiful weather with some decent vintage.

7th

Nothing special today, just class, a short jog etc. Victor and I picked up Visili in Chisinau and I got to check out his Semi. It is huge! And I think he just pulls it over when he needs sleep on the road, because he brought some bedding out with him. I can't imagine driving for ten days across the Ukraine and Russia and sleeping on the side of the road!

8th

Today wasn't too bad; language class for three hours. I have to go to the hub-site school today at 1 p.m. and the lunch Luba made was very light noodle-ham soup, thankfully. I haven't had much of an appetite the past few days. It is amazing what a week can do; last week I was very optimistic and content and I'm definitely struggling to find reasons to feel this way at the moment. I'm feeling very homesick this week (sorry for making whoever you are listen to my issues). I hope the feelings pass because I was having a lot of fun and I need to snap out of this mood. (If you are all completely confused at this point, I understand. Ranting is cathartic though, learn to like it.)

On a lighter note, we find out where we will be spending the rest of our time here – as in our permanent sites. I actually am pretty sure I will be living in Cearda Lunga, so Mom, you can mark it on the map! It seems clear because it is one of the possible Russian sites and it is the larger of the two. The girl I'm taking classes with has voiced a concern about safety in bigger towns and I think she will be in the village. Anyway, there is a significant chance that I will get DSL in my house *and* I will live very close to a horse farm, which is pretty cool. The south has less relief in its landscape, but as you all know Moldova isn't really big enough to have significant geographical change by region, so this isn't much of an issue. On Friday of this week, we have our first language assessment, which is a conversational based test on the progression of our skills. By week nine we should be up to par (that's gonna be the biggie test), so I'm not overly concerned about this week's test, although I wish I was in better spirits to tackle it.

There are some funny photos from Sunday. If you are wondering, the striped shirt is Pat's dad's old navy tank top – he was in the Russian navy years ago. There is a great video of us singing some Russian song with the whole family, but I seriously doubt that the bandwidth here can handle a video being uploaded…you'll have to come see me soon and I'll show you the videos!

I love you all and miss you as you know and I am thankful you are all behind me supporting me; good days are good and bad days are severely amplified, as I am almost half way around the world. Я лублу вы и до сведаня!

(Oh yea….where the hell are my Skittles MOM!) Just kidding I got them.

July 8 through 11 - week before site visit

Hmm, not much was happening through these days. We had had class on Tuesday morning and then we had a hub-site visit for the rest of the day. Wednesday was a 5 hour language class and then nothing else.

On Thursday we had hub-site all day which consisted of a tech session about internet viruses and spy-ware and then a very graphic sexual safety health session. I won't go into details, but it involved lots of detailed pictures and some demonstrations on how to keep safe (this was a little much, in my opinion). We then had lunch (what an appetite we built looking at diseased genitalia!) and then more TEFL stuff (if I've been saying TEFL and if you don't know what I mean, TEFL is the acronym for the English teaching program).

After TEFL, the program director pulled me aside to tell me that my village had changed; my partner teacher had some pretty serious family stuff. So I will now be living in Sarata-Galbena, which is a 6,000 person village southwest of Chisinau. On the upside, I'm less than an hour from the capital, but because it is a village, I may not have DSL! I think I'll have a different and better experience, considering I live in a larger town right now and it will be nice to switch it up a bit; go a little bit rural you know. I don't have any more facts about the village other than it is about ten or fifteen minutes south of a pretty decent sized town. As I mention before, the PC worked up some nice packages of information about our towns, but my change was very last minute. I do know that it is a half Russian and half

Romanian speaking village, which bothers me as I want my Russian to be immaculate at the end of my service; I guess I'll just have to avoid those Romanians.

As you can guess, I will be visiting this new site on Saturday and not Cearda Lunga, obviously. By the way, an issue I am predicting I will run across is that because the switch was so last minute – leaving me, in part, wondering if this new village *actually* wants a volunteer – that I may not get a choice in housing. Formerly, I was going to be given the choice of four families, but I may get one now, not too sure. I only make this point, because there is one other volunteer named Katie, who is actually being placed in Iaolveni. She is not getting a choice in living arrangements because her site was changed last-minute as well. Эта Жизнь right?

I found a fellow volunteer who had a Tom Robbins book she is going to swap with mine, so hats off to the Phoenix Public Library system – I couldn't have done it without them. I'm reading a Phillip K. Dick novel right now called "The Crack in Space." It is very Vonnegut with a more science fiction oriented plotline; less Kilgore Trout, more "Blade Runner." Thanks to my wonderful mother and father (фамйля Scheurich да?) I am wearing a Ducati T-shirt as I type, and I have introduced my host family to the wonderful world of Starburst. Still a little confused on the boxers you sent though…

So, there is my entry. I've been running up a storm to keep myself from going crazy, so don't worry in that department. I find that if I can run three or four times a week I can wear myself out enough to stay sane and, the physical exertion is a relief from the twisted world which is my thought process. This week has definitely put me on a strange tangent and I need to regain keel evenness. The first three weeks here almost seemed to level me out and raise my tolerance level for everything. There was so much to take in and deal with, it made the things that would have normally bothered me seem very inconsequential. I'm sure I will get my lone-wolf mental interior back soon and stop this yellowed belly-aching! Owen Meany would claim providence in this situation and suggest I follow suit.

July 11, 2008

Today we all met our site school directors. Mine is a very witty ball of fire who managed to crack a joke or interject a missile strike of a comment during the whole meet and greet session. She speaks fluent Russian and – as far as I can tell – fluent Romanian. I am a bit concerned that I will not be getting the total immersion I want with Russian, because of the Romanian population, but there is not a lot I can do and as Dad's co-worker Kolby said, one needs to go with the flow. I am also guessing that signs and things will not be strictly Russian, which sucks. My other town's motto was going to be "Go Russian or go Home!" Such is life I guess. Being about 40 minutes from the capital should make up for it; I've been told many volunteers frequent the capital – as in every weekend they are in Chisinau. I don't know if I need to be there that often, but it is definitely an option now. I also left a person down south that I would have liked to be around, but I gained two more that I am happy to be closer to.

As far as I know, the breakdown of it all is:

Population 5600

School Population 740

Safety Level Normal (Great, what does 'normal' mean?)

Teachers 47?

English Teachers 3

And one French teacher

I will post more information when I have time to transcribe it and I have definite things to post. You know inaccuracy is not my thing. Precision baby, precision…

I was told I may actually get a house with DSL; I believe one of the choices will have DSL inside. I had said earlier I would get no housing options, but apparently I do get them now, we'll see if this holds true. Regardless, DSL will not be my priority – I think that family functionality is much more important in the long run Aa?

###Disclaimer###

That's all I've got for now. This big blog may not be posted until much after the fact (try Tuesday the 15th) because I will be away from my PST site until next week. Sorry if questions are posed and I answer them later on in the blog.

It is more fun to present my thoughts as they come to me than to edit a week or two into one neat package.

###Disclaimer###

Also, I`d like to point out that I just got back from my site visit. This is a previously written entry, but should give you some really great bloggage to read. I`m going to update with photographs and more print as soon as I get the chance - most likely tomorrow. TAKE EVERYTHING WITH A GRAIN OF SALT.

Incorrect site visit 12-16

This has been a very eventful week; I will go so far as to say that some happenings have been unique. As you know from my last entry, my site changed because of a partner teacher's personal life; things have changed again, but I will go into my weekend in Sarata Galbena before I get into the newest pile of dirt I have to offer you.

Saturday the 12th

Today's priority was to get myself to Sarata Galbena, my then permanent site. I had made a plan the day before to meet with two volunteers, Gretchen and Josh at the southern-most bus stop in Chisinau. Ialoveni is so close to this stop that it is questionable whether the station is outside of Chisinau or Ialoveni but, in any event, I met them where I was supposed to be on time, with few hiccups. We were met at the station by Gretchen's (she is in Cahul, four hours south of Chisinau) school director. Josh and I ended up splitting off into another person's car and started the journey south. It only took 35 minutes to get to the school on Sarata Galbena and from there, Josh stayed aboard for the rest of the trip to Leova.

I was met by the school's vice director and director immediately and was shown around 'campus' a bit. I met my partner teacher and walked around inside, getting the lay-of-the-land, as they say. I quickly realized that everything printed in and around the school was in Romanian – which was just awesome.

After checking out the school, I walked to my host dad's house (I had three choices, but I only had one choice, if you know what I mean) and ate lunch. We hung around for a little while and then went to look around town and meet the other host families. Our first stop was his vineyard. Our second stop was supposed to be one of my host family options but, when we arrived, we were greeted by half of the married couple – the male half specifically whom, much to my dismay, spoke not a lick of Russian. This housing option went swiftly out of the window.

The second 'option' was with another family pretty close by. The house was very rural, what with the pigs and chickens running around. We happened upon the family and their neighbors eating a Saturday meal outside and stopped to sample the wine, chat and try some food. It was good and the wife was very friendly and younger than I was used to. I wanted to give this site some serious consideration because, while they did not have three television sets and two computers like the first house, they were friendly and welcoming. I told the wife that I would be spending my second night with she and her family.

The rest of the day...

Let's say, for the sake of brevity, that the rest of the day happened and leave it at that. Nothing extremely interesting to report on it except – forgot to mention – that the school had a large soccer stadium with astro-turf.

It turns out the host father in the first house is a photographer/cinematographer by profession. He decided to take me along with him (He wanted me to wear one of his shirts and ties, but I declined – My fashion sense is immaculate after all.) on the job. I obliged of course, not fully sure what the night had in store.

Things did not seem promising right away because when we arrived at seven in the evening, I was told to sit on a stool and watch as he set up and prepared to film guests filing into the small banquet hall handing gifts to the birthday boy. Things started to get a little better, when the 'birthday boy' handed me a beer and a glass, which he had gotten from a mini-fridge nearby, and then pointed at said fridge, indicating that I could drink as much beer as I wanted. Not too bad, I can deal with this situation. As guests began to arrive, my house father filmed them; all the while the tables were being filled with plates of food – lots and lots and lots of food. Eventually, as dinner was about to begin, I was asked to sit at a table by some of the guests. After an initial shot of cognac to get the appetite up and running, the dinner was off and I gorged on salads of mushroom, meat and corn with mayonnaise; meats, vegetables and the like. Beer and champagne was flowing and general merriment was being made by all. Eventually dinner broke into song and song broke into dance. I was asked to join in on many traditional dances (some embarrassing as I had to kiss my partner once) and was even asked to dance by my school director, who was in attendance.

As the dancing died down – or I died down from the dancing, rather – I found a quiet little part of the room and some beer to sip on. I was chatting away with a couple people in broken Russian, when the staff started to bring out more and more food. I was forced to try everything, even though I was already to the bursting point from the first feast of the night. At this point it was around midnight and I was ready to get some much needed sleep.

At around 12:30 or 1 a.m., cake was distributed and the director of the school made a speech. Apparently the party was also held in honor of a fallen family member which was an interesting twist on a birthday celebration, for me. I need to mention that I talked to my potential house mom at the party and she basically told me I shouldn't live with her, as she didn't have a shower or running water in her house.

I didn't end up leaving the party until 2 a.m., when my host father had finally gotten all the footage and still photographs from the party that he needed. I was asleep before my head hit the pillow upon arriving at home.

Sunday the 13th

I woke up at ten or so and hopped on the computer to write some Emails. The rest of the day was lazy and boring; I managed to buy some water to cure the slight ache in my head and wrote a lot in my journal. As five and then six in the evening rolled around, I told my host father that I would stay in his house for the second night because I had decided it would be pointless the check out the other house; the owner had warned me off at dinner the previous night. It was a fun night. I got to help out canning juice with the husband and wife. Mom, you would be impressed; we filled about 20 one gallon jars full of fruit, sugar and water and then placed wax lined caps on top of them. We then filled a long, shallow, metal basin with water and lit a fire underneath it. The jars heated in the water bath and the bacteria were killed inside. I then had the task of lifting them out of the bath and setting them down so the caps could be sealed with a jar-sealer dealy/thingy.

Monday the 14th

I woke up at eight and made my way to the rutiera stop. It was to be a journey divided into a rutiera ride into Hincesti and a bus ride from Hincesti to Chisinau, where I was meeting some PCV's for beer and lunch. I waited at the stop with my partner teacher for an hour. She then left after telling a Romanian man that I was a lost American and he promised to help me find my way; I would have been just fine alone but, she felt responsible for me, I guess. When we got into the van, the Romanian speaker began talking to a younger man, who spoke some English and Russian. The older gentleman got off, but informed me that the younger man he was chatting with would help me find my way around. I immediately realized that the younger man was sweating, dirty and severely drunk – or hung over. His eyes were listing back into his head and he was questioning me on everything from my motives to my salary; needless to say, I definitely didn't need his help. When we got to Hincesti he showed me which bus to board, which was helpful. Then he asked to borrow money to buy a drink. When we got on the bus (yes he was going all the way to Chisinau, yippee!) he asked me for money for bus fair. I ended up giving him only one lei, which he needed to get to Chisinau. There were no seats on the bus, so I sat in the stairwell and read. My new friend obviously needed to know what I was reading, so he asked about the book and then asked to hold it and look at it. At this point, the scowl which had been etched into my face for hours deepened as his glazed eyes scanned the pages – which were, oddly enough, filled with Hunter S. Thompson's personal correspondences, irony?

When I finally got to Chisinau, I met with some friends and we had a great lunch at a Syrian restaurant and drank some much deserved beers. I got back to Ialoveni around six and showered and ate a dinner of Borsht and cheese.

Tuesday the 15th

On Tuesday, we had an all day TEFL session, which was pure and unadulterated hell… Learning about teaching is rough when you have to do it for 8 hours straight. I also realized that morning that the best parts of my day are my run, and the walk to school with my I-pod and cup of coffee. Music and caffeine rule my life and when they run out, I'm bored again!

I also spoke to the program director, to help me solve the Romanian problem in Sarata Galbena. I told her some comments locals had made such as:

"The last two volunteers here spoke Romanian," and

"It would be better if you spoke Romanian," and

"Don't worry! You will learn both languages!"

I explained that all signage in the school was in Romanian and dealing with it as a prevalent part of my service would detract from my integration into the community (In addition, I really want to be very good at Russian at the end of my two years; a little self-interest doesn't hurt too bad right?). She made some calls and now I am going to be teaching in Cearda Lunga, once again. There were some tragic happenings with the first school and they actually resolved themselves in an equally tragic and weird way. There were also some questions I had as to why my situation in Cearda Lunga couldn't be solved in the first place, without switching my village. Anyway, it is a relief to know that I will be living in a Russian speaking town and teaching at a Russian speaking school. I'm very happy about it and when the coordinator told me it was going to work out, I was skipping around the school house for joy – I literally hugged her and skipped away; I get weirder and weirder every day.

Wednesday the 16th

Today's language lesson was fun and informative and I am speaking a much better Russian than I did a month ago. I didn't do so well though on last week's language assessment, as my marks were in the middle — about average for volunteers going through the Russian program but, as you all know, I get down on myself for everything, even when I succeed. Anyway, we have another test in a couple weeks and I am speaking limited but useful Russian to my family, so I shouldn't worry too much. As far as sanity goes, I think that last week was a fluke as I am in much better spirits going into week five. I'm sure every volunteer has trouble with distance and the difficulties we are all faced with; that or I'm just a big wuss.

If you've made it this far, it means you have gotten through this poorly written, extensive — hopefully coherent — description of my last couple days in mighty, mighty Moldova. You were with me as I canned fruit and heard pigs being slaughtered next door. You woke up with me as large roosters made it known to the world: "I am the most unfortunate animal to grace this earth God!" Pour a Sierra into a tall glass Dad, and think about what a relief it is to have your credit card back in your pocket and not in my clammy hands as I wait in line at the supermarket with said pale ale tucked under one arm and a grin plastered on my face.

I miss you guys and don't worry Willie, the next time I hear a pig scream and gurgle out its last breath of life, I will think of you, you little weirdo. Now all: go do, that voodoo, which you do, so well! Ciao.

The 17th..

Today it the 17th of July and you are on the cusp of an important and life-changing Blog. It is an emergency blog that I was forced to write by my nagging conscience. It could not wait another day (although by the time I actually post it, the 'other' day will have taken place).

I found out yesterday evening, while picking up a translation of an advertisement for practice school (more on this later), that my co-Russian learning PCV is leaving the Peace Corps for good. Very shocking news, as she and I are the only two people in class and I didn't expect a thing! Apparently we didn't click well enough for her to inform me that she would be taking that big plane home (A pity, we had been bonding in the last few weeks. She was privilege to all of my problems and complaints!). This leaves me as the one and true king of Ialoveni. It also leaves me with what will amount to a private tutor. I had a discussion with my LCF (language teacher) and we have decided that during five hour sessions, it will be best to take short breaks every hour, as opposed to three breaks throughout the class. We shall experiment tomorrow and, as I remarked to a friend today at hub-site, I will either end my time in PST fluent or frustrated; either way I am in store for a much more personal language-learning experience.

In other news: I should be making my way back down south to check out housing options, now that I am back in Ceardar-Lunga. We'll see when this takes place, but I think it makes sense so I can avoid choosing my residence for the next two years before I move to said city. I am going to put off the aforementioned trip for as long as possible though, as I plan on utilizing my next few weekends taking day-trips to neighboring volunteers towns; now that I am truly alone in my town (oddly enough Сэм is my name in Russian and Cам means 'alone'). I am also the only volunteer who is allowed to spend the night out of his/her site; this is a sympathy move on their part and I assume they believe I deserve to bond with other PCV's. All-in-all though, I am officially quite happy with everything at the moment and am very glad that I chose to spend my time here perfecting the Russian language. This has been a very good week for me, especially compared to last week (which I know isn't the last time I'll feel unhappy, etc., but I'll get over it, every time). I believe it was Dad's co-worker Kolby who mentioned that the highs and lows in the US are much less pronounced, say east coast swells, and the highs and lows here are higher and lower, say north shore Hawaii. This is very true and we have all had our ups and downs; although apparently we don't all talk about them.

Today at hub-site we had a seminar on blogs, where we were told what shouldn't be said, most of which was fairly obvious. I would like to remind you all to try and keep wall comments as culturally sensitive and appropriate as I try to keep the blog. It will all come back to haunt me I am sure (Nate). The only threat I can offer up is that, when you all come to London to celebrate Christmas with me (yea right!), I may forget all of your presents…

Dad, please say hi to Grandma Kate for me. She hasn't been commenting on my blog, so I assume she isn't reading it and is obviously missing when I used to drop in to say hello and argue with her.

I'll make this one short, but remember, I am the true king of Ialoveni now, so I can make my blogs short and you will have to learn to like them. Also, you may want to get started on sending over those teaching supplies Mom and Dad; we're about halfway through PST and who knows when they will arrive (I'm going to Email the two of you a 'wish list' of extra things I may need for the classroom). I still haven't gotten the package with the small music posters and magazines but I did get the Skittles, which may have been a mistake because I'm sure eating that much candy every day cannot be good for my health – not to mention the sheep cheese, oils, eggs, pastas, rice, potatoes, etc. I think it is important though, to ingest everything I see, as a means of integrating into a culture successfully. Ciao?

The weekend

July 18, 19 and 20

Somewhere in Yellowstone National Park: An adolescent leads his cousins around, in search of the elusive Moose that has been haunting said relatives' dreams for the past month. It was a long and treacherous drive for the two of them. As twins somewhat advanced in their young adulthood, their thoughts intermingle in an almost telepathic way. Weird waves had bounced around the cab of their vehicle as they slogged through the 20 hour drive to Wyoming.

In San Francisco: A young social worker drives to see a patient; she doesn't know what to expect, as this is a first time patient. She hopes for the best.

In Ialoveni: A rather witty and handsome young man sits at his typewriter and confuses his family with his pointless – and sometimes raving – rants. One day they will know him as the next Hunter S, but for now, his musings are but a small aspect of their respective lives.

Your son had a fun and eventful weekend past. On Friday I met with my resource teacher, who will work with me as I make my way through practice school (real students in a classroom setting, to (duh) practice with) for the next three weeks. We planned the lesson together, somewhat, and tomorrow morning, I will put me ideas into visual and verbal form as I attempt to impart some knowledge onto my students.

On Saturday, I had a short language class and then my LCF and I went to Costesti for a cross-cultural session regarding Moldovan family life. I went home after the session and finished up my lesson plan. Following this small bit of work, I contemplated my potential actions for the weekend and decided upon paying my colleagues in Costesti a visit. At around 6 I dropped in on Patrick's family, with a gift of beer and peanuts for his host dad (he bought me a replica of the sweet shirt I am wearing in the photo with him). I ate a dinner of boiled oats and meat before meeting with a gang of volunteers at Pat's house. After finishing a bottle of beer between the five of us, we all made our way to the 'café/bar' – as they all put it – and settled in for some peanuts, beer and conversation. Towards the end of the night, a Moldovan man solicited us for conversation and – somewhat luckily – he did not speak much Russian. He bought us all coffee and tea and hung around our table discussing football with Pat. This all took place towards the end of the evening and, we eventually made our way home.

I awoke at 8:30 in the spare room and made my way downstairs to eat breakfast with Pat's parents. I caught the 10 am rutiera to Ialoveni (I realized 5 minutes before the taxi was leaving, that I had left my cellular phone on the bed; I ran both ways and still made my ride). Once in Ialoveni, I picked up some mushrooms, sausage, and tomato paste because Sunday is – from now on – Italian night. After getting a haircut, I got to work cutting and sautéing. Next time I won't use the tomato paste as my house Mom commented that the sauce tasted like ketchup….(Ouch!)

Later on in the evening I made my way to the internet café, picked up an ice-cream cone and stumbled onto my computer, where I am sitting currently (as you may have guessed).

Wish me luck for Monday's class. No matter how much confidence I have, I am sure I could use some good fortune; there must be some difference between substitute teaching and teaching English to Moldovan 7th graders da?

I hope the trips to Yellowstone and where ever Mom and Dad went (sorry mom, I forgot) were fun; I assume you were all gone on Sunday afternoon because I called the house to chat and no one picked up. I hope you are all enjoying the heat as I am not missing it (bwahaha). Thank you to everyone who is keeping up with my story. All I can see is hits on article, so I don't know exactly who is reading, although I have a pretty good idea.

Love,

Сэм

P.S.

Dad, the new 'noroc' is 3a – pronounced 'za' – followed by anything. It is a toast meaning "To health/wine/family/Sam/dad ('to' whatever you add onto za). Use it copiously!

July 21,

While I sitting here, I thought I`d add that my first class went ok today! My resource teacher taught the 1st class of the day to give me an idea of some methods, but I will be taking care of the rest of the lessons. It is an odd format right now because I have to cover 7 lessons in seven days. I teach 2 classes a day to the same students to cover all of the material. The Wednesday after next, we will have a hub-site day and on the following Thursday, we will be teaching with our partner teachers for the remainder of practice school. Anyway, besides the lesson I taught, today has been your good old fashioned Monday; everything is its bleakest on this tragic day of the week - just as everything peaks on Fridays. CIAO!

Today (The 22)

I am at a loss at the moment, as to what was keeping me so busy last week…and I am hoping I can find whatever it is soon, as I seem to be awash in a sea of boredom. Last week, I vaguely remember days filled with activity and a much deserved beer at the end of these days at the local bar, where I would study up on my Russian and afterwards, make my way home for dinner. The past two days on the other hand, have been taken up by the occasional morning run, language class and practice school. After practice school I write my lessons plans for the day and make my way home at around 3 p.m.

For some reason, I was extremely tired all day today and, after writing my lesson plan, I came home and snacked on some pretzels and promptly fell asleep while trying to read in bed. It is now around 5 p.m. and I am trying to find the energy to do my homework and again, contemplating how and why I was so content during the last few weeks here. I am certain that my lack of energy is a problem, although I'm not sure of what this deficit is being caused by; I have been sleeping well and eating plenty (I awoke to the sound of voices 20 minutes ago and had a mid-afternoon bowl of borsht). I will write more on this topic when I find the source of the problem.

In other news: today's weather was pleasantly rainy and cloudy and, despite my lack of energy, I enjoyed feeling chilly for once while walking to class this morning. But, in a truly perplexing manner, the weather spiked to the high 80's or low 90's this afternoon and is now back down to a agreeable 65 or so.

Class has been going well and I give myself a timid round of applause at my first go in the teaching world. My lesson plans are working out well and the only problem I had today was that I didn't put enough of the effort onto the students – with the activities I had planned – and my timing fell short, forcing me to 'wing it' for 10 minutes. I am in the class room with a resource teacher who tends to speak with the students in Romanian. This will change when I move to Gagauzia, but for the mean time may remain a proverbial thorn in my side. One point of concern is my coffee intake: I consumed two cups this morning (rather weak in my opinion), one cup during my language class (I've taken to instant in class, for convenience's sake) and another cup during my planning period. Despite this rather copious amount of caffeine consumption, I found myself tired enough to pass out briefly while reading – as I mentioned earlier. Maybe I am like my father and am somewhat unaffected by caffeine (although, frighteningly, my heart was feeling a little off-beat…).

Now onto the important stuff: I really must find a good way to bring lunch to school. Today for example, there was no meat in the house, so I brought some cheese and two tomatoes for lunch. My host father gave me 10 lei to buy bread or meat at the market but, I bought a sprite and a bag of *sour cream and dill* (yes DILL and not CHIVES like we have in the United States. These are fantastically tasty chips. Очен вкузно!) Lay's instead. In effect, my lunch today was soda, chips, cheese and two small tomatoes. Yesterday, lunch consisted of two tomatoes, a Coke and pasta and sauce that I had made on Sunday night for dinner (by the way, there was so much sour tomato paste in the sauce, that Visilli took it upon himself to wash it out of the sauce with tap water and strain it, rendering it somewhat edible). Who knows what tomorrow will bring. I have to say I miss bringing a good, old-fashioned cold-cut sandwich to work and chasing it with and ice-cold bottle of Squirt. I also miss the pantry at home which was stocked with a variety of familiar foods. Don't get me wrong, there are days that I am in sweet bliss because I finally discovered brinza (I have mentioned this product before but, just in case you forgot, it is salty and similar in texture to feta. I have convinced myself that it is low in fat, — maybe akin to cottage cheese? — as I eat a great deal of it.), but occasionally, I get tired of this salty sheep-milk based cheese and wish I could snack on some corn tortilla chips and Herdez Salsa Casera (medium in intensity of course).

That is all for today. Wish me luck with tomorrow's class and also, wish me luck explaining the passive voice to 7th grade Moldovan students when, I have trouble grasping the concept myself! Ciao…

July 25-27

Today was a big day for your volunteer; he has finally made contact with his new host family and will break down what he knows about them if he can. But, let us begin at the beginning, as it were:

As you know, I will be engaged in practice teaching for the next three weeks. This so far, has been an interesting an enlightening experience filled with ninth grade Moldavians and copious usage of miming and gesturing (it is English as a *foreign* language, after all). My class time is going great and – I may not have mention this – I am teaching solo, whereas at site and for the second half of practice school, I will be team teaching for at least a few hours per week. The idea behind this teaching method has to do with sustainability of the information and general 'help' we are providing Moldova. Working with host country national's in class will give them time with a native English speaker and most likely some lesson plans written by volunteers – this is the idea at least. Anyway, I will teach on Monday the 27th and then write a test on Monday evening for Tuesday's class. On Wednesday I will collaborate with my current resource teacher and a partner teacher from my future site. Because of some 'personal logistical issues with my specific partner teacher, another will be working with me for the week and a half following hub-site on Wednesday.

I am concerned with the set-up of partner teaching, to some extent. First of all, I got the feeling that I would be working with 4 English teachers at site, whereas I was under the impression we all had one partner at site. Secondly, if this is the case, it would seem to me that I would be bouncing around from classroom to classroom and may not feel that I have any real territory of my own.

This being said, my partner teacher (according to my research teacher) was under the impression that I would be solo teaching and would have my own classroom, etc. I know we have to have a certain amount of partner teaching hours, so I am not sure what my future will entail, work-wise. My main concern is that I want to feel that I am on staff at the school in Cearda-Lunga; not some bouncy-ball hopping from lesson to lesson (a bouncy-ball with an immaculate grasp on the English language, mind you).

On to the site visit: I ended up choosing the second house I visited and for the sake of their protection and in an effort to keep myself from publishing something that a certain governmental agency (Dept. of Agriculture, of course) may not want to see published, I will just explain why I am quite content with the house I did end up choosing.

Here is the layout:

Mother at home

Father working in Moscow (will probably be home every three months, I believe this is the trend)

3 year-old

7 year-old

Indoor toilet/shower

Modern washing machine

Optional малинкий дом or casa mica (guest house you uncultured humps!)

Sunny kitchen where I can drink coffee in the morning

10 to 15 minute walk to work

5 minute walk to central part of town (shops, bars, etc.)

I will begin by living in the house I think; the room is towards the back of the house and has a locking door, so as long as the kids aren't too loud, it will probably where I end up living. There are two advantages to living in the main house, as opposed to the guest house. One is that the bathroom and shower are in the same building and the other is that it will probably be warmer in the main house, during the winter (the guest house would have to be heated with a wood burning stove and an electric heater provided by PC). So, that is the general lay-out and I met the woman of the house briefly and she seemed young and friendly, so I hope we get on well.

So, this all took place on Friday the 25th and it is now Sunday the 27th. What has happened since then – I am sure you are all dying to know. As you know, all of Friday was spent on my site visit with Gretchen, a volunteer who had to switch her site house. On Friday night I came home and ate some food; Victor and Bacilli were working on the big-rig truck near the house and I was asleep before they came home. Much to my disappointment at the potential boredom to come, Victor is going to be learning his father's trade and, beginning yesterday morning, will be gone for two weeks, trucking across Russia, Belarus and the Ukraine. My house bro is essentially my only contact in

Ialoveni who is around my age. On the upside, my Russian will be put to the ultimate test, as I have only Luba to converse with (I was home late last night and had to call her and explain in Russian that my maxi-taxi would be late).

On Saturday, some of us went to Chisinau to eat - ...Mexican Food!... – and let off some steam through ice-cream and beer. The Mexican restaurant in question actually had chips and a sweet, almost Indianish salsa – but to order more than one tiny bowl of aforementioned chips was outrageously expensive. I ordered the burrito with meat and vegetables. It was covered in the same salsa and melted cheese – Swiss I think. It was served with sliced cucumber and tomatoes. Interesting to say the least, but I think that all of us Southwesterners enjoyed the idea eating Mexican food, if not terribly impressed with the replication of the dishes (for example Lanie ordered fajitas and they were made with lots of dill).

After eating, we made our way around to various shops and cafes. I discovered a store called No. 1, which was essentially a modern grocery store. I was very impressed, if not discouraged by the high-prices in light of my meager allowance (Illy Coffee was 155 lei per can!). I will undoubtedly go back though, because they sell tortillas and other objects I cannot find throughout the rest of Moldova.

Today is Sunday and it has been uneventful so far. I woke up around 8:30, ran a few miles, came home, made and egg with bread, cleaned my room, ironed some clothes and am now sitting at my trusty lappy, regurgitating what I can, in a brief manner. Among news that may interest you all is that I will be giving a small speech at swearing in; one health volunteer, one Russian TEFL volunteer and one Romanian

TEFL volunteer all give mini-speeches. This excited me because I had already thought it would be fun to say some words to the crowd. What I didn't realize though is that the speech has to be given in…*Russian*. This should be interesting. I think I may make printouts for my fellow volunteers as, they don't really understand Russian.

Ciao, Sam

P.S. Mom: The package came in, but I haven't been able to open it yet as it had to be delivered from Chisinau to Ialoveni (this was on Friday) and I have to wait until tomorrow to claim it.

Dad: I get the guitar on Wednesday, keep your fingers crossed that it is at least partially worth the $150 I am paying for it.

Charlie: How are you my brother, have you and your other brother found jobs yet, or have you given up. Feel free to call me and tell me all about it. Go to Miracle Mile or, better yet, El Bravo for me soon. Maybe I'll be able to smell the beans from here..

Willie: Ditto to everything I wrote Charlie and, who is your roommate next year? Will it be that little snake Jake again? Also is Warhammer out yet, DIII? Keep me informed on these things. I can't even access the Blizzard site at the internet cafes. It must be some weird European thing.

Michelle: Eat some Thai food for me and, I will know very soon when my breaks are next Spring. I WILL be attending your wedding and I don't want you to have to move things around or anything, for me. Hopefully things will co-inside.

Hello to everyone else as well, I miss y'all (Grandma, I've made sure to watch my Tomato spelling; my ego will sure crack and crumble if another Dan Quayle joke is made at my expense!)

Ciao II,

Samuel J

The sickness (July 28-31)

Things have been rather boring since my site visit and weekend in Chisinau but, like every week for everyone on earth, something was bound to have happened, right? Yes, to answer your question, things did happen; I will explain all of these things as eloquently and interestingly as possible in the next few lines.

Monday started with a lie-in until 7:30 – I skipped the run because I ran the day before – and a decently big breakfast of eggs and bread (if I haven't mention it before, I will now; there is no toaster, this is why I never refer to 'toast' in the morning…FYI!). Gulping down my last cup of coffee which was made with love in the new coffee maker I received in the mail, I then trotted down to my language lesson and taught some kids a little English with all the expertise that a young and inexperienced teacher can muster.

Tuesday went almost exactly the same, except I went for a run in the morning. Now, I do say 'almost' for a reason because, Tuesday will mark the date in my history where – after a run – I realized I was coming down with my first Moldovan illness! I now officially have a cold, or some such bothersome affliction, and am currently fighting it with allergy medicine at night, and anti-histamine, Emergen-C and acetaminophen during the day.

Wednesday was a TEFL day in Costesti and I felt somewhat miserable all day. I forgot my lunch to top things off but, I went with my friend Caleb to his house for lunch. At the very end of the day, I planned a bit for the next session of classes I will be having with one of my partner teachers from down south. I didn't end up getting home until that evening – around seven thirty. I also finally got my hands on a guitar today. The instrument seems to have a shorter neck than a steel-string, but I think that A: it will be a good thing due to the modes of transportation I will be taking it on and B: maybe classical guitars have shorter necks than their steel cousin's; I don't really know as I don't really play the classical guitar, yet. I got home and got the 'Led out' as it were (Zeppelin reference, come on you dolts) in the kitchen. Luba was around, so I made her appreciate how talented I am – I think she appreciated it.

Lately I've had quite a lot of work to do, so I kept the playing to a minimum.

Today was a good day. Despite my illness I was, dare I say it, elated as I walked to class this morning (this may have to do with the de-congestion medicine I'm taking, it really gives you that "Yip-Yip!" feeling), listened to music and sipped on my mug of coffee. Things went slightly downhill, as I don't feel 100% and writing lesson plans with another teacher can be difficult; I tend to dislike group work. That being said, everything went rather smoothly and as you know, I am fairly good at 'winging-it,' so class has been going well. I have two lessons on Friday and ten more next week. We then move onto week nine and ten and then site and then I'll be back home in two years to talk about my experiences in depth....

I will try, at some point, to include the speech I will be making during swearing on my blog, with a translation if you would like (you won't be able to pronounce anything, unless of course you have taken a look at the Cyrillic alphabet that I so painstakingly transcribed onto the blog). I also have to perform some sort of 'entertaining act' at the PST site going away party. I'm not really sure what this entails but, once again, I am alone at site, so I may have to recruit friends to absorb the embarrassment with me. As the twins know very well, I cannot sing for shit, so while guitar playing may be a part of my repertoire, I will stay away from the vocals (all of this is assuming that I will be performing a musical act, at all). I've also decided to grow a bit of a mustache, as if the striped shirts and Cyrillic alphabet weren't weird enough.

Finally, I'd like to add that I wish I could be a part of the Scheurich family's summer vacation – this will be the first of two I will definitely be missing but, I assume you will get-on quite well without your opinionated and, sometimes, unbearable/problem-causing son. Mom and Dad, I got the package of teaching supplies already – somehow; it's a friggin' miracle! – and I will use them will however, DO NOT send any English teaching books or anymore books in general, unless they are fiction for me to read. We have been drowned in so many grammar and English books that none of us know how to swim to the top. Also, you may want to reconsider sending packages, as they seemed to be post-marked between $30-$50 a pop. I don't want our family to go broke because I like drinking 'Starbucks' coffee. As always, feel free to post any comments or suggestions on how I can make this boorish and unoriginal blog better.

I love you <u>all</u> and have fun on vacation! (I love anyone who reads this blog too, unless you are creepy and enjoy specifically targeted blogs that are not targeted at you, you creep. (People like you fill me with fear and loathing, you filthy fink.(whoever you are)))

1st-6th

August 1st thru 6th

On Friday I taught class with my current partner teacher. Everything went to plan and I ended the day with some food. On Saturday morning, I went on a run, per usual, and walked to language class to perfect my already immaculate (at the moment I am working on adding a bit of Dostoevsky French to my accent) speech. After class I did something I've wanted to do for a month or so. It was sunny, so I bought a can of Chisinau draft at the local market and sat outside with my newly acquired guitar and played some tunes; my speed and skill is lacking (considering I have to slog around on silk string!) at the moment, because it has been a while since playing. However I did print out the full tablature of 'Classical Gas' and…I still can't play the whole song! At least this will give me something to work on when I feel like frustrating myself.

The weekend was fun; most of my fellow volunteers came into Ialoveni and drank some drinks with me at the café near my house. At some point, I got rid of these much needed distractions and got some sleep. Sunday was, as usual, spent doing a whole lot of nothing.

The rest of the week was spent partner-teaching with my partner-teacher. I have discovered that if I listen to 'Flogging Molly' I can really get into the right mood for the walk to school; maybe it's a pseudo-Irish thing. Anyway, it is now Wednesday – 'hump-day,' as we say over here – and practice school is nearing an end. I am now thinking about what my role will be in my new school. I am worried that I will not have a class room of my own. If I don't, there go all of the cool posters I wanted to hang-up around my room. At this point, I tend to sit and wait for the inevitable, because – as 'they' so precisely say – it is inevitable. I am very happy about my Russian though, it has given me a definite mental fall-back when everything else doesn't have my 'back' when my backside needs catching, as it were.

But...to get to the point...HAPPY BIRTHDAY MICHELLE! I hope you have a fantastic and eventful birthday and be sure to drink a Racer 5 for me before the day is done! ДНЁМ РОШДЕНИЯ!

Oh, by the way, it is really hot in Moldova at the moment and – due to my temperature related incarceration – I have been sequestered to my house for a good portion of the day. The pictures I may, or may not, post are of me exaggerating the ridiculous heat. Such is life.

I've also included some pictures that I took while viewing a church in Costesti. Most of them are of the dome which was beautiful. Eastern Orthodox churches seem very similar to Roman Catholic churches, in that they contain vast numbers of beautiful paintings and artifacts.

7th - 10th

August 7th thru 10th

Hello all. Michelle, I hope you had a wonderful birthday week and if I could have gotten you a present, I would have. When I come home for your wedding, I will bring you something!

This has been quite a week for me in many different respects. It was week 8 in pre-service training and, the last week of practice school. We have a week 9 and half of week 10 and then we move to our sites. Everything seems to be changing very quickly and it will not be long until I am sitting in my room in South Moldova, writing my musings out on screen for you all to read. Due to the move, I am trying to stock up on reading materials because, as you probably know, I am stuck at site for the first three months during 'lock-down.' Luckily there are some people I will want to visit near-enough that seeing them won't necessitate an overnight trip. We all – English teachers – have two days during 'lock-down' that we can use to spend the night places though, if we need to. (Lock-down, by the way, is the first three months of service before the first IST – In-service-training – when all of our volunteer group gets to meet again in Chisinau. There is a rumor going around though, that the IST's will be held in Rayon centers and not in the capital in an effort by the PC to save money... This would be очен плохо because if we don't all meet in the capital we don't get to get back together as a group and converse about life at site, as a whole. Additionally, – I thought about it for a while –if we meet in different city centers, we may *never* all be back together again as a group after the swearing in ceremony! Once at site, it is totally up to volunteers to decide whom they are interested in maintaining friendships with. There are people – this goes without saying, with all of us (but there I went and said it anyway) – that I will never get in contact with, unless I am put into a room with them as a part of a PC training session, lesson, seminar, etc. Leave it up to me to find the worst case scenario possible and play it out in my head with different variations – which brings me to my next topic...

I feel that divulging any more personal information on the big-bad-world-wide-web would be wanton (God, alliterate much?), so, suffice to say that I think the worst is over for the time being.

Moving on…

The following week should be easy and fun, if I can get my head screwed on straight again. We all have language classes and seminars and on Saturday, there is a farewell party being held for the host families in my town. I have to give another speech at this ceremony; I guess my public speaking skills are being put to the test – in a new language! I also need to start focusing on Russian more this week. I've had trouble concentrating on studying this past week and I really want to come out of the Peace Corps with excellent Russian that I can use later on in life (I already have some fairly grand plans). I've made a pact with myself to study my note cards every night. Learning a language in this environment is very interesting because it has it's sharp spikes in the 'high' and 'low' ranges. (I had mention Peace Corps mood spikes being much more pronounced due to our relative seclusion.) I go through weeks where I feel like my language is going very well and am proud of myself and go through weeks where I seem to have hit some sort of 'language-block.' Whereas it is quite normal to get excited about conversation in Russian, some days it is also frustrating and exhausting to deal with expressing yourself in a different language. As most of you reading probably know, I put a great deal of emphasis in expressing myself mentally and emotionally through – often convoluted – speech. It maddening to try to express problems and emotions to others because, without an excellent knowledge of a language, it is nearly impossible to elicit the correct feelings out of your subject. That being said, I am impressed daily with my house-mom's knowledge of different languages. It turns out that she actually grew up speaking Romanian and it would be her language of choice if it were not for her husband and son, who speak Russian, primarily. I found this out one morning after a particularly chilly run, where I explained that I could see my breath. I used the verb 'to breathe' (дышать). Luba had to think about how to say the word for 'steam' in Russian. I'm sure she knew the word in Romanian without a second thought though.

Anyway, the weekend was fun and Mike (the guy with the guitar) and I finally got together to play some music. We brought a jug of beer out to the woods and sat around and played some tunes. Earlier that day I was in Chisinau and the day before I went to Costesti to hand out with everyone.

Today, Luba came in and asked my help in installing window shades. This small task turned into an ordeal, but after my work was done her and I ate a huge lunch and I'm about to meet some friends at the bar/café to make an attempt at watching the U.S. play basketball… I'll keep you informed on how this turns out; I have to hear the Olympic theme at least once, so I hope we can figure it out.

That's all for today folks. I'll try to update you all later this week, but it will depend on the direction and force of the wind and the amount of ivy I am wearing at the time. Everyone stay safe! До Сведания и мир!

August 10 - 21

August 10th – 21st   It has been quite some time since I wrote a blog and I apologize for this! I have also been informed by my mother that my grammar skills are slipping! I will try to avoid any more errors as I can't afford to lose any more respect on these grounds – maybe I can hire an editor here in Moldova. The past week or so has made it very difficult to take the time to sit down and write, but I have finally arrived at site and I think I need to dump my thoughts and feelings onto my laptop, so you all have something to do at work – I know that Mike S plays solitaire all day… So, last week was a good week and I had a great time on many different occasions. Many of my fellow volunteers came to Ialoveni quite often and I made it to Costesti a couple times to shoot the proverbial 'breeze.' The night before the language assessment was one of the best I've had in Moldova – although considering I had a test the next day, I might have been better off staying home. Anyway, Gretchen, Виктор and I all went to the woods near his house for a birthday celebration. I'll try to get some pictures online for you all to look at because it was amazing. I had no idea that this area existed in Ialoveni, but it does; the trees look laid-out or planted by hand – very European. Everyone present basically sat around and talked and ate and sang and played guitar, until it got dark. We brought the dog, Donna, and met quite a few interesting characters – these included one Moldovan who was the spitting image of Mick Jagger. I am not kidding, the guy even had the same haircut as our favorite antiquated rocker! At one point, I sat and played the melody to 'Over the Hills and Far Away' while he ad-libbed something in Russian over it. If there was a way to post videos I would, because his crooning is definitely worth hearing (or just come visit me and I'll show you the video).

Oh, and I did very well on my language assessment the next day to boot, so don't worry. I don't mean to boast (here it comes though), but I am in the top half of all of the Russian speaking volunteers who have come through the program and I achieved the required level of intermediate low – Romanian speakers are 'required' to reach intermediate mid, but many don't. There has actually never been a Russian speaker to reach intermediate mid during PST so, while I didn't break any records, it seems like I am in good company anyway, да?   With all this Russian though, and taking my 2 week break from blogging, I do feel that my English is suffering. I need to get back on the 'horse' which is my laptop and 'ride' it much more often (did that make sense?). I've also noticed – today mostly – that when I form sentences I often use odd sounding English because the phrase I am using is actually just a Russian phrase that I am used to saying… For example the word поэтаму means 'because of that,' in English. I would rarely or never use this phrase, but had to catch myself earlier on in this particular journal entry.   As I mentioned earlier, I am now at site! I arrived today (the 21st), a day late, because my family had an obligation near the Capitol. It was for this reason that I had another night of fun in Chisinau. Another volunteer had to stay behind with me and she and I wandered the city and eventually ate some pizza with Marion, whose site is Chisinau. The two of us also ran into some American travelers and hung out with them for a while. It is amazing how different I feel than non-Peace Corps people and, even though they may not have wanted to listen to us, it was great to explain what is going on in our lives to someone outside of the 'fish-bowl' (36 people living very similar lives can generate problems and there is never any real need to explain things to them because, they already know) The two had actually been

traveling the world for the past few months and had more time away from home under their belts, but I'm fairly convinced that 2 months here is more challenging in different ways (at least I feel more seasoned than them). This was also the first time someone needed me for my Russian skills – I had to figure out when they could get a bus to the Ukraine at the hotel desk. I realized though, while I was speaking to the concierge, that I speak very loudly and probably annoy people. But hey, Russian is fun to speak and it is a great language to get angry and argue in (Я не знаю, Я не знаю, ничего! Sing it: I don't know, I don't know, anything!), especially when you suffer from 'Loud Sam Disease' (very similar to another viral strain by the name of 'Loud and Obnoxious Michelle Disease,' though not as severe) and you don't have a firm grasp on the language...   Well, to the present we will fly...
The swearing-in ceremony would have been enjoyable if it weren't for the extreme-death-sweat heat. I was wearing a dark blue suit, sunglasses and a tie and I almost fainted. This was mostly because we were seated on a small set of stairs facing the sun while speaker after speaker got up to give their bit. At the very end, I gave my speech in Russian and it went rather well. My language trainer was present and I made a point to glance at her while I spoke to make sure I wasn't saying anything glaringly wrong. For a second – while on stage – I had thought I left out a whole line of the speech, because reading Cyrillic isn't quite like the Roman alphabet just yet. I didn't though, luckily, and everything went without much of a hitch. I was, however, interviewed *in Russian* by a Moldovan news team. This was difficult and at one point, the anchor basically told me to rattle off what I will be doing and where I will be living in Russian, which was easy. I can generally answer people and

speak well, but I have a difficult time comprehending things verbally.   I am at site now in Cearda Lunga and have been so for a few hours. It is hot outside and I am sitting on my floor because, as of yet, I do not have a desk. There are some interesting complications with my hosts. I don't think it is anything serious, but I am now living with the parents of my potential host family while they work on the small house that I could potentially live in. Apparently the guest house will be done in 2 months and, at that point, if I want to move into it, I have the option. But, if I feel like I am close to the family I am living with now and want to stay, that is on the table too. All of this was probably rather confusing, so call me if you need any clarification. I hope I'm not put in any awkward situations, but I'm sly and smooth and will grease the situation with my Russian prowess (and I'll get my partner teacher to translate). In any event – at the moment – I would like to live in the first house (where I thought I'd be) because it is a walk to school, not a bus ride, and it might be nice to have a little Casa Mica for myself. At the moment I actually have AC, which is very surprising. There is also a television in my room, which I'd like to avoid if at all possible. I don't need to get in the habit of watching animal planet and American DVD's everyday; it's not really why I decided to leave everything in my life behind for two years (what a whiner).   Well that is all I think, for the present. Your official – as of yesterday – Peace Corps volunteer is signing off for the day. Remember that I love you all and thank you for the support – even if the only form I can get is through peanut butter and coffee! It is amazing how fast the summer has gone by, but it left us all right on the cusp of the next 2 years (as of now we have 23 months left). I got so close with my Mama and Papa and Brother that it was very difficult to leave them in Ialoveni. Now I miss two families! I hope I can visit them and will make it a goal of mine – Виктор called me today making sure that everything was going ok for his little bro. Once life gets going here in my new town, I can only imagine that in a year I will be sitting here wondering where the time went, as I am doing now after a whole summer has passed me by – но, эта жинзь baby.   Your faces are all bouncing around in my head as I'm sure mine and my new mustache is sitting on your frontal lobes, waiting to come out in the form of rhapsodic waxing. Wax on, wax on people and, Ciao!

Random Things

2008-08-24

Hey everyone:

I happen to be at a cafe right now, so I thought I`d drop in for a bit...

My new site is craziness and I definitely miss the old family, but I`ll get accustomed, per usual. Michelle and Mom....My `gift` of language isn`t all too great now that I`m living with all Russian speakers! I feel like I don`t know anything! I want to thank all of you for reading and writing comments to me; they make me laugh and that is very important right now - lots of turmoil in life at the moment. (For instance, I may be moving to a new house that is closer to school; the walk right now is almost an hour, down a hill)

I am finally to the point where the weather here is worse than Phoenix, especially because I have to walk everywhere. There hasn`t been any recent rain, and I think there is less precipitation down here in the south. It is also warmer as a general rule. I live in a bigger town than Ialoveni, but it has less pavement. I visited the bazaar today and it was...interesting. What I thought was a fish out for sale was a skinned rabbit! Then there was the pigs head staring at me with blank eyes - the butcher was nice enough to stick the pig`s tail through a hole in its ear for the lucky purchaser.

Anyway, I`ll make this one short. I can`t put any photos on right now because a friend of mine has my camera at her site. I went to meet her in Cahul yesterday, but she forgot it. By the way, Cahul is beautiful and I`m going to try to get there for my birthday; I know a volunteer who entertains at her house quite frequently and some others are planning to meet up with us. I might get to cook some food and, of course, drink wine. Anyway, I`ll keep you all informed on everything and thanks again! I`ll add a link to Romanian TV where you should be able to see me...(I shaved the stash btw, so don`t worry)

Distantly yours,

Samuel

Hello Again!

2008-08-31

Today is Sunday and I popped in the check an Email while waiting for a potential family to have lunch with me. This new family is a bit closer to school and to my work life, so while I wait for my partner teacher to get in touch with me, I`ll fill you in on the weekend.

On Friday, the students came to the school and I met my 10th grade homeroom class; seemed like a good group of kids. On Saturday, I woke up at 4am to take a Rutiera to Chisinau to pick up a package(it turns out that only the poster has made it so far) and eat Mexican food. This day takes its toll on the wallet; I think I spent 300 lei on transportation and food. It was worth it though and my meat burrito with weird sweet "Mexican" salsa on top was delicious.

I managed to get home around eight and watched Hancock on my laptop. It was a relatively early night, but seeing as I had been up since four in the morning, it was quite a long day.

The `space` bar here is sticking badly, so I am going to make this blog very short. Next weekend, I am going to Cahul for the birthday - apparently Jennifer, who is the volunteer down in Cahul, has truffle butter. It should be fun and I will go into greater depth later on in the week. My first day of school is Monday as well, so I`ll try to keep the WWW updated about how that goes. Ciao, and talk to you soon.

AT SITE

September 9, 2008

You are all privileged to be reading the first official blog that has been posted on this website since it's author and subject moved to his semi-permanent (permanent is such an everlasting word – two years isn't permanence is it?) site; Ceadar-Lunga! From this day forward though, the aforementioned word will be referred to as Chatty or Chaddy or Chatty-Loooonnga or something similar. Maybe even Chat-man-do, if I'm feeling adventurous.

I want to begin by saying thank you to my family – you guys make life sticky with peanut butter, spicy with hot-sauce and properly hydrated with electrolyte rich Gatorade (not to mention beautiful with artwork, warm with down jackets, etc...) – and my friends for recognizing that I had a birthday last week. I would also like to congratulate Grandma Kate for sharing my birthday; it was great to hear from her when she called. The 10th of September also happens to be my good friend Steve Chard's birthday and – while this has been an on-going battle since the fourth grade at Orangewood Elementary School – I would like to point out that I am still 5 days older than you are Steve. Thanks for everyone who called me and yes Mom and Dad, I forgive you for waking me up at four in the morning because you can't do math. Thank you to Michelle for not only giving me birthday wishes, but assuring me that being tall isn't everything (that one is inside, joke-wise) and of course, thank you to William and Charles for choosing to call me while either at or on the way to a party; part of me can't help but miss the college days boys. Finally, thanks to Grandma Arline, the Herrings and the Sherrick's for the money and thoughts.

Now that I have finished thanking everyone I can for making me feel like a birthday is still a birthday (if I forgot anyone I am truly sorry), I will move onto my life at the moment.

I moved down to Chatty in late August, but was living with another family. Certain things, including distance from the school where I teach, caused problems and I now live in another house with a fantastic family. The father is away three or four days at time and home three or four days at a time. There are two hilarious daughters in the third and eighth grade. The eighth-grader is actually in one of my classes, which is fun and now I have the protection of a 12 year-old girl when I walk home from work. Mama Ninka is funny and smiling most of the time – she even cooks food in a Wok…

Since we're on to school, I will explain what I can about the first week and a half I've had at work. It has been tumultuous and random. There is still no set schedule and

– per PC rules – we are all team teaching in the class room but, my main partner is out for a few weeks while her broken arm heals, so I have been solo-teaching many of the classes. I have three English teachers that I work with though, and I have been teaching with two of them every day. The solo classes are challenging but fun, as I have to explain grammar as best I can in Russian – which isn't great. The team-taught classes are good too, but can be frustrating because my partners often resort to Russian, which is difficult for me as it makes me feel somewhat worthless as a teacher, at times. That being said, I definitely contribute a great deal in pronunciation and a reference for the teachers who are unsure on some English rules and phrases. This doesn't always help though, as the books are written from a British perspective and certain phrases just don't add up – for example, during a grammar exercise, the books says that a person will "make a report (as in for homework)," but if I were to use the phrase I would say something along the lines of, "I'm going to go home and do a report/do my report." Not too huge of a problem, but new and strange anyway; it is not like the English teachers here have enough English to understand every little quirk about the language. So, I have been working everyday and getting tutored by a – wait for it! – Russian speaking-only woman two days per week. As you can imagine, this is difficult and mentally taxing but, I hope the beating my brain takes on Tuesdays and Thursdays will pay off. I am now re-learning the grammar rules (things such as dative, accusative, etc.) in Russian instead of English and I trust that this dive into the deep-end will pay off – you know how it goes, I'll either die or learn to swim…

This weekend was my birthday and I had a great time. The birthday started at school on Friday, where the director and teachers held a small party for me with cake and wine (at 11:00 a.m.). The director gave me a desk lamp, which was actually perfect, because I need a reading light. My partner gave me chocolates and so did my sixth grade class. Two girls in my eighth grade class also gave me a card in Russian! I have to say, it is the first birthday card I have ever received/seen in Russian.

Some friends and I stayed with a volunteer in Cahul, made food and drank lots of good wine. I actually found a brand of wine that I really like and will share it with everyone when I can (and when I remember the name). The fare included your basic Northern Italian: lasagna for lunch (there is a very comparable Ricotta in this country, not to mention eggplant, tomato and mushroom), and for anti-Pasto/dinner, crustinis with various mushroom and truffle pasties, fried rice cakes and pasta with an eggplant, tomato, onion cream sauce. As I said the wine was a-flow and your birthday boy made it to bed at a very early hour!

A very notable gift that I received (very thoughtful because I had mentioned buying it for myself earlier) was from Marion, a fellow volunteer. It is a copy of Harry Potter, in Russian (Garri Potter i filosofskii kamen)!

It is awesome for me to read through (it's gonna take me like two years anyway) because I recognize all of the names and I know the story well, if not embarrassingly well. It is now the book I bring in to tutoring sessions to read aloud.

As I am writing on this Tuesday afternoon in September, there is a small animal making very upsetting noises out my window; be it a pig or dog, complaining or actively dying, I am not sure. It is strange to be at my site because there was a great deal of build-up in us all moving apart and starting the *actual* volunteering that we came for. I'm not sure if the real challenge is yet to come or not; we'll see I guess. I do know that now that it is official and I have started the work which will keep me busy for the next two years, my goals and 'check-points,' if you will, are stretched-out over longer periods of time. Where it was the end of PST that I was looking forward to, or the fourth of July party, it is now the end of lock-down (the period where we cannot travel or spend the night out of site) on November 20th and my sister's wedding which I am looking forward to. I am also ambivalently looking forward for the winter to come whistling into Moldova, as I have never spent more than a week living in the cold. I have been told it is the hardest time though; it is dark a lot and you never really warm up. Today may mark then end of summer in a way, because there were some clouds and it was actually pleasant outside all day. We experienced a similar weather shift two weeks ago though, and the temperature climbed right back up on us (I've got a good feeling this time around…). When winter does descend like the dark and dreary nightmare that it is, and you don't hear from me in months it is because I have succumbed to the phantom of the cold wet clouds. If I may quote Kurt Russell in closing, from his finest film, "Captain Ron:" "He's going storm crazy, I've seen it before! Hold his tongue!"

If you have made it this far, you deserve to be the recipient of my heart-felt thanks and admiration for making it through this addition. I hope everything was written coherently but with enough bounce to keep you interested

– also with enough gravitas and weightiness to keep from sounding too cheesy. And, as usual, if you have questions, post them up on the message board (but somebody remind Brian that it is a public message board).

Photos

2008-09-12

This is a mini blog to signify the new photos I added (it's over now(the blog, that is)).

I would also like to point out that this site adds lots of weird characters and things when I copy and paste (I noticed that the Russian didn`t translate this time). It also adds words like helllip etc. which don`t actually mean anything.

THE NEXT ONE

September 16, 2008

I would like to begin this entry by apologizing for whatever program is causing my writing to be skewed into words like "hellip" and turned into smiley faces; I have a feeling this same program is turning my Russian characters into gobble-dee gook as well. I *also* have a feeling that somewhere between me copying from word pad and pasting onto the website, microscopic computer organisms, shaped like cork-screws are burrowing their way through various print and shaping them into their own incoherent creations. Once again, I apologize from the depths of my apology-well. In any event!   School this week has been up and down and the language barrier has its own sinister way of causing me frustration and confusion. I taught two classes on Monday and was supposed to teach none today, but I received a phone call last night that I would be teaching the 12th grade the next day. Unfortunately, it has been raining profusely and first period was cancelled. This cancellation didn't rule out my class, but as a result, only four kids showed up for school. Needless to say, not a lot happened as I felt it necessary to wait for the other 12 students to be present to move on with the lesson (I use the phrase 'move on' loosely, because it was the first time I had taught the class). The day wasn't without its small victories though, because yesterday (this may be why I received the last minute phone call) I told the Director of the school that I wasn't getting many classes to teach and that I was living in Moldova and working in the school to teach. As a result – maybe – I am teaching five classes tomorrow. Now I am hoping they didn't take me too seriously, because while it is important to feel useful at your place of work, you will end up kicking yourself for becoming too useful, if you catch my meaning. I think the proverb of the day is: "When a request is made out of self-vindication, the requester will undoubtedly be left with more than he bargained for and, as a result, will regret his request, which was made out of his insecurities in the first place." (You've heard that proverb right?)   Life will go on and we'll see how tomorrow goes. I am teaching the same class that I taught today and so I didn't really have to plan anything additional because there will be 12 new students in class. As far as the school as a work place though, it is very difficult for me to find my 'niche,' if you will. As of now, I am still teaching most of my classes without my partner, because she has been out for three weeks with a broken arm (sounds like teaching is a contact sport or something, eh?). She and I actually have a classroom, and I even have a key for it, but it seems to be in use most of the time. This is somewhat irksome because another one of my partners also has a classroom and she seems to get to use her classroom for all of her lessons – I tend to ping-pong around the school all-day. I have found a room where some of the teachers hang-out where I can sit, read, write, study and generally relax but, on occasion, the room is locked, leaving me in search of an empty room to utilize. I also frequent the director's office because she has DSL. In fact, I will probably be using her computer to load this very blog onto the World Wide Web. As far as day-to-day food consumption is going down here in Chatty, I tend to eat foods similar to those in Ialoveni, but different in some respects. The fried meat patties called 'Culetta' are different in that they tend to have less eggy breading and their 'patty' shape tends to be more of a 'ball' shape. During my first night in my new house, we ate what actually resembled fried rice and sautéed vegetables with chicken. My house Mom actually has a wok that she uses ('used' may be a better term, as in once) which I believe was purchased in Jolly 'Old England. Woks and other goods that can be found in England can also be found in our house, because the father of the family flies to London and drives cars to Odessa, for work. Apparently the cars

are pieced out once they reach the Ukraine and he takes a
bus back to Moldova. It is not uncommon to find Tesco
products, Toblerone and Capri-sun in the house, as a result.
Another wonderful food that we tend to eat here is called
"ãðè÷êà" (greeshka). It is essentially rolled oats with pieces
of carrot, chicken stock (I think) and other miscellaneous
vegetables. It is the kind of food you can't really stop
eating, if you try – it is somewhat dangerous really. I'm not
sure if it is this time of year either, but this will be served
tomorrow…

September 17, 2008   …because during lent, those
who observe cannot eat meat. It turns out that ïñò is short
for "ïñòíûé,"the former standing for 'post' or 'observation
post' and the latter meaning "Lenten." I don't know a
whole lot about lent, but it seems to be falling every
Wednesday evening in our family, as we eat sausage for
breakfast, but eat no meat-products after lunch-time.
Tonight's dinner, in fact, consisted of greeshka, canned egg
plant and garlic and stewed squash. This may sound like a
small child's worst nightmare, but I'm not a small child and
it was one of the most enjoyable meals I've had in
Moldova. The southern area of the country is also famous
for its spicy Dijon-style mustard and it goes great with the
greeshka . Other fairly common-place foods are: salami
(prolific amounts of visible fat), cold sausage, boiled-eggs,
bread, butter, brinza-style cheese, canned vegetables, fresh
vegetables (it is getting towards the season where these are
going to be a luxury), Nutella (thanks to England),
meat/vegetable/mayonnaise/egg salads, soups, etc. I am
fortunate enough to eat bananas as well, which can be
purchased at the market *and,* oddly enough, cocoanut. I'm
not sure if this milk filled imitation of a bowling ball is
bought here or brought home from England, though.

Seeing as I did drag you into a new day of my life, I'll go into how school went today, and what I am in store for tomorrow.   School went great today. For the first time, I had a full day of classes and I was allowed to use *my* room and sit there during breaks reading *The Call of the Wild*. I think the reason why I wasn't really grounded in the room was because the school administration wasn't sure whether I was going to be taking all of my partner's classes while she was out. I am going to be taking the classes and, now that they are wise to this concept, I seem to be teaching more. Tomorrow, in fact, I have six classes and a free-day Friday. I'm under the impression that this is going to mirror a normal week for me: Full-days Monday through Thursday and an off-day on Fridays. My partner even suggested that my 'planning day' be on a Friday, allowing me an extra day for traveling, which is common among volunteers (traveling in country, when out of lock-down). Some of you – mom – may be interested in my lunch today too – I found it rather amusing at least. I made myself a peanut butter and banana sandwich and packed it with an apple. When lunch rolled around I ate these and purchased a áûёё÷êà (boo-leech-ka), which is a sweet roll, stuffed with òâîðîðîã (tvorog) and a Joy's Cola (coke is too expensive). This may not amuse you all but it was a very odd, yet tasty, assortment of food. On normal days, I walk across the street to the corner store where they make sandwiches of bologna and ketchup for 50 cents, so understand that as mundane as banana and peanut butter sounds, it is quite a delicacy! Also, keep in mind, that in the United States, a common work-lunch for me was usually a sandwich consisting of turkey or ham with lettuce, tomato, mayo, mustard and cheese with a Squirt a bag of Sun Chips and some skittles (if I was in the 'taste the rainbow' mood). I will leave you with a quote which, in no-way applies to me (or you, I hope), but is worth reading, none-the-less. It floated from the pages of *The Call of the Wild* today and wedged itself somewhere in the creases of my frontal-lobe: "The two mongrels were without spirit at all; bones were the only things breakable about them." --Jack London

September 23, 2008

There is one thing that I realized today: it is possible to make excellent pizza in Moldova. In fact, I will go so far as to say that the pizza I made today was better than ANY pizza I have eaten in this country. Although you may have no interest in food, food preparation, or what I eat in this country, I could care less. I plan on going into extreme detail as to what led up-to and transpired surrounding the creation of this magnificent cheese-covered, disc-of-dough. Nick herring if you are reading, I think I may have finally one-upped your famous, double-decker, "Pizza-Pie." Here is how: On Saturday, I went to Chisinau and did the usual; drank beer, saw friends and yes, ate pizza. The week before though, I had promised my house mom Nina that I would be making my own pizza at some point. After days of me proclaiming, "Tomorrow I will make pizza!" she started to nod her head in sympathy; she felt that I had obviously started to lose my mind.   Well I made it home from Chisinau in one piece. The pizza wasn't great, as usual, but at this point it does the trick for all of us. I went for a run Sunday, taught Monday, went for another run Monday night and decided – while reading a novel in bed – that Tuesday was the day that I would be making my pizza. I taught Tuesday and then walked to the center of town where I pulled some cash out of the ATM and purchased yeast; the missing ingredient... I arrived home and began making dough. The recipe I have calls for dry yeast and I had wet yeast – it didn't matter, nothing was going to stop me. I boiled water and let it cool. I added yeast, I added sugar, I added oil and I added flour. I started mixing and realized that I didn't have enough flour! I screamed into the house, aiming my desperation at my host sister Valeria: She got the idea and sprinted to the garage, producing another bag of flour for me; she could tell the pizza was going to be a hit. I dumped the dough out onto the counter, applying flour to my hands to keep from creating a fantastic mess. It didn't matter: a mess was made and it was glorious. I placed the dough-ball in a greased crock pot and put it in the girls' bedroom; they have a heat lamp which was necessary to help my baby-ball incubate and expand. Then it was onto the sauce. I cut up tomatoes, garlic and onion. I sautéed said vegetables, added sugar, salt, pepper and a dash of cayenne and let it simmer. When all was said and done, prepped and waiting to be splayed out, sauced, cheesed and baked, I walked back to my room, in the hopes of getting some work done. After twenty minutes of doing nothing but obsessing about how everything would make more sense if I went for a run, I went for a run. When I got back, I began typing up a test which will be administered on Friday, saved the file, opened a tall bottle of beer and walked back out to conquer the crust. I spread the dough thin, grated cheese, cut peppers, cut sausage and cut onions. I slathered the sauce on (thin enough to make the cooks at Pizzeria Buffato proud) and dumped on the toppings. It was a beautiful site. While all this was going on, I had the presence of mind to make bread sticks with the excess dough – while the pizza preparation was taking place, the sticks were turning a golden brown in the oven. When they were done, I pulled the sticks out and slid the pizza in; it was a perfect fit. I ran to the shower to wash off my post-run grime and dried off quickly enough to leave my cheeks rosy and my hair wet. I made my way to the kitchen and pulled out what can only be described as: Pure Joy. I ate far too much pizza. I topped it with hot-sauce, sour- cream and excess tomato sauce. I even tried to make my own ranch with the aforementioned sour-cream, pepper and salt. In true pizza form, my house mom and I split another beer with the gorge and by the end of it, I could barely get up from the table – but I had a huge smile on my face. The pizza was good. It was actually *really* good. I didn't have any measuring spoons or cups and I didn't have mozzarella (the hard cheese we have is basically pizza mozzarella anyway). I didn't have basil or a wood burning oven but, my house mom said from then on, I had to make pizza every week. I took the compliment in stride, but it was more important to me that I truly felt it was one of the best homemade pizzas I have ever eaten. Next time I suggest that all of you out there make your own sauce from tomato, onion, salt, pepper, red-wine, sugar and garlic. That's it. I hope you enjoy the photos I posted and if you don't like reading about food (Brian Gavan) I'm sorry you had to go through this with me. It was cathartic, in any event… I realized while I was eating though, that maybe making familiar foods isn't great to do all the time. I couldn't help but think about the family pizza-making sessions we used to have at home with the Craig's and Brian and Ted. But, considering these little parties took place no more than twice or thrice per year, I can't say that I can justify terminating my service early on their behalf. Just promise we'll eat some pizza at Michelle's wedding. Ciao. (On a side note: the fountain I am posing in front with Morgan is outside of the train station in Chisinau. If you are surprised at how pretty everything is, I was too. It looks like a tiny little slice of Italy. Also, we are drinking beer at an establishment by the name of "Beer Haus," which brews their own fairly decent ales. Unfortunately, they are around $4.50 each, which is way out of my budget. The children sitting in the class-room are my 8th grade boys; they look a lot nicer than they are... I am sitting at my desk in room number five, which Sylvia – my partner – and I share (Granted, she has been out since the beginning of the year with a broken arm so, I guess it is *my* room at the moment. I will, in fact, be teaching six classes in it tomorrow.) Finally, the dog in the photo is "Taki," my house-dog, and the girl he is chasing is Valeria, the youngest sister.) (I am also including the dictionary I made for myself; if any of you ever decide to learn the Russian alphabet to the point where you can sound letters out, you can go impress your friends.)

September 29, 2008

It's about that time for a recap, now isn't it? Well, I'll do my best.

Last weekend turned out to be quite an experience for your 24 year-old volunteer, as he participated in the tried-and-true practice of picking grapes at a near-by village to help aid another time-honored practice; making house-wine. This dark-red and – sometimes - delicious drink is, without a doubt, the national past-time and beverage of Moldova *and* Gagauzia. You may question why I would add this small region of such a small country in my description but, remember that the aforementioned autonomy prefers to be considered…autonomous! Most products and traditions are either referenced as Bulgarian, Turkish or Gaugauzian around these parts – the nick-name for wine, in fact, is 'Gaugauzian Chai' (chai is the Russian word for tea). Interestingly enough, I read in Newsweek that around 4 percent of Moldova identifies as former-Soviet but, this is only in reference to the region to the east, Transnistria. Russian is the spoken language where I am from but, it is not uncommon to hear Turkish and Bulgarian being spoken, especially in outlying villages.

Speaking of outlying villages, I picked grapes on Saturday in Òâàðäèöà ('tvar – deet – sa') and one of the most common languages spoken in this village is Bulgarian. There is a volunteer living in the village right now, but she will be leaving for the United States – having completed her service – soon. She mentioned that, when she moved into the house, her – at the time – three year-old house brother didn't know a lick of Russian; he only spoke Bulgarian. Two years later, thanks to her, he now speaks very fluently – don't expect *fluency* out of me though; you know kids are like little sponges.

The grape picking started off with a bang Saturday morning and I was greeted with the site of two gutted, hanging goats within the gates of her house. I was lucky enough to catch her host-brother pulling the stomach of the second unlucky animal; what a site to see that was. After posing next to said carcasses, we made our way to the grape fields where we did a whopping two hours of work, covering about two rows of grapes each. The method was to go in pairs, fill-up buckets and dump the buckets into larger plastic bags, which were then hauled up a hill into the animal-pen and wine-making area. The house was pretty incredible: there were cages full of pigs, chickens and geese and a large storage area for hay-bales. Towards the rear and around the corner was the cellar for the wine barrels and preserved foods (I actually discovered a similar cellar in my house yesterday and, while my family doesn't make wine, they preserve lots of meats and vegetables for the winter.). After grapes are harvested, they are placed into some sort of grinding mechanism, which churns them through and spills their contents into a trough, of sorts and drains into a bucket. The mashed grapes are then put into a second trough, where what remains of their juices spill out into a second bucket. These sufficiently drained grape-skins are then put into a 40 year-old wine press, where they are squeezed until nothing is left but dirt, skin and stems. I was lucky enough to taste the juice as it came out of the presses and, despite the fact the grapes were not cleaned before going into the contraption, the juice was delicious. It basically tasted like you were eating grapes, sans-skin. That being said, there was also a bit of an earthy-taste to the juice – no doubt from the dirt which clearly attached itself to many of the grapes.

After witnessing the process, we were all treated to a big dinner, served with grape juice and a neighbor's 'young' wine. Everything was delicious and, that was that.

On Sunday, I didn't do a whole lot except go for a run and lay around. Unfortunately, I had started to get ill on Friday and by Monday the feeling seemed to be returning with a bit more of a vengeance. My stomach has felt odd for a few days and I am feeling some 'flu-ish' symptoms. I have decided to lay off of the running until Wednesday (tomorrow), even though this is difficult to do with my obsessive mentality about running and, well, everything.

That has been about it as of late, with the exception of a few odds and ends I feel I need to mention:

Apparently you can purchase full Moldova track suits (I believe they are black) in Chisinau *with* stenciling for around 600 lei in Chisinau. I feel this is a purchase I will have to make in the next few weeks; how could I give up a chance like this in good conscience? Not only would the track suit be great to wear around the house, I wouldn't have to buy any more sweat-pants for running in the cold weather (that being said, some cold-weather running gear would be a great present to send me for Christmas or Halloween or...).

October 12th is 'wine-fest' in Chisinau and many of us are going to be using a night out of site to partake in the merriment. Pray for sunny weather and pray no one spills wine on my camera.

Patrick, Mike D. and I have decided to fly to Turkey over the winter holidays. This decision was made not two days ago and, at the moment, I am rather excited. Everyone loves planning for trips. As of now, I think we'll (I haven't actually discussed this with my travel-mates) spend Christmas Eve in Chisinau, hopefully eating at a decent restaurant and drinking some eggnog-brandies and fly out on the 25th or 26th. Plane fare is actually pretty cheap and the ultimate goal is to spend New Year's in Istanbul. This week and the next will be devoted to internet research on hostels and spots to travel to. I am hoping that most lodging does not require some sort of reservation because I don't feel like being the person who has to deal with using a credit card online, more than is necessary (I am the only one of the three of us with access to high-speed internet). If any of you people back in the states would like to accompany us, feel free to let me know (shot in the dark?)

I discovered the 'American Corner' at the Chat-man-do public library yesterday, which was interesting. It is a small section of a small library devoted to THE UNITED STATES OF AMERICA. There are old newspapers, books, and a row of computers *with* internet; the internet is free as well as long as you are …ahem… American. I ended up spending three hours at a computer yesterday and was forcefully removed from my seat as the librarian attempted to go home to feed her children (she was actually very polite and I kept saying 'ten more minutes' until I racked up around thirty). I was trying to Email my program coordinator when the internet went up and died on my computer. I had to save a rather large WORD document on my flash-drive, upload it onto another computer and then send the message. It turns out that I was asked to do some documentation a little while back that I somehow missed looking at in my inbox…oops.

That is it for now.

There is a screaming child outside my window. He/she has been screaming off and on for three hours. Taking this into account, I will leave you with a quote from The Bible:

"When he hath tried me, I shall come forth as gold."

-Job

and another from *Breakfast of Champions (Good-bye Blue Monday)* by, Kurt Vonnegut Jr.:

"Trout did not expect to be believed. He put the bad ideas into a science-fiction novel, and that was where Dwayne found them. The book wasn't addressed to Dwayne alone. Trout had never heard of Dwayne when he wrote it. It was addressed to anybody who happened to open it up. It said to simply anybody, in effect – "Hey – guess what: You're the only creature with free will. How does that make you feel?" And so on.

It was a *tour de force*. It was a *jeu d'esprit*.

But it was mind poison to Dwayne."

Last week

October 8, 2008   I actually have a few interesting occurrences to report this week; some including wine-drinking at school and some including large dogs performing a 'bladder-check' on me (e.g. they made me pee my pants).   Friday was teacher's day at school and it began with a ceremony involving dancing, singing and speeches. The singing portion was, borderline, hilarious at times – to me, being from a different culture? – because the students (mostly boys) covered popular pop tunes - solo. They performed faithful covers to the 'T,' even going so far as to whisper at the end of the song, when needed (for instance, "I love you," but whispered in a really creepy Justin Timberlake voice).   The fun sections of the ceremony were those including traditional Bulgarian dancing; the tenth grade girls were pretty good and were fun to watch. By far though, the most impressive part of the entire morning was when the sound system cut out and the vice-director promptly pulled out her *accordion* and fired-off startlingly exact renditions of certain songs. Every grade had to perform in some way, and many stood up as a class and sung traditional Russian folk songs, with accordion accompaniment.   After the ceremony, the whole school walked to the nearest park for the 'health' section of the day. This consisted of every grade competing against each other in a 500 meter run. The lower classes competed in games of soccer (as it turns out, everyone is better at soccer here than you, Charlie…), which was hilarious to watch, especially when pint size footballers got into pint-sized rows. The 6th vs. 7thgrade match got heated at one point during a shootout, and I was worried little 7 ounce punches were going to be thrown.   Following Moldovan field day was a party for the teachers. We all retired to the school house where we feasted on traditional food and wine. I, not surprisingly, ate so much that I had trouble standing up... The food, if not astounding, was familiar and the wine – being homemade – was actually very good. The physical education teachers tried their hardest to get me to stay and finish off the jugs but, I showed restraint and made my way home. On Saturday morning, I took a bus to Chisinau to what I thought was a seminar on how to organize secondary activities in our respective communities. It turned out that it was a sort of game day, where we went to a spot by a lake and were taught how to administer group-building games. The games were fun, but we all knew most of them. I wouldn't say it was a wasted trip (mostly because the lake where the session was conducted was on a neat little lake – there are camp sites and spots to bbq right on it as well – where I am dead-set on going someday to have an overnight lake/bbq event) but, it was unnecessary. I will be going to Chisinau again this weekend though, for WINE FEST! After the day at the lake, I took a bus home and walked to my site-mate's apartment. She had invited me to a 'party' she was having. This involved a very tasty soup she had cooked, another volunteer from Comrat and...wait for it...Turkish truck drivers whom she met through God knows what network. They were fairly pleasant fellows though, – despite the fact that only one of the bunch spoke English – and when I became tired of sitting and watching them eat, I retired to the kitchen to eat ice cream. Sunday was a normal day, with one exception: I discovered an amazing new running path. If you leave the house from the opposite direction of town and take a left, you end up on a tree-lined dirt road in the middle of (what appears to be) nowhere. It is pretty amazing. I'm not very used to sparsely populated farming areas that look a little bit like English countryside, but I am now. During the run I only encountered two houses and they reminded me of some story by Dickens, where the main character has to take a carriage to a secluded farm-house to meet with an old alchemist (I may have mixed a few genres there). As soon as I can, I will go for a walk and take some pictures. On Tuesday, after a heavy rain that began right after my run on Sunday, I did the route again; this time even farther, clocking in at an hour. On my return journey, I was accosted by three gigantic dogs. If you have ever read "The Call of the Wild" or "White Fang," then you might have an idea as to what these animals reminded me of. They were roughly my size (or would have been if their owners fed them) and ran up to me barking, drooling and performing other panic-inducing actions. I could see their ribs, they looked rabid and the owners were 100 yards off sitting on donkeys, waving their hands at me. At one point I literally had my arms wrapped around a near-by tree, waiting for my cue to start climbing. I waved my arms around like a fool and screamed in Russ-English until one gentleman rode up on his donkey and told me to keep walking – they weren't going to hurt me. In any event, they *didn't* hurt me, but before the donkey-man came to help me out, there was no way I was going to turn my back on the vicious beasts. The rest of the week has been somewhat boring. But, other newsworthy items are: My partner teacher is back. She has taking over the classes I was covering and I finally have a schedule that doesn't shift day-to-day (maybe). Apparently my pizza was good, because my host mom requested that I cook it on Thursday. My hair is getting long again. That's it! ποκα

NEWS

2008-10-17

Hello, I have some fairly relevant news to impart unto all of my dear reader(s).

The Tucson Citizen (a paper I interned at in Tucson, AZ - the Sherricks and the Scheurichs might be familiar) has expressed interest in me blogging for them. If this goes through, I may abandon this blog and write only for the Citizen, given my internet and time constraints (I'm a busy guy! I'm like Bruce Wayne here in Moldova!)

The new format would be 4 blogs a week with some photos and blogs would only run about 400 words, every entry. Hopefully I either find a humorous niche, or interesting things start happening here...laughter...

I hope it works out and when I begin writing, I will provide a link! There is a chance my family will be getting DSL at the house as well, which is disconcerting because I will probably start playing WOW again - Mom, freeze my credit card. ποκα

A bit of a weekly update

2008-10-21

I don't have a lot of new information to dump on to you all at the moment, but I'll give you what I can:

Last week was fairly routine, with the exception of Friday at school, when the upper classes taught - at least it was a great way to get out of doing any real work on Friday. (For the last two Fridays, at least, the school has found some way of getting out of any kind of work...I love it. Last Friday was "teachers day." I can`t wait to see what will happen on Friday`s to come.) The students only acted as teacher for the first four periods of the day and then they were analyzed by the staff on their performance. During this hour, I was not present but, I came back to the school because there was a mini-market/fair held in the front of the school - which was amusing. I ended up leaving with a big bag of walnuts (unshelled) and 15 lei less than I had at the start of the day.

On Friday night, I played basketball with a student and his friends at a nearby school. His `friends` turned out to be two other kids his age and five other full-blown adults who were - just like my student and his friends - fairly talented at the game; a skill I am severely lacking. We played a 100 point game - I was ready for dinner by 50 but, I agreed to play and I couldn`t think of any suitable excuse in Russian, so I stuck it out...

On Saturday morning I went for a run and was, again, chased down the road by a pack of huge dogs. This time there was no farmer to tell me they were not going to bite me, so I assumed they were primed to attack. I ran into the woods and they seemed to back off a bit. When I got back onto the road, however, they resumed their pursuit, making me wish I had a safer hobby. The worst part was running away - quickly - and hearing their barks get louder and louder as they gained on me. The trio abated eventually, leaving me with a racing heart, jello legs and another two miles to cover. I can only liken it to getting a shot of adrenalin and then continuing to run after the euphoria wears off.

Later that day, I went to my tutoring lesson which was actually very enjoyable. I explained my running predicament as well as I could in Russian and even managed to crack a joke about my legs feeling like macaroni after the fright I had with Hitler and his two brothers.

Saturday night came and went with some Cricova cabernet and the film "Babel." The wine was actually fairly good, as was the movie. I managed to get a full night's sleep and wake up around 7 a.m., a good two hours before the rest of the family so...I: drank coffee and finished "Mr. Norrell and Johnathan Strange" (thanks for the book Michelle), went for a walk and took some photos of ravens (if you`ve read said novel, you would know why) and waited around until ten, when my sisters wandered outside. I had mentioned `omelet's the night before so, upon waking, they requested these French cheese-filled egg packets for breakfast and I obliged - making sure to make mine with tomato *and* cheese (gotta one-up everyone). The omelet's were good.

The weather has been beautiful, as of late, which I am pretty happy about. We went through almost a month of off and on rain and clouds but, the past two weeks or so have been sunny and cool. It is perfect weather to run and be outside and it nice because, unlike Phoenix, I get to wear a sweatshirt on a sunny day. I was running today in a sleeveless shirt and wondering when the big-bad winter will descend upon our country; needless to say, I am not looking forward to the day. As of now though, it is a chilly, sweater-wearing, see-your-breath walk to school in the morning, and a pleasant walk home. The distance is great enough though, that I end up feeling pretty warm by the time I reach the high school.

That`s all for now. Пока! (I will update you on the Citizen blog when I get an update)

Photos and such

2008-10-27

Hello everyone. I decided to walk around the area where I go for runs last Saturday and take some stills. I tried to take a video and post it, but apparently videos have to be under 10 MB and somehow the video I filmed was 101 MB...go figure.

Anyway, the roads I photographed are of where I run around. They should be in a logical order to explain my route but, as you have never been here, it won`t make too much sense, I imagine.

This weekend was borrrring. I watched "Big Trouble in Little China" though, which was strange and humorous. I also discovered that I am a Zen master and my Zen involves listening to Pink Floyd and playing solitaire. It might help that I have had a terrible head cold for a week.

It is turning me into a philosopher. Anyway, I'll try to write more later this week. Hopefully my section on the Tucson Citizen will be up some time. The next couple weeks should be pretty interesting, but I'll explain later. ποκα

November 9th

Last week was very long and fun. We had an in-service-training last week in Chisinau and spent our 9 hour days sitting through seminars and our nights eating-out and going to bars. I have to admit it was enjoyable and none of us were used to the faster pace that it offered. Needless to say, the week flew by...

School has been going well, but I am struggling to begin clubs and activities outside of class. As of now, the first English club meeting will be Friday the 14th – if anyone is interested – and it should be enlightening to see who shows. I was working on getting a group of boys together to play some rugby but, it doesn't seem to be working out; I will keep on it though and see what happens.

As far as personal interests go, I have been upping my distance on runs (I measure this with time, because there is no way to get a concrete distance), the furthest lasting one hour and 17 minutes. I also have two more running stories to share: both took place while I was running near the fields in the valley behind my house. The first instance was over a week ago when I took off for a run in an absolutely blind fog. I could not see more than 100 yards in front of me and almost got lost at one point because I took a wrong turn! I managed to run to the top of a distant, leg-killing, hill and – it must have been some trick of the fog I am unaware of – when I reached the top, the sun suddenly broke through and the air temperature rose 10 degrees. It was an eerie feeling. After a stop and a stretch I descended back down into the thicker and colder fog which was lining the "valley" (using this word stretches its meaning). I was literally standing on top of the hill looking at a sort of soup bowl that I had to run down through. If this wasn`t weird enough, as I made my way home, I heard Mussolini and his cronies (the dogs) barking in the distance and spent about 20 minutes expecting to see three large hounds break through the fog and go for my throat with their mighty maws. Luckily they had as little visibility as I had and the only sign of them came through as – literally – white noise.

The second story took place yesterday when I ran the same route in a rather strong wind. This too, was an odd feeling because I couldn`t hear anything except the wind in my ears – a disconcerting feeling because cars and motorcycles frequent my favorite back-country road. A little while into the run, two boys rode up next to me on their motor scooter and promptly began to laugh and point at the weird guy in blue running shorts and a wind-breaker. I began speaking with them though, and I found out they went to Turkish school in the center of town (promptly explaining that I knew the director of the school in case the boys decided to get shifty on me). They ended up pacing me for 20 minutes or so and it afforded me the chance to practice my Russian and gave me some sort of company. I didn`t run out of breath speaking either which is a good sign, eh? Whenever people ask why I am doing something as stupid as running for an extended period of time, I now explain that I plan on running a marathon next year. This is a generally accepted response (my only subjects have been 5 drunk neighbors, a goat-herder and two seventh grade boys, so far) and now I have to run a marathon because nobody likes a liar.

That being said, I do plan on running Athens marathon next year and, while training this early may not be necessary, I enjoy running and I can keep up a base right?

Finally, among my random thoughts and events yet to come:

1. I swear, I was asked to blog for the citizen, and am waiting on a response from the editor. In fact, as I post this very blog, I am simultaneously writing an Email to the online editor politely asking, "what is going on?"

2. The photos I am posting are from the week in Chisinau and other random images I chose to capture.

3. I learned last night that what I thought was the word for `disgusting` in Turkish was actually what the next-door-neighbors` baby says when he doesn`t like food. I found this out because I was explaining to my family and my neighbors that I knew the word for `dog,` `disgusting,` `I` and `hello.` It turns out that I only know three words in Turkish...

4. In a couple weeks, we will all be off `lock-down;` a term used to explain the first 90 days of service, where volunteers have to spend every night at site. After lock-down ends, we are allowed to wander the country like hobos whenever we want on a whim (just kidding). Some of us ate at a very nice restaurant in Chisinau during the

week and the plan is to celebrate this momentous occasion is to make a big group reservation at said eating establishment.

5. Two more volunteers have decided to terminate their service early. If my math is correct, we started out with 38 and have so far lost 7 or 8, including the married couple. It is very difficult to predict who is going to take-off and it is very different from group to group. For instance, the M19`s, who just completed service only lost one or two members. On that note, I made a few friends in this group and it is too bad they left right as I began my service. One of the volunteers actually lived about 15 minutes from me, and her family loved to have volunteers stay at the house. Said volunteer bequeathed Cool Hand Luke to me, so at least I scored some treasure. "WHAT WE HAVE HERE IS A FAILURE TO COMMUNICATE," as it were.

That's all for now, except for a quote that I included in the mass Email I sent to all of the M23`s about the party we will be having for the end of lock-down. It was greeted with a mixed response because I explained that the author was the official author of our group. Some agreed and others explained to me, in so many words, that said author is something along the lines of a `pompous wind-bag.` So much for world peace and acceptance I guess...

"`There are things that I like,` Amanda exclaimed upon awakening from her first long trance. `These are: the butterfly, the cactus and the infinite Good."

Later, she amended the list to include mushrooms and motorcycles.

While strolling through her cactus gardens one warmish June morning, Amanda came upon an old Navajo man painting pictures in the sand.

`What is the function of the artist?` Amanda demanded of the talented trespasser.

`The function of the artist,` the Navajo answered, `is to provide what life does not.`"

-Tom Robbins-

November 15

Three three-inch-long centipede extracted itself from the floppy fringe of the throw carpet and began to make its way, ascending the bedroom wall. His brother had come this way days before and had yet to return to the family nest of slimy, tentacled bodies, writhing underground.

Just as he had made his way, not more than a foot above the base of the Persian rug, a courageous ray of sunlight nuzzled its way through the cloud cover, blinding our centipede in a shower of radiant, yet diffused light (the bedroom window was covered in a steamy film). Simultaneously, a large, lumbering object began to stir on top of the bed wedged in the corner of the room, near the night stand. A large bipedal creature with startlingly wild tufts of unkempt, blonde hair was stirring from his night`s slumber. Surely, this could mean nothing good for the light-sensitive centipede.

Suddenly, an eye-lid parted and an almost perceivable line could be drawn between the monster`s gaze and the centipede. There was a fierce hatred behind those icy-blue eyes and the centipede had a notion as to why his brother hadn`t made it back to the nest the week before.

"Arrrrgggg," cried the beast as he lept from his bed, picking up a stone-grey bedroom slipper. "You must die! I alone am best!"

The centipede let out a centipedish shriek as he saw the bedroom slipper flying towards him at an incredible rate of speed. Just before the object closed the distance between the blonde-beast and the insect`s perch, he swore he could see the remnants of his lost brother.

The now fully-roused creature let out a deafening roar as he did a sort of victory dance around the room, made all the more terrifying because he was wearing knee-high winter socks, shorts and an fiercely striped under-shirt.

"I am Sam...," he proclaimed in a bold voice, "...keep coming centipedes! I will conquer your kind!"

Once again I have a running story to begin with, which may or may not keep you amused, depending on your interest in such things. This story begins on the usual running trail, two days ago. I was making my way up the road in shorts, ankle socks (this comes in to play, I promise) and a wind-breaker, when I saw three *new* attack dogs coming to rip out my throat and play doggy games in my blood. So, I did the only logical thing and took a 45 degree right-hand turn, leapt over a stream and began running up hill through a field. It took me 5 minutes to get away from the animals, but during that time, my legs were sufficiently cut up by prickly bramble, including some good-old-fashioned Scottish thistle (that one was for you grandma).

I eventually made my way back onto the road, but at the this point, I was nearing the half-way mark which meant that the whole detour took place during a hill climb. This particular run turned out to be the farthest I have run yet, clocking in at one hour and 26 minutes 19 seconds. When I run around that distance, I make my way up a rather steep hill, which eventually levels out. When the hill does level, off to the right, I can see huge fields of wheat, which are still very green and nice to look at (`nice,` what a weak adj. God...).

It was also on this run that I have decided I can no longer venture out into the wilderness in shorts. During the away journey, I am usually warm enough because I have a hill to tackle and the wind is at my back, but on the return trip, it is almost impossible to warm up. I also have a theory that at the beginning of a run, the body heats up tremendously, but after an hour or so of running, it reaches a `robot-zone` where it doesn`t need to heat up any more. Don`t ask me what a robot-zone is though, I just made it up (and if I read it in a Runner`s World, I`m going to sue for royalties).

School is still going well although, we are in the middle of an inspection that takes place at all schools in Gagauzia every five years. Essentially, there is randomly an inspector in class, watching us teach and everyone is annoyingly nervous. It is really pretty funny to see how the dynamic changes in class while I am team teaching. Where it is normally pretty smooth and relaxed; when there is an inspector, the mood is bumpy but, by no means, bouncy. I try to add some of my Sam humor to the room though, which keeps things squelchy.

Last night was fairly interesting too, because myself and three of my co-workers had a mini `TGIF` party in the teachers room involving bread, pickles, sausage and that dreaded clear rocket fuel made so popular in Russia... I made it home though and ended up going to sleep by 9 p.m., waking at 8 a.m. I made some eggs, drank a bunch of coffee and am now sitting in my room trying to bore you all as much as possible.

So, I will conclude with my usual "hang onto your seats," "don`t panic," "put on a five-point racing harness," list of new and exciting things that have or will be taking place in my life:

1. This week has gone by very quickly and as of Wednesday next week, we will be off LOCK-DOWN and free to do as we please on weekends.

2. Next weekend, we are all eating at a restaurant and then going out to Chisinau bars to celebrate aforementioned event. Mike, Pat and I are all going to attempt to split an apartment so we can match

our Turkey itineraries and turn them into the office. This is a necessary step and should be completed soon, as we have all already purchased $400 plane tickets; it would be a shame if our vacation was not given the `go-ahead.` (I wrote that last comment just so I could imagine the look on my Mom`s face as she reads it. Don`t worry Mom, it`s gonna be okay.) The trip has been dubbed "Project: Gobble-Gobble," by Patrick. I was opting for "The Big-Bird Debacle."

ПОКА

New blog site

2008-11-18

Soooo, I can actually start posting on the Tucson Citizen website. I Think this may turn into my new primary blog site, and here is the link to the blog section (I believe my blogs will be posted under the `life` section):

http://www.tucsoncitizen.com/blog/

The Cold has Returned – Report from Moldova

2008-12-11

It was a was a dozily cold-morning, as I slogged my way to school. The birds in the trees chirped, mocking me with their ability to break the bonds of gravity and flit through the air. The cold had come back to haunt us; it was mother nature getting back at us for her slip-up last week. No more 50 degree, December-weather and no more jogging in shorts; no more dry roads and no more clean footwear. Confusion ensued this week as well, due to the fact that 'winter session' tests have begun at Lyceum M.P. Guboglo. On Monday, Wednesday and Friday testing will begin at eight and classes will be shortened to 35 minutes to accommodate. I worked all last week, typing up tests for my students and those of some of my colleagues. Tomorrow, the 12th graders have their English exam and the 10th graders on Friday. To complicate the week, my partner is out for the mean-time with various illnesses and so I am covering for the classes I teach with her and some of her eighth grade classes (which I don't normally teach). I am not exactly sure where she is in the book and so – given the fact that the eighth grade classes fall on test days – I think we'll play some English games in class.

Goal!!!!!! The countdown is still going for Turkey and, by the time you read this blog, it should be around 15 days to goal... I am rather excited, as you can probably tell by the ellipses. Speaking of Turkey; my host-mother's sister-in-law is in town from Istanbul and I have been chatting with her about her hometown, seeing as I will be visiting said city soon. Apparently, Istanbul is rather 'dead' over the New Year, due to a major Muslim holiday (Please don't make a comment about my ignorance or cultural insensitivity; I barely know anything about my own religion as it is). Our plan is to be in Istanbul and welcome the new year in style but, it appears that there is going to be a bit of a 'cramp' in that style. The sister explained that the place to be over the night of December 31ˢᵗ is Antalya... that or Moscow, Russia. I explained these problems to one of my travel-mates and he responded by pointing out that we should be able to find *something* to do in a city of 14 million people, not to mention we are staying in a youth-friendly hostel. Hopefully it all works out because, for some reason, I had a wild image of Istanbul over New Year`s Eve... Just read it in italics: *New Year`s Eve in Istanbul.* Sounds pretty sexy doesn`t it?

That`s it for now. Пока !

It`s still winter in Moldova

2008-12-15 to 2008-12-17

Today is December 15ᵗʰ and there was a light snow last night. The ground was dusted with powder and it was pretty to look at this morning. As the day wore on, some melted and the roads muddied a bit, but they managed to stay much more firm than they had been.   My main partner is still out – and will be for the week – so I am covering her classes, as needed. I also looked at the schedule today and apparently I am covering for another one of the English teachers. Working in a system that operates without the aid of substitute teachers is interesting (not that the schools systems from town to town are big enough to warrant a substitute system), and the whole faculty helps out quite a bit – or students have a `free period.`   While we`re on the subject, school life is crazy right now, and fun. There is definitely that "end of the semester" feel going on right now. I had to teach my 11ᵗʰ graders for two periods in a row today and, needless to say, I don`t really think their hearts were in it. There were tests three days last week, in the morning, as I mentioned earlier, and they will continue this week.   I also found out that the last day we can give grades to students is on Thursday the 18th but, we don`t get out for break until the 24th... I can`t imagine that next week is going to be very scholastically productive but, seeing as I am hopping on a plane the day after we break for break, I`m not too upset about it.    Running today was interesting. I`ve taken to wearing my only hoodie sweatshirt under my only windbreaker/rain jacket with my running pants. I felt okay on the run, but I can`t seem to find my wool running gloves (the ones I bought for a dollar fifty) and so I went with naked hands. It was cold enough to where, for the first mile or so, they were REALLY cold and hurt a lot.

The weekend was fun; we went into Chisinau and played around on the town. We actually ended up going bowling, of all things, which was fun (I also discovered that my bowling skills have disintegrated quite a bit). Martin, Pat and I also got into poker games later on both nights in town and I made out pretty well on the second game. It is pretty fun to play with lei because they are the equivalent of ten cents apiece, but we get to play with bills, instead of dimes.... Nice.   That's it for now my people.   10 days and counting until I am boarding a plane to the great land of the biggest bird!   **Пока!**

Report from Turkey; December 27 2008

Today is our third night in Turkey and I am currently sitting in a living room, in a pension in Selcuk. Today we saw the ruined town of Ephesus, which is reportedly one of the greatest in the western world. After walking through the ruins we paid 25 Turkish lire for an official Turkish bath. This basically involved stripping down to nothing but a carpet-like towel, washing with water and laying on a large circular marble slab until our turn came up. Our turn consisted of getting scrubbed down with a coarse sponge and then switching stations and getting soaped up with what resembled a foam filled pillow-case. During the latter part of the bath, our calves, feet, backs and ankles were cracked and massaged by an extremely strong Turkish man - clothed in nothing but a towel and a large handle-bar mustache of course. The bath ended with a towel on my head and a cup of hot Turkish tea and me, feeling like I had taken a handful of muscle relaxers.

During our brief stay in Istanbul two days ago (we will be getting back to Istanbul for New Year`s eve and the following 4 days until our flight) we glimpsed the Blue Mosque and the Hagia Sophia, both of which were breathtakingly large and amazing. We`ve eaten some interesting food and are, at the moment, discussing whether we should change our travel plans to see the Capadoccia, which are cave-dwellings worth the 12-hour overnight bus ride. At the moment though, it is high-time to see what this milky anise flavored liqueur is all about - I`ve heard it is referred as "lion`s milk," by some...

Istanbul; day 1

2008-12-31

Today is our first day in Istanbul, but it began by de-boarding a 12 hour bus from Cappadocia at 8 this morning. Needless to say, I slept like hell on the bus and ended up napping for three hours at our hostel. It's around 1 pm now and in addition to adding a short entry, I'd like to give a pre-emptive apology for the grammatical errors in this blog; I am forced to use a Turkish keyboard which differs from English to some degree.

While in Cappadocia, Mike, Pat and I took our second day to get our beards shaved and partake in our second Turkish bath. It was about negative 7 Celsius the whole time, but the sun came out on the second day, which made for some beautiful views. The odd formations studded with dwelling carved out of the stone, covered in snow, makes for a very surreal image - I was half expecting a couple hobbits to pop out and yell at me. I'll try to post some photos on www.getjealous.com/samuel.scheurich when I have time, but they are kicking me off soon to prepare for some sort of yearly celebration in the hostel at the moment. Onto said celebration:

Because of the missile attacks in Israel, there will be no New Year's celebration in Taksim square and we are trying to figure out what we're going to do this evening. I'm sure it will involve Efes (virtually the only beer available in this country) and a late hour. I'll let everyone know how the night unfolds and don't worry mom, I'll watch out for those pesky brothers and fathers... Also, Ness, I won't drink the Kool-Aid

2009

Istanbul

2009-01-03

Today is our second to last day in Turkey and we are attempting to use these last couple days to squeeze every site in that we can - today we saw the Blue Mosque, and the Palace. We had planned on seeing the Hagia Sophia, but Patrick and I lost Mike in the Blue and went back to the hostel to find him. As luck would have it, Mike went into the Sophia, took in all the majesty and consummate arches (there are a lot of arches) and went back to the hostel. This leaves Pat and I in a bind, but I'm sure we'll figure something out.

In any event, the mosque was amazing, but difficult to photograph due to low-lighting and sheer size. They hang hundreds of small lights very low, which also obscure the view of the ceiling with wires. They close off a lot of the floor for real worshiper types and, in that respect, it is very odd because there are no stool, benches, pews or chairs of any kind. I don't really know anything about what goes on inside a mosque but I was surprised that there was nowhere to sit... The ceiling was amazing though and was covered in ornate patterns and Arabic cursive.

We ate an excellent dinner last night that stung our billfolds - I had a bit of a pasta primavera and we all split some decent house wine. Tonight we are supposed to meet another group of travelers from Italy and head to Taksim square (where New Years is usually held) to witness some nightlife; I believe we are eating under a bridge in an attempt to get some fish - I'm not leaving Turkey without eating any fish.

Speaking of fish, we ran into a specialty shop that sold caviar covered in wax (it vaguely resembled a waxy sea cucumber), which was odd too me. Apparently it was a pretty good deal, but I don't know a whole lot about caviar and didn't really feel like experimenting.

That's all I've got for now; I'll try to make my blogs more extensive when I'm back in Moldova and have some time to write.

Turkey; the whole shebang

2009-01-12

It was a crisp January morning when I awoke and, if not

sunny as well, there was light diffusing through the thin cloud cover. Today is Christmas morning, if you are Greek Orthodox, and therefore today is not Christmas for me, but I think I`ll do what I can to get in the holiday spirit (I`m wearing a red hat...)

I landed at Chisinau International Airport on January 5th and missed the last mini-bus back to site. I arrived at site yesterday afternoon and promptly went on my first run in two weeks. I got in a solid hour (it was rather painful – realized the thing about running is that you can`t just up and quit for two weeks and expect to be tip-top immediately) but, over the course of my vacation, my site went from rainy and muddy to frozen solid. While this was definitely an advantage from the perspective of my lower-most, shoe-wearing appendages, it was really cold. At one point, I went to scratch my neck and couldn`t feel anything, so I assumed I was feeling my jacket – turns out it was my neck, it was just numb.

I have been significantly more bored in the last couple days than I was in Turkey – surprise, surprise. I gave myself a day of unpacking, movies, reading and rest yesterday and would start on some more productive activities today – like studying for the LSAT`s, which I may or may not be taking in June -  but, today is Christmas and from what I have gleaned, it is primarily going to involved walking from house to house, sampling wine, followed by a big dinner at the Grandma`s house.

Instead in summing up the latter part of the vacation, I`ll just give a brief description of the whole thing – everyone get out your maps! Every number represents a leg of the journey. It takes many, many legs to create such an epic period of travel – or something...

1.   Left for Ialoveni on December 2nd, where I met my old host brother Victor and spent the night, sampling Cognac and all the foods I missed from that region of Moldova.

2.   Headed to Patrick`s site, Pitusca, on Wednesday and stayed the night with Zan where myself and a few other volunteers had a Christmas eve celebration. The night ended with a chili-eating contest with myself and Mike Mathers. I won.

3.   Took a scary mini-bus to Chisinau, where Mike, Pat and I waited around for our flight at the Peace Corps lounge (I ate McDonalds). Flew to Istanbul and found our hostel. Ended up meeting a group of Americans and Canadians and celebrated Christmas with them by drinking beers and smoking Hookah (I felt like the caterpillar from Alice in Wonderland).

4.   Took off that morning for Izmir. The mode of travel was a ferry across the channel and then a train to Izmir. We found a terrifying hostel in Izmir and naturally decided to sleep there. This was also the first day/night we tasted some terrific Turkish food. The three of us basically pointed to dishes and the owner brought them to our table.

5.   Left for Selcuk that morning. Arrived and checked out the ruined city of Ephesus, ate some kebabs and went to the Museum. After the museum, we took our first Turkish bath, which was sweet; that is if you like seeing your dead skin come off in rolls, while a burly man with a mustache treats your body like a muddy SUV. That night the owner of our hostel, Muslim, prepared some mezes (appetizers) and demonstrated how to properly drink Raki. Later, we

went to the strangest bar I have ever seen in my life. The general idea was that you order a beer, you sit, a woman comes and sits next to you. If you talk to her, you buy her a $10, much smaller beer. Apparently some gentlemen ...cough... make some sort of a verbal agreement during the conversation...

6.   We left for Cappadocia the next evening and spent the 12-hour bus ride attempting to sleep.

7.   Arrived in the big C at eight in the morning and promptly got into another bus for our tour. Because of the snow, we missed out on a beautiful hike through a gorge, but it was a very interesting area of the country none-the-less. We spent the night in the best hostel yet. We were the only people there. (I also forgot to add that during these last three days we ended up meeting a guy named Juan who hails from Buenos Aires, Argentina. We just tended to refer to him as "That guy" (like, "Hey why is that guy over there yelling at a scarf salesman?") and he was the best haggler I've ever met, not to mention he tended to live like a cat. As in, all he did was eat and sleep and speak with a funny accent.))

8.   The next morning, the sun was out and we lounged around sipping on coffee and eating the breakfast prepared by the host. Around noon, we decided to get shaves and partake in our second Turkish bath. I forgot to mention that we met three Italian women in Selcuk who also headed to Cappadocia. Our plan was to meet with them, but we couldn't find them. The three of us sat getting scrubbed down in the bath saying things along the lines of; "Man, what if those Italian girls were here...that would have been awesome!"

9.   We took another completely horrible overnight bus straight back to Istanbul. We got in pretty early on New

Year`s Eve and took naps. That night we went to a party at
our hostel, which was fun.
10.   We spent this day (rather over-hung) walking around
the city and eating.
11.   Today we saw many of the sites, including the
Topkapi Palace (90 carat diamond and all) and the Blue
Mosque.
12.   Today we did more sight-seeing – the photos I post
will do a better job of describing everything – and then
went out to eat with two other travelers. We actually ended
up running into the Italians again at the restaurant and were
supposed to meet them for a drink. Mike and I ended up
back at our hostel rather late, drinking tea, when they came
in to find us. It was weird.
13.   More sight-seeing followed by dinner and dancing at
some weird club. I hate dancing. We were with the Italians
and two of their friends. I`ve decided that Italian people are
the coolest most stylish members of the world community.
There language sounds cool, they dress cool, the men even
have cool facial hair! (Whereas mine is pretty shifty.)
14.   Our last full day was spent sight-seeing and eating fish
at the fish market. It was delicious and fresh, fried-up in
front of us and served on a bed of greens and onions, with
rolls. The sardines had a light batter and you could basically
pop the whole bony fish in your mouth and crunch it down
(my stomach felt funny later that day). We saw the aqua-
ducts later on and then went out for a dinner and glimpse
at the Taksim square bar-scene. We happened upon a bar
with an great band rehearsing and doing sound checks.
Later we found a metal bar called `Old School` and stayed
to listen to rock and sip on $3 beers.
15.   Spice bazaar and home...Damn!

I after re-reading the schedule, I think days 11 and 12 are

actually one day, but the auto-formatting on WORD is impossible to use, so just do the math yourself.

So, that was basically it. I`m back in Moldova now and getting ready for the new semester to begin. I`m hoping this will bring a change to my mood because, while the prospect of my 2 years wasn`t daunting while I was counting down the days to visit Turkey, it is a bit more difficult now that I am back. I try to divide it into semesters; one down, three to go.

I spoke with my brother Willie last night and he is worried about the 6 months he is about to spend studying abroad in Budapest. I told him that I`ve already completed what would be his entire stint abroad and have three times as much to go, so... yeah. I am definitely excited to have him come visit me and REALLY excited to meet him in Budapest before we fly home for Michelle`s wedding. Oh and Ness, get a job and buy a plane ticket. :-) Just kidding...

If anyone is still reading this jibber-jabber, I`d like to throw some verbal thanks towards everyone who sent me things.

Michelle, your pants are coming in very handy, what with the cold weather and, because it is so cold, my sweat dries or freezes while running, so I don`t really have to wash them!

I got some DVD`s and a book on Russia from my brothers – are they hinting at something?

Grandma, the shirt you gave me is awesome and the book is weird...

I`m listening to the I-pod player right now Mom and Dad and the passport holder actually came in handy; I just carried all my ID`s and passport in it the whole vacation.

Oh, and I just realized that I always speak to my dog in Russian. I wonder what language he speaks, you know? Maybe he hates Russian...

School`s back

2009-01-17

www.tucsoncitizen.com/blog

It is Thursday and I am on the cusp of yet another weekend in Moldova. It has actually been a somewhat significant week for two reasons:

One is that, as of Tuesday, every one of the 23rd group of volunteers to enter Moldova has been at our respective sites throughout the country for 90 days (how were my tenses in that sentence?). This may not seem very unusual but it is! Let me explain: We all flew into Chisinau in early June and the 30-ish of us were spread out over three villages near the capital to partake in technical and language training. On August 20th (I believe it was) we were spread out throughout the entire country to serve as health and English teachers.

During the first 90 days at site, none of us (this is a Peace Corps-wide rule) were allowed to spend the night out of our sites. Moldova is a small country and there are a whole bunch of us serving. We are all very excited to be able to travel around and visit our friends. In fact, we have a sort of celebration planned for Saturday in the capital. This is one interesting aspect of serving in a country such as Moldova. Most of us live in villages ranging in population from 3,000 to 15,000.

That being said, we all also live within three or four hours to the capital (most live much closer than this – I live about three hours away). Because of how small the country is, it is easy to do things like meet up on a Saturday to eat food at one of many restaurants throughout Chisinau. I can't imagine that Volunteers in Morocco are afforded this opportunity.

The second piece of news - that I found out about just today - is that the 10th graders will officially be лицей (this the Russian equivalent of 'High School') students today and there will be a ceremony after school. I'll inform everyone what this consists of but I can only assume it will include dancing, singing, speaking and balloons.

Mooooooldova

2009-01-27

Mud. Rain. Clouds. Dreariness.

The weather has been less than stellar for the past few weeks; the roads are serving as messy slip-and-slides for all of us pedestrians. As far as I can tell the Modovan "Winter" is a bit of a myth - with the exception of a couple weeks where the temperature actually dropped enough to form snow and harden the ground. I haven`t seen the sun for about two weeks (with the exception of a brief glimpse yesterday) and its starting to wear down on my soul. A friend of mine mentioned a movie, "Wrist-cutter`s, a love story," which is about people who commit suicide and are slated to an after-life in purgatory (don`t get the wrong idea here, I`m not depressed). Apparently said mythical land resembles Moldova, during the winter, in many ways: it is dark and gray all the time, no one is really smiling, it's not good, it's not bad.... I guess it is right in the ... middle.

School is progressing well and I have made a pact with myself, that I will get my school club going before I head home for my sister`s wedding (more on that later). The concept - yes, it is only a concept right now - is going to stray from the traditional English club. What I would like to do is to hold a meeting and offer-up anything and everything I possibly can to participants, whether it be running, environment, politics, debate, writing, English, weight-lifting, typing... I`ll let you know if it works out.

The wedding is approaching rapidly. I have numbered the days in my planner and I believe I`m on day 51 right now. My brother should also be leaving for Budapest soon, where he will be studying abroad for the 2009 spring semester. I`m excited to have one half of my favorite group of twin brothers studying two states over from me. I am sure that William can profit from having such a witty and sagacious human being only a thousand miles away.

Moooldoooova (February 2nd)

2009-02-02

I have little time! - to write today...

This weekend was interesting for various reasons. Primarily, because the first meeting of mentor coordinators took place on Saturday morning. Three other volunteers and myself whom were chosen to be mentor coordinators, all representing the four groups (agriculture, community development, health education and English education), discussed our responsibilities and plans. If you are curious, a mentor is a volunteer who works on greeting new volunteers when they land in Moldova for the first time and generally helping them out, thereafter. The coordinator tends to coordinate these activities, which includes picking the actual mentors.

This June, we will have a group of 60 odd volunteers coming in and I am excited to be the jaded, "old guy," giving advice and buying beers in Chisinau... There are twice the amount of volunteers in the new group, because, in the past, agriculture and COD volunteers and English and health volunteers all came in groups together. This will be the first year that all four groups will be starting service together, which also means that there will only be one group coming to the country per year.

The super bowl took place on Sunday - as some of you probably know - and the marines stationed at the embassy threw a super bowl party. There was pizza and a reasonably priced bar and their house is ridiculously big but, the only catch was that the ball flew off the tee at 1:30 a.m. and the game ended at 5 a.m. I decided that I would forgo a good deal of sleep, in an effort to see the Cardinals win a super bowl but, I ended up falling asleep at 2:30 in the morning; not that it mattered, because the Cards lost (I did hear it was a good game though...). I managed to hop on a very early bus, and make it to class on time.

I`m being kicked out of the library now, and I`m not really feeling very creative to boot so, I`m going to let my intrepid reader go and start walking home.

Musings

2009-02-12

Monday morning leaves me sitting and writing about the days that have passed. My school schedule is constantly changing although, I was told that last week`s schedule will be permanent for the rest of the year. Monday`s are great as of now, because I don`t have class until 3rd period, giving me an hour so of extra sleep.

I would like to address a comment I made in my last blog (two actually). I believe I described myself as `jaded,` and how I had interest imparting my road-weary wisdom to the fresh and excited volunteers – or something along those lines. In actuality, I am not jaded in the least and hoped that, as a mentor coordinator, the reader did not leave my last entry feeling like I would drag down the spirits of group 24. I promise that my improper use of the English language was done in to put across an image of a grizzled war-veteran, telling stories. It is not the case, but it was the image I was going for, however false. Lastly, I also mentioned cheating in class rooms. This was a generalization and I am sure is not the case in every classroom. In reality, I don`t know much about other volunteers test-giving experiences but, even at my school, every class and every student varies greatly. I have some classes where students rarely cheat. Regardless, as we all probably know, cheating is something that is done in most institutions around the world.. (Again a gross generalization....)

I am very excited for the next few weeks to come. My brother Willie, who is finally alone and depressed in Budapest (just kidding) is most likely going to visit me in the next couple weeks. I have a spring break coming up in early March and I`m doing my best to bring him here – if for nothing else, my entertainment. The weeks are flying by and in less than 40 days, I`ll be flying to the USA for my sister`s wedding. I`m getting more and more excited to eat some pistachios on the couch and eat chips and salsa.

In other news:

I have a language training coming up in Chisinau in two weeks, which will be nice. I actually miss the language classes we had this summer. They moved me from the southern city of Cahul to the capitol, mostly out of pity, as far as I can tell – I would have been alone in class in Cahul, whereas now I am alone in class, but many other volunteers will be around. The only nerve-wracking part of the weekend will be the LPI (an oral exam) on Sunday afternoon. I left pre-service training with a score of intermediate-low (where I was supposed to be) but I don`t have any real idea where I am at now (I am assuming intermediate-mid to high). A lot of the score will depend on the topics we discuss and how my braining is firing that day.

That`s all I have for now; Пока!

Moldova (pronounced like R --iii--cc--oolllaaaa) - for all you yodelers..

2009-02-19

The past week has shown me that it is possible to improve; that is, if you are the Moldovan weather system. The ground has been drying up and I even saw the sun a few times. Unfortunately, I woke to rain, turning my roads back into soup.

I held a film club last week, cookies and all, and two students showed to watch "Stardust," in English, with Romanian subtitles. The two enjoyed the film (I could tell) and it was fun translating what I could, when their expressions were south of `blank.`

I made a break-through in the culinary world last weekend, making Samosas for the family (deep-fried dough pockets, filled with peas, potatoes and onions with curry.) I think everyone like them, and there was filling left over for me to eat for lunch on Monday. Plus!

Willie lands in about a week, kind of excited.

Among the projects I am attempting to get done (or started) is the digitization of all lesson plans, to post online and save for my partners, in electronic form, of course. It is mindless data entry, which I don`t mind, but I am one unit into seventh grade - essentially I`ve got a ways to go. Hopefully it is worth the effort.

I`m very limited for online time today, so I will leave you with an idea: Read `Catch-22,` it`s really funny.

Yo yo Ma - Mo mo dolva

2009-02-23

The frosty air lingers in the south of Moldova, making life chilly.

My original intention was to walk across the width of the country next week, during our first spring break, but seeing as the ground is frozen and I sleep in a sweat suit, under a goose-down blanket, I don`t think camping outside would be wise. The first week in March sounded warm, to me in October, but I am the wiser now and won't make assumptions.

My partner is out sick all week, so I am teaching solo until she gets back, which isn`t a huge deal but having her class tends to add a bit more control to our lessons. Lets factor in that this is the last week before a holiday and you can probably imagine that feistiness is at an all-time high (I`m even excited for a week off). That being said, classes went fine today and I had an especially fun time with my 11th grade group. While writing sentences with vocabulary words, one of the girls in the class asked how to translate the word for `bosom,` because her vocabulary word was augment... You can imagine where that went.

Willie comes in a couple of days, and as I said before, I`m excited! Time to show him all downtown Chisinau has to offer. Should be a good time.

The whole winter has been a roller-coaster of meteorological changes. January brought us rain and mud but, now late-February has come and it is frozen again. It is actually cold enough that powdery snow falls throughout the day and sticks on the ground like white-flour. It is almost ideal though, because it is cold, the clouds aren`t *always* present and the roads are dry and hard, instead of incredible messes of mud and rocks. If the weather stayed like it is year-round, I think I`d be content. I can`t stand extreme heat, and I can`t stand dirty, cold, muddy, rainy weather, but I enjoy the cold. I even like running in gloomy and cold weather the most - if it weren`t for my pants, fleeces, windbreakers and hats I had to dry of sweat at the end of every run. That being said, I complained about the heat this summer, but I`m excited for a change. I`m sure by July though, I`ll be rife with anticipation of the coming fall.

I am waiting to get the names of the incoming volunteers now that we have our team of mentors picked out for June. As I mentioned before, I`m excited to meet them, especially because there will be twice as many new people as there was in our group last June. It is amazing that this much time has flown by; I remember thinking about visiting Turkey last summer/fall and now that vacation is over and I will be flying home shortly to see my sister`s wedding.

We were all required to be in Chisinau last weekend for language training, which was helpful but unfortunate because I missed out on my host Mother`s cousin`s wedding... I was pretty bummed that I didn`t get to take part of one of Moldova`s finest traditions - which are notorious for going all night (literally until the early hours of the morning). I assume there will be more weddings to attend in the next year and a half, so I will keep my suit pressed and hanging on the wall (I`ve actually only worn the thing once, at swearing in... Kind of wish I had left it at home).

The dogs are back! (and so is the sun)

2009-02-26

There isn`t a cloud in the sky today, and I can`t say I mind it.

I went for a run this morning (it is my planning day, which means I only have club meetings) and if I didn`t feel wonderful, at least the weather is wonderful. And, my best friends are back; the dogs... I was running in the middle of a very wide-open area, near a sheep-herder and his animals when four dogs came bounding after me. They were fairly large but, seeing as I have yet to be bitten, I wasn`t too concerned. They followed after me barking for about a 1/4 mile and I couldn`t help but break into a huge smile - looking back over my shoulder every few paces of course. After my run, I sat down to eat: two eggs fried with jarred eggplant, onions and peppers, three pieces of toast with chocolate spread or butter, crackers, brinza and two cups of coffee. Should keep me going for a couple hours.

Willie gets in tomorrow and I am ready to give him a low-five and call him a cod-fish at the top of my lungs (the airport is really small, no one will care). We are also on the cusp of a week off of school, which almost makes me feel guilty because I will be missing a week of school to attend my sister`s wedding - darn guilt... Anyhow, I`ve planned a bit of `bar-golf` for him on Friday night, where I plan on showing him a few of our haunts.

I am holding my second movie club today after school gets out for my 12th grade class and will be showing the new James Bond movie; hopefully someone shows.

I`d like to finish on a sad note; I received the news that a very close family friend of ours died yesterday and I will miss him. He was an amazing person and my family and I enjoyed spending time with him a great deal. Bart was the kind of guy who was always ready with advice and smile and I swear, he had a twinkle in his eye.

Spring Break I

March 2nd – March 9th Spring Break I   The illustrious William Scheurich flew into Chisinau, Moldova on the breath of a gale-force wind – clad in ivy, of course – last weekend to amuse his older, yet humble brother. At first sight, it was obvious that the boy had been concentrating on growing his curly locks and I was happy to see his angelic face beaming down Grigore Ureche Strada. We spent the weekend dining in Chisinau`s finest restaurants, playing darts and sampling various lagers around the city. I also managed to take him to a Moldovan restaurant with a large group of volunteers, where he tried the local cuisine and even took part in a traditional wedding dance called the hora (this involves being selected from a circle of people, kneeling down and kissing a random woman; I'm sure he loved it.). I have to give myself some credit, because if it weren't for my employment by the government, I am almost sure that he never would have made the voyage to our beautiful country. Alas, his time here went by like a candle in a hale-storm and, come Monday afternoon, he was back on a plane to Budapest, Hungary where he is undoubtedly wowing professors with his engineering acumen.   While in town we managed to make our way to various landmarks, including an old soviet statue and a WWII memorial. I had a slight scare because I read the Cyrillic on the statue out-loud to my comrades and realized that I didn't understand a word of it... It wasn't until I saw the word 'pentru,' and realized that the inscription was from a time when Romanian was written in Cyrillic, that my mind was set at ease. I hope he had a fantastic time and it was great to see one sixth of my family for the first time in nine months.   I spent the rest of the vacation making my way around Moldova. Among notable actives (and the the bulk of the week) were: Going to a house in Glodeni, where Mike, Martin and I purchased a live chicken at the market and turned it into roasted chicken stuffed with lemons and onions. The meat was tough, but it was an insightful experience none-the-less. My host family informed me that we probably purchased an old chicken which isn't surprising – it couldn't have been too tough for the vendor to realize that we were not locals and we would buy anything they threw at us. I also played Russian billiards for the 2nd time, and quickly found out that I am as bad at the game as when I played it for the first time. On Friday, Saturday and Sunday, we had a mentor coordinator meeting and peer support network training. The meetings were actually fairly enjoyable, and I tried to inject as much humor as possible into them for my entertainment, if for no one else's. The week went by very quickly and now I am back at school, teaching. I went for a run before work today and found that after a week off, my body digressed somewhat, which is understandable. After eating different and flavorful food for the week, it was also hard to go back to my usual diet at site but, I love food in all forms, so I should be able to get over this quickly.

Before I go home for my sister`s wedding, I have one task that I would like to accomplish and that is writing a small grant for new linoleum on my classroom floor. I will be missing a week of school as well, which leaves me feeling guilty but, she is only getting married once and I am sure school administration can understand the importance of this. I am excited because I will be seeing Willie, Charlie, Mom, Dad, and everyone else soon. This leaves me feeling elated but it will not be until after the wedding that I can get my mind back into work-mode. The next two weeks are going to fly-by and I am sure it is going to difficult to think of little else, while I attempt to wrap my mind back around my life, which is living in a small town in Moldova.
The weather was great all week and is quickly improving – it`s happening as we speak. The days are warmer, sunnier and longer and for the first time since winter enveloped the country, I am waking to sunshine, instead of starry skies. In an odd way, I will miss the blanket of darkness. I am not really sure why, but there was something comforting and getting my run in after work and sitting in my room as the sun set in the late afternoon. My friends think I am crazy, but I have gotten used to the winter hours – of course, I`m the kid in the family who had adjustment problems when we got a new refrigerator in the kitchen so, it is expected. I look forward to the drier and warmer summer weather; the only thing that worries me is that I will be forced to change

my running schedule around. I can take off down the road at any time of the day right now, and this summer the heat will prevent me from doing so come May.

Home

MARCH 23 – April 2, 2009

As I predicted, the wedding came and went very quickly. It was exciting to have the build-up to my vacation home, but as I said it flew by. This `build-up` began with William visiting, my own Moldovan spring break, followed by a flight to Budapest, where I met aforementioned brother and we flew to СIIIА together. So, to recount: I arrived in Budapest and from what I saw, it is a beautiful city – more to come on that later though, as I am going to visit Willie again over second spring break with "The" Mike D. The cherub and I flew out of Budapest, through London to Phoenix, AZ, where we promptly ate a cheeseburger at Houston`s and went out to 16th Street Bar and Grill to meet with our Phoenician friends. The night was fun and it was great to see everyone again. The oddest part about all of it though, was that it wasn`t odd, at all. I forced my parents to let me drive the car home from the airport – despite tremendous concern about my current driving skills – to get a feel for driving again for the first time in almost a year. Rolling down the 51, I felt like I had never left my hometown. The feeling continued throughout the vacation and when it came time to leave, I felt like I was leaving home for the first time again – disconcerting to say the least.   I woke Sunday morning to what was probably the most pleasant part of the trip: spring in

Phoenix. For the nine days I was home, we had nothing but sunny skies and temperatures around 80 degrees. Seeing as I left Moldova a cold, wet, muddy mess, it was enough to make me strap on my running shoes and skip around butler park with a gigantic grin (I only skipped once or twice). Michelle arrived on Sunday and it was great to see the bride-to-be. The rest of the week progressed well: I ate more than is humanly possible at restaurant`s including Chino Bandito and El Bravo. The fridge was constantly stocked with an assortment of IPA`s (a beer that is unheard of in Moldova and, unfortunately, my favorite) and I made sure to sate my hoppy appetite. Brian Stratton arrived early on in the week and subsequently moved in to the house, just as God intended. Most of my other friends, including the illustrious Brian Gavan had work or school all week, so I didn`t get to see them as much. Ness arrived on Wednesday and it was awesome to see her again. I bought her the usual soy chai latte with a single shot of espresso at the airport that she used to get in Tucson; I think the last time I ordered this obscure drink was in Tucson, come think of it. My family was happy to see her again and she was one of the factors that my time at home wonderful. On Thursday night, I crafted a full-on Moldovan feast with Mamaliga, Sarmale, Holodetz (chicken in natural aspic) and Cognac and Pickles; the works. As far as I can tell, it was a big hit. Michelle`s friends Rudy and Josh were at the wedding. Rudy is a hair stylist and I actually convinced him to give me a "whisper cut," as he called it, for free... I`m sure the cognac had nothing to do with it. As you can see, the week was sunny and relaxing. There was the stress that the wedding planning put on the household but, for the most part, it didn`t cause too many problems (although my dad did threaten to stay at work all day when the arguing got out of hand on Tuesday).

On the day of the wedding, Brian, Brian, Ness and I went to float the lazy river at the Point Pool. After the float, I went to meet up with Michelle and her bridesmaids. At four, Gavan and Teschner went to the bar for a pre-wedding drink and my brothers and I went to the church to prepare. Our main task was to usher people to their seats and stand up front while my sister was married. It was a short and sweet ceremony and it was unreal to see my only sister get married: Молодец Michelle! After the ceremony, we made it back to the house for the dinner and reception. Without a doubt, the reception was not only the best wedding I have ever been to, but it was one of the best dinners I have eaten and the best party I have ever attended. The tables were set, the dance floor was out, lights were strung above everything, and there was enough champagne to kill a baby blue whale (In fact, the same Josh I mentioned before made a bet with the bar tender that he and the rest of the wedding-goers could finish every bottle. While this task was not accomplished there was plenty consumed – enough to make me cut a rug out on the dance-floor, which is something I have never enjoyed. Lets also not forget what Josh said to the bar-tender, after deciding that he wasn`t going to let a guy with a bad hair cut tell him that finishing the champagne supply was impossible. Josh: "Give me another glass flat-bangs!"). My favorite/most awkward part of the night, was when I requested Michelle and I`s favorite song "November Rain," to dance to. I am positive less than 1/8th of the guests knew the song; all they saw was Sam and Michelle dancing to some odd slow song. I picked up the mood though, by motioning to the DJ that it was time to throw on "Shout." At one point, we had everyone on the dance floor touching the wood as the artist whispered "A little bit slower now."

It was better than a movie.   Among my fondest memories from the week are: When the Scheurichs, Ness and Stratton went for a post-Moldovan, beer-soaked journey through the neighborhood. Laughter is the best medicine and is even better when you aren't sick (did that make sense?).   Our Wednesday night journey to the bars with Michelle. We started out at the Rokerji, where Brian and I convinced ourselves that we were sitting in the bar where Frodo and his friends discovered strider in "The Fellowship of the Ring." We migrated to 16th Street, where we promptly took over the juke-box. Nate decided to treat us all to a drink called "Surfer on Acid" and Willie, Charlie, Michelle and I spent the rest of the night waxing on how awesome we all are, how much we love each other and how great our family is. At one point, someone tried to interject and we quickly shut them down - assuring them that the Scheurichs are elite, etc. The night ended with a refrigerator-routing session of eating. Notice the pictures I've posted of us in the kitchen, very intent on food (be sure to pay special attention to Ness who decided that she needed the biggest spoon in the drawer to eat her carton of ice-cream).   Let's also not forget that it takes a great home and set of people to make someone miss home. The only reason I had trouble leaving again, was because I realized how much I enjoyed growing up the way I did (in addition to living at home for the last six months before I left for Moldova). In a way, it made leaving easier; it would have been far worse to be happy to leave my friends and family behind again. The year or so I have left seemed daunting but, seeing as I have been here for the better part of a year already, I know that April 2nd 2010 will come and go, just as the last year has.

April 13

The past two weeks have gone by quickly and I have involved myself in some fairly different sorts of activities...   I will begin by saying that school is still going, but it is obvious that teachers and students are getting ready for the summer holidays. The weather has been sunny and fairly warm, leading to students out in the yard talking and kicking soccer balls around, as opposed to drinking hot coffee and chocolate in the dark halls of the school. My guitar club is thriving with three students, one of which is fairly decent, making my job a bit easier. I just submitted a grant to Peace Corps, to get the floors and lighting fixtures in my main class room replaced; we`ll see if that works out. Patrick and I are also trying to get a mini-baseball camp going around various villages in Moldova this summer, the idea being to teach Moldova boys how to play and then possible play a few games with them. Luckily there is a set of equipment that we would be able to use if the camp actually works out.   Our second spring break begins at the end of this week and I`ll be visiting Willie in Hungary. But, seeing as this will be much more interesting to hear about after the fact, I`ll stick with my rabble-rousing in Moldova: Two weeks ago, I played some baseball with the Peace Corps team. My original intention was to go root the team on, but I was conned into playing, because they were three players short – we ended up using two Moldovan players, to complete our team. I didn`t do horribly – hey, it's been 15 years or so – and I got on base once. I missed a pop-fly in the outfield, but I did snag a line-drive while playing second base. The best part was that I got to wear a baseball uniform though; at least I looked like I knew what I was doing.   On Tuesday, the family and I went out to the woods near my house to grill fish and have a bonfire. The fish was great and I was informed that it was a fish not available in America. I find this fact difficult to believe but, I ate the fish with cabbage salad none-the-less. My host sisters introduced me to a game called "Duck," which is basically six person dodge ball. The night ended with house wine and a very large fire; I have a feeling my host father was trying to fight a war with the local flora, because I am sure there was the better part of a small tree burning at one time. On the way home, the car actually ran out of gas, so I had to hop out and push, which was actually the funniest part of the whole night. At one point I was running to catch up to the moving car trying to jump into the side door.   This weekend, I attended a joint Bulgarian/Moldovan dance recital at my site, and it was pretty funny to see all of my kids up there in costumes jumping around like Irish jiggers. Pat and I visited his old host family the following night in Costesti and Miha brought the old family vintage – we ended the night in the actual wine cellar, which led to some pretty funny photographs. Bcë!

Budapest

April 27, 2009

April has come and gone with some speed and, in the last two months, I have been home, to Budapest twice and am coming up on the last five weeks of school before summer. From today (mini-Easter) on, I'll try to recount my second spring break– and trip to Budapest– up until this very Monday afternoon.

Mike and I arrived in Budapest last week, very early in the morning, and spent our first day in Hungary seeing the castle district and Fishermen's Bastion (a tower/walkway area named such for no apparent reason; maybe it was simply a poor translation). Because we got into Hungary very early in the morning, we got a lot of sight-seeing in on the first day. We even had some time to enjoy the sunshine at a cafe up in the market district, where we drank some beers, go through an underground labyrinth and witness a Hungarian Nationalist's rally; which essentially amounted to a neo-Nazi rally, protesting a recent holocaust memorial (I know I shouldn`t take sides in reporting my `news` but, come on guys, have a little empathy (that was directed at the protesters, not you)).

We went home to nap a bit before our big night out, rather unsuccessfully, and headed out to eat at a German restaurant Willie and I discovered around 8 p.m. This was the second time we patronized the place, because they serve something called a `mixed-grill platter.` Dinner consisted of a duck, cheese and potato casserole, a mixed platter of meat, potatoes and cheese and another plate with goose, polenta and a very heavy cream and paprika based sauce. We topped the meal off with liters of German beer, just for good measure. Needless to say, I ate until I thought I might deposit the meal back onto its respective serving trays. Later in the night, we went to a club where I met some of Willie`s more colorful classmates (one claimed to be in med-school, play for an international, semi-pro football team and own real-estate) and we stayed up far too late.

The first day was the best, but I'll recount the rest:

We took a river cruise on the Danube and ate a fairly good meal that was provided by the staff. We ended up getting lost on the way to the boat and were literally running to climb aboard as it was getting ready to shove-off. The humor in all this is that there happened to be a marathon that day and we ended up cutting through the race twice. When we finally arrived at the boat, the hostess actually handed us glasses of champagne and showed us to our table; I felt like I had just finished the Tour De France. Later on that day, we saw the House of Terror, which is a recounting of torture and other various atrocities, committed in a specific building in Budapest, and went home to make dinner. That night we watched "Captain Ron" for what was probably Willie and I's seventh time and got to be early.

Mike and I decided to go to a bath the following day, which was an excellent decision. If you have read any of my previous blogs– specifically referring to Turkey– you will remember that we have quite an affinity for these places. The day started with coffee, a light breakfast of two eggs, bacon, coffee and bread at a sunny, outdoor cafe and a game of chess. We made our way through the city and discovered that: The Hungarian bath was unreal. It had spas and saunas indoors and the outdoor pool made me feel like I was swimming in Mr. Hearst's backyard. We lay around getting tans sipping on beers and at one point– we try to live like Sultan's when possible– we were eating a plate of french-fries and a bag of potato chips (I'm used to a diet rich in carbohydrates). It turned out that Will didn't have class for nearly as long as we thought, so he and I were bummed that he couldn't join Mike and I but I guess that's life, the way the cookie crumbles, the cat's left paw, etc. We ended up walking around Margaret Island around dusk and ate a fairly good Mexican restaurant, even by Arizona standards.

The next day, we went on an excursion to a botanical garden and got somewhat lost along the way. We ended up in a small, but pretty town over-looking the Danube and met a man who agreed to bring us to the gardens. Before leaving in his car, we ate lunch with him and his friend, which was interesting. It was there that I found out that it is very common for Hungarian restaurants to offer a set menu for very cheap, affording eaters the chance to sample the local fare. That days menu consisted of fruit soup and meatballs with a white sauce with rice. The soup was very good and went well the with warmth and sunshine. When we did make it to the gardens, they turned out to be pretty un-impressive and, while the excursion to said gardens was my idea, I'll take no blame for this. When we got back into the city, we had intended on going to the statue park— which has old soviet statues on display— but we found that it was much more difficult to get to than we thought. Later that day, we went to look around the city with Willie and even made our way to a shopping-mall. That night, we went to an apartment party with Willie's friends which was international to say the least; at one point there were kids from Greece, Italy, Turkey, USA, Finland, Poland all conversing in some degree of English.

Mike and I went off on our own to Lake Balaton the next day and enjoyed its magnitude, vastness and sublimeness (new word I found). The lake itself if forty miles long and not too narrow. It was a long train ride though, and on the way, the train attendants apparently thought it would be funny to attend to us in an unfair fashion and we ended up taking the wrong line; the trip turned from a two hour jaunt on a direct train to a four hour slog with three connections. In any event, we had a great lunch, and the lake was beautiful. We went to bed early and...

On the final day, Mike, Willie and I went to the Alphonse Mucha exhibit near hero`s square. After the exhibit, Mike and I wandered around the square and made our way to Gerret Hill, where we climbed to the top and later met Willie near his school. We went home, relaxed and then made a pasta with spicy dry pepperoni, mushrooms and tomato sauce for an early dinner. Our flight was later that night and we finally arrived back in Moldova around 1 a.m.

That pretty much sums it up. I`d like to add that after the vacation, I have decided that Budapest is probably one of my favorite cities on Earth. It is an old, city, with amazing architecture, but is also very modern and clean. The people are extremely kind and helpful (we were given advice and directions without any prompting on more than one occasion) and have their own interesting and artsy sense of style. Speaking of people, it seems as though the city-dwellers had many varied aspects about them; it was fun to see a broad range of interests. We all also noticed that everywhere we went was fused with something artistic and progressive— even the graffiti tended to be bearable. Even the cafe where I had my two coffees per-day was very modern, with all white walls and a weekly photo exhibit. The food was amazing and that alone would have been enough to make me go back (okay, that was an exaggeration).

Back in Moldova, I was around in time to experience малинки расах (that may not be spelled correctly), which is a lot like Mexico`s "Day of the Dead." The whole town goes to the grave-yard to drink wine and eat food on tables which have been permanently installed in the ground. I had heard that this was a particularly boozy event, from other volunteers, but luckily my family seems to avoid excessive, excessive amounts of drinking– which is good for me, because it is Monday and I wasn`t really in the mood to tie one on in a graveyard.

This week should be a light work-load, because Friday is also a holiday and I should be making my way to a village near Stefan-Voda, where a friend of mine is having a Cinco De Mayo party. Summer is on the way, the sun is out, and I`ve almost forgotten what it was like to live under the oppressive hand of winter. It is four in the afternoon and I`m happy the sun isn`t down, as it would have been if it were still December.

On a more serious note (before I let you go) I`ve developed the dangerous habit of watching a showed called "Battle Star Galactica" (BSG, for all of you who aren`t noobs). Big mistake. It is a great way to waste two or three hours, finding out what those damn Cylons are going to do next...

Spring in Moldova

2009-05-14

The pernicious weather Gods have decided that instead of giving me and Moldova a steady ray of sunshine, they were going to clot up the sky with rain and clouds. Luckily, it is warmer out as of late, making the foul weather bearable.

I am on the verge of the completion of my first year as a teacher in Moldova and I am ready for the break. I've noticed that things start going, dare I say, downhill towards the end of the semester. As is true with every institution on earth. That being said, I am ready for a summer of relaxation and youth activities, in preparation for my last school year in service. It is pretty amazing how quickly things have gone. Last year at this time, I was freaking out in Phoenix, AZ, and getting ready to board a plane.

The grant I am writing has been sent back for some editing, and I am hoping I can get it submitted soon, as I'd like to spend the end of the summer using the funding to improve my partner's and I's classroom.

There are rumors of a Chisinau marathon and this prospect has given me new reasons to run everyday - as if sanity and emotional stability weren't reasons enough.

Finally, in actual news, there is a PC baseball game (not officially PC, not affiliated, etc.) in Nisporini on Sunday, and I will be standing out in right field, picking my nose with Martin for the entirety of the nine innings. Root us on as we bring "America's national past-time," to Moldova. (In actuality, all the Moldovan teams are much better than the American team but, who's counting?)

Last Saturday was the day of victory in Europe, and my town celebrated by gathering in the center and listening to speeches being made at the local war memorial. As tradition would have, later that day, families and friends gathered in various spots in the forest to drink house wine and eat food.

Later that day, I went to a neighboring village, to participate in a barbeque with European Union workers - specifically those whose job it is to watch and inspect the Ukraine/Moldova border. The food was great, and the night was long, but I made it home alive.

Monday came to me feeling mildly ill, and now I believe that I have the full-blown flu, cold, Ebola or something equally unpleasant. I ran three times this week (if Sunday counts), but I think I am going to give it a rest until I recover.

Today, I took a day trip up to Chisinau, to try and get my tourist visa to Russia sorted out, but it turns out that a copy of my invitation will not work. I need a passport sized photo, and *original* copy of the invite and my passport. Luckily I have a few weeks to get my hands on an original; the only problem is that I am assuming it will have to be sent from Russian - I hope they don`t mind paying for fed-ex.

I`ve gotten myself involved in another grant with my site-mate, to improve the resource center at the school. I am attempting to do about half the work with her but, because she will be completing service within six months, the grant is under my name and, as far as I know, I will be presenting it to the committee (officially, the "SPA" committee - let's just call them "The Committee Who Lets Volunteers Know if They Get Money or Not").

I`ve gotten interesting opinions on the new flu. My host family refuses to eat pork because of it, which surprises me to some degree - I`m honestly not sure why. I was talking to a friend who pointed out that people die from the regular flu too... right? Not that it is a pleasant or especially worthwhile strain of influenza but it seems like its hyped up - like the new Star Trek movie, for example. Anyway, my opinion on said flu is complete speculation, as I haven`t any idea what I`m talking about.

T - minus 2 Weeks

2009-05-19

We are coming down to the finale. The last two weeks of school at Lyceum M.P. Guboglo. At the moment, I believe there is some sort of sewage problem outdoors, but I will try not to let the stench affect the tone of this article.

I had a fairly eventful weekend, hanging out at McDonalds on Saturday night, watching some sort of live performance in the center of Chisinau. The Eurovision finale was also on Saturday night, and we watched Norway take the win (if you didn`t know *Eurovision* is a Europe-wide competition - held in Moscow, Russia this year - to find the best pop act). Moldova came in 14th place with their song "Hora Din Moldova," and it was pretty fun to hear the cheers of locals, as we sat sipping our beer at "Napolis."

This coming summer will be hot and fun. The only problem I have, is that there are a few people I know, who will be leaving service early - a disheartening activity, quitting. I joined under the impression that I was volunteering 2 years and I was going to commit to those two years, not give up. In any event, everyone is different. I`ve turned over a new leaf and now will pretend that I am some sort of weird Zen master/yogi (I actually tried a few yoga moves, on involved a sort of crouching hand-stand. I ended up falling on my head and I don`t really remember the rest of the afternoon.), in an effort to make light of everything. I had already had the `weird` part down, now I just have to read some literature on the topic, and I`ll be 100% into my new hobby.

Students at school have stopped giving it their all and, oddly enough, almost every class I teach is working on essays all day during lessons - something which motivation-lacking students don`t appreciate all too well. Another interesting practice in Moldova is that we cannot give grades to students for the last two weeks of school. This, as you can imagine, doesn`t give students a whole lot of drive. That being said, I have a lot of fun in lessons, as we are all but done with books for the year. I teach a ninth grade class alone and I finished the lesson by playing hangman with students and talking about their summers.

On another note, I just finished re-reading "The Great Gatsby" and I am following up with "The Rum Diary," by HST. I have heard that Mr. Thompson based a lot of his style off of Fitzgerald (actually I know this, after having read "The Proud Highway"), even going so far as to copying the book word-for-word on his typewriter to learn Fitzgeralds cadence... or some such nonsense.

Unfortunately, the carousing life-style of the journalist and main character "Kemp" makes me wish I had taken the life of a reporter a little more seriously (Although, there seems to be some more glamour in taking your type-writer with you to San Juan to work at a newspaper, than working for a newspaper in Vail, Arizona on an Apple computer - is it just glamor I`m looking for?). Всего хорошого людей.

What Would Capt. Ron Do?

2009-05-28

It is Thursday in sunny Cedir-Lunga, and the crows have finally began to shut-up. There was nothing worse than running or walking through the fields, with a portentous sky and a thousand crows mocking your mood (not to mention it was downright creepy).
Speaking of running, I have decided that I have completely lost my mind in some respects. I got about an hour in yesterday and I realized, when I got back that I accomplished the following: ran with no shirt, in a country where no one runs and people are generally pretty modest (and I have long hair...weird), chased down a herd of goats while bleating at the top of my lungs, sang three consecutive songs, also at the top of my lungs (including

"Leningrad" by Billy Joel), and finally, followed up the goat-chasing with cow-chasing while fantasizing about the course of events if/when I get gored by an angry cow. All very strange indeed.

Another problem I encountered was whether cows kick... It turns out they don`t, but I was running up behind a herd of bovine in the fading sunlight, on a narrow dirt road and I felt it wasn`t wise to run up from the rear – mostly because of what I know about horses. It turns out that cows are scared of everything, and generally didn`t notice me until the last minute. When they did notice me, then ran away with fear, sometimes knocking into each other – very funny stuff; lets also not forget they are rather top heavy. I honestly thought a couple of them were going to topple over.

The last day of school is coming up on me pretty damn quickly (tomorrow) and while I haven`t been in the greatest mood all week, I am feeling somewhat excited. The kids all come to school in light, summer clothes these days; which is a huge change from the coats and caps they wore all winter. They same general things happen here, as they do in the states: kids turn in books, skip class, etc. The only major difference here is that because grades are given out on the spot, usually during class, during the last week of school teachers make a `total` of the grades, with the class. This basically involves a teacher calling out every grade for the year and having students add them and then average them. I still haven`t figured out how kids just can`t add the odd point here and there but, I can only assume the method is tried and true.

As I mentioned, tomorrow is the last day of school and we will be having a ceremony in the morning, followed by a picnic sort of thing in the woods. I hope it doesn`t last too long because I will be having a little celebration of my own, in Chisinau with my friends. Luckily, I met a man who drives to and from my town everyday or every week (I don`t bother with specifics, in general of course). Last week, I spent the journey up with him working on my Russian and discussing politics, religion and drinking habits. He taught me a lot about the succession of deeds during the post-Soviet era (as in, some people just happened to be lucky enough to own large factories after the SSSR fell). My driver also told me that it is illegal to drink and drive, period. In the states there is a limit, but in Moldova, there is no tolerance. He also poked fun at our lenient system of driver`s licensing. In Moldova, there is a mandatory driving school and you cannot obtain a license until the age of 18. He then joked that in America you can drive at 16 after taking a simple written test but you can`t drink until you are 21 – whereas in Moldova, the driving age is 18, but you can drink at any age (His words, not mine. I`m simply reporting the news).

In any event, the alcohol explanation ended with him explaining that it is quite possible to drink a liter or more of distilled liquor (Vodka, Cognac, etc.), as long as you don`t mix it with any other boozes. Apparently you are not supposed to start dinner with an aperitif, have wine with dinner, and a Scotch afterwards. I let him know that I took the tradition of Cognac and pickles home with me, and that was wrong too. Allegedly, you chase cognac with an orange slice, dipped in sugar and instant coffee. You ONLY eat pickles with vodka. Food for thought Michelle, Josh, Nate and Rudy (and whoever else you guys have your cognac and pickles night with)

.Anyway, it was a great ride and it was fun to practice Russian while gaining an hour that I would have lost sitting in a bus. Thanks Oleg.

We have a few interesting activities planned for our summer weekends. One of which will be walking across the country, with tents and sleeping bags. It may end up being just Pat and myself, but we will see who else is feeling adventurous.

I have also started to (as I mentioned earlier) play baseball on the Peace Corps team and, after playing a couple games, it turns out I'm not too bad. We lost last game, mostly due to pitching but, I had a triple and slid into base. It was pretty funny because I've .... yea, never slid into a base. I was running thinking "Don`t F#$% up! Don`t F$%^ up!" but I not only did it with some semblance of form, I even have raspberries on my knees to prove it. JT hit a single on the next play, getting me into home. The best part of all of it though, is that we have uniforms. Apparently when they bought the uniforms though, they could only get them with "MC" stenciled on the breasts. This limited the team-founders anachronism options and so the team has been dubbed "Mamaliga Corps."

It is almost nine in the morning and today is LSAT practice-testing day. From here on in, I am going to try and complete one test a week, until the big show in late-September. Wish me luck Michelle, because if I don`t do better than last time, I don`t think I will be attending Hasting`s and living near you in San Francisco...

I`d also like to add, that a great way to get through life, is to ask yourself, "what would Captain Ron do?" In most cases, he would simply reply, "nobody knows!" wearing an eye patch the whole time.

Poka!

Schools out

2009-06-08

Moldova has stepped into June, like a poodle walking through a pool of burning tar and it has left my fellow ex-patriots and I sweaty, to say the least.
It has been a while since I have mentioned anything about life here, mostly because I have been traipsing around the country for a week or so, since our last bell ceremony at school. On that note, the ceremony went well, but it rained the whole time; giving my white shirt a definite disadvantage in opaqueness... Among the funnier parts of the ceremony, was the end, when students came up to dance with the teachers. This left a rather confident 12th grader, asking a rather awkward feeling 24 year-old school teacher dancing in the rain.

Later in the week, I ended up in Drochia with some friends, where we roasted a whole pig on a spit. I arrived the night before to help with the slaughtering of the pig, etc. The following day, two friends and myself made our way to a field, where we began roasting the thing at 8 a.m. Liters of wine and lots of sun later (about 8 hours later), we had 30 kilograms of pork and really bad sun-burns. The meat was delicious and, thanks to some relatives in Phoenix, we had a large bottle of BBQ sauce to slather on the meat. The best part of having an entire pig in front of me, on a spit, was taking off the rib bones, one by one, and eating them (obviously).

I made it back to site yesterday, where I promptly laid down on my little couch and slept for two hours (three hours on a boiling hot bus takes it out of you) and dreamt about snow. The ride back reminded me of last August, when I first started using the bus to get back and forth from site. The most frustrating thing about riding on public transportation in this country is a little thing called "the current." The current is air that comes down from vents in the ceiling of the bus. It is well-known, that this ventilation, causes you to be sick. Not to generalize but, generally, the older a person is, the more they hold true to their mistrust of the current. Unfortunately, in June, when it is 95 degrees outside, it feels pretty nice to have some breeze in your face, while sitting on a crowded mini-bus. The woman next to me sat up and shut the vent, just as we were leaving the southern bus station and I looked at her with my best air of incredulity as she sat back down and I enquired rather loudly, "Why!?" She explained that there was no need for the extra fresh air, as the driver's window was open. Too bad we were both sitting at the back of the bus.

I'm gonna end this little thing by saying goodbye. I have my first day of work at the orphanage tomorrow and I'm excited to get back into a rhythm, now that my primary assignment has ended for the year. More on that later though.

New group

2009-06-17 to 2009-06-18

June 11, marked our group's one year in Moldova and it was also the date that the newest group of volunteers landed in Chisinau. We spent the weekend helping the new group out with adjustment and getting used to our glorious city, in between their mind-numbing seminars and language classes.

We had a good time meeting people and taking them out to bars in the city before they took off to their training villages on Saturday afternoon. It was an experience I was looking forward to, for a couple reasons; one that we have been here a year with the same people and it was nice to see some new faces in the country and two, that I can remember when I was in the same position as this new group, wishing I was the volunteer who had been in country for a year.

I have officially started working at the orphanage at site and for a couple hours a day, I play sports with said orphans, essentially acting as a camp counselor. It is fun and interesting to be a part of an orphanage for the first time.

One definitely notices the disparity between those who live in the community and the children who live at the orphanage. For example, some philanthropist donated T-shirts, most of which are marked with World Wrestling Federation logos. It was pretty funny to see students sitting at a ceremony (last week) and listening to the first lady of Moldova speak wearing clothing bearing the slogans "Ass-Kickers Anonymous," and "Drink or Fight!"

Children are also decidedly funny, innately. Sitting in the grass, speaking with a seven year-old girl yesterday, I was asked about where I live, etc. The girl asked if I spoke Romanian as well. I explained that I speak Russian and English. The little girl looked pretty surprised when she heard this – keep in mind the whole conversation took place in Russian. I went on to tell her that, clearly I speak Russian, given the recent conversation. I can only chalk it up to her being a tiny-little seven year old and my Yankee accent.

As I mentioned before, June 11 marked our group's year in country and we are going to be celebrating next week at a group of cabins in Val Lui Voda; drinking beer, burning wood and cooking meat. Should be a good time.

Late June in the DOV

2009-06-28

"I am tired, I am weary. I could sleep for a thousand years. 1,000 dreams that would awake me. Different colors made of tears."

The last couple weeks have been a dull din of activity, leaving me back in the south, sitting and writing. Unfortunately, I came back to a less-than welcoming greeting yesterday, with my host father in a rather bad mood (I'll refrain from expanding much on this). Because I have been traveling around quite a bit, and haven't had constant access to a computer, I will try to sum up what has been going on since my last entry:

As I mentioned before, we celebrated one year in country last week by the Nistru river. It was a very pretty spot; somewhere I definitely plan on visiting again. We rented small motel-style rooms to sleep in, but spent the majority of the day on the sandy beach. Most of us went into the water to swim, which was nice for once – swimming pools and oceans aren't easily accessed in Moldova. The current was strong enough though, that it made getting back to shore rather difficult. Patrick is an asthmatic and at one point, he and I were holding onto a buoy in the middle of the river. Pat got swept away and had a pretty rough time getting to shore. I'm sure he was being a baby (weak asthmatics), but he said he had to lay on his back and float along for a while, because the river had stolen his will to live.

I had planned on crossing over to the Trannistria side (there was dispute as to whether the adjacent bank was in fact Transnistria ,since the river had a delta, or was still Moldova on the other side), but I was yelled at by the life guard – and yes, there was a life guard patrolling around in a little white boat.

A friend whom I will not name (starts with an M) rented a jet ski for 25 lei per minute and roared up and down the river, which seemed like fun, if it weren't for the ridiculous price...
Later that day, we retired to the motel area and did some cooking over open flame.

The next day, we made it back to town, laid-low for the night and then took the new group on a tour of Chisinau. The tour was fun, and ended in beer and Pizza, just as God intended. That night, I stayed at a friend's house near-by and on Monday, made my way up to Glodeni, where a couple of us (Pat and Martin) camped in the forest for a few days.

On Friday, I had a question and answer panel with the English teachers in Costesti, assuaging their fears and giving them a fair portrait of life as a volunteer – I hope.

As of now, I am back in dear old Chat-man-doo, waiting for my family to make their way to malevolent Moldova. This week I will be reading, running, studying LSAT's and playing at the orphanage. I have to be back up in the city – or nearby – on Wednesday or Thursday to be on another panel, but I will squeeze as much as I can out of this short week. I am extremely excited to see Michelle and Mom and Dad. I will actually be participating in the panel in Ialoveni; the town where I lived all summer. Apparently my old host family has a new volunteer and Mama Luiba talked about me for a week straight to the new guy. I am rather proud that I had such an impression on her (Hopefully she wasn't complaining about how unbearable I was. That being said, I'm sure the language barrier we had between us led her astray, to believe that I am a gentle and kind person, worth waxing niceties about.)

As lucky as I am to have a family who is willing to visit me, I also found out yesterday that my other brother will be going to school in Turkey next semester – clearly, visiting me will be obligatory. This also means I may get to spend Christmas with at least one member of my family. Maybe in two years, the whole family will finally be back together for the holiday.

To top this off good old Brian Stratton has informed me that he has acquired a ticket to Portugal and will be extending his vacation a bit to stop off and see me. If Mr. B-dog can pull this off, getting through the next year will probably too easy. If he comes, it will be right in the middle of my last month before the LSAT's, but it will be worth the sacrifice in study time. Speaking of Stratton, make sure you all watch his YouTube video. It is some sort of a mock-up survivor deal and I would like everyone to watch it and make fun of him.

That is it for today because, as the Velvet Underground said it at the top of this text, "I am tired, I am weary," and now I have to take a bloody three-hour practice exam! See you soon Scheurichs!

ПОКА, МЫ СКОРО ПОЛЕТЕМ В САНКТ ПИТЕРБУГ КУШАТЬ ИКРА!

Without a hitch

2009-07-04

As awe inspiring as coming into the "gates of Moldova" is, from the airport, my family wasn't able to do so until 1 a.m. Their flight was delayed and, instead of landing at 7 p.m., it landed in the wee hours of the morning. None-the-less, I am very happy to see them and they were very happy to relax, finally, and drink the wine I bought for them. On that note, I was a bit perturbed, because I did some fairly extensive shopping for said relatives and they weren't really able to enjoy much of it. Also, seeing as we will be eating out a lot and be out-and-about a lot, there won't be much time to consume the perishables I've managed to acquire (including 2 Kilos of heirloom tomatoes I bought from a fellow volunteer who is growing them at his site).
Seeing as we all went to bed far too late, everyone continues to sleep and will probably do so until noon, whereas I am on a normal, non-jet lagged, schedule and I am up. The weekend has the potential to hold various amusements for us – the only definite activities being the 4th of July party today, visiting my first host family tomorrow and leaving for big bad Russia on Monday. That is all for now; I'll keep more updates coming as we attempt to take on Saint Petersburg (Oh, and drink the 4th of July celebration dry...)

POKA

Back in the Doldrums

2009-07-16 to 2009-07-17

July 16th finds me back in Cedir-Lunga, reflecting on all
that has happened in the past few weeks. My family has
come and gone, Russia has come and gone and now it is
time to re-adjust to the slow-paced life of a volunteer.
Hopefully I can sum up what has happened since I entered
an article last:
I spent the few days before my parent's and sister's arrival
helping out with the new group in Chisinau. I had rented a
nice apartment in the center of the city for my parents to
stay in and in the subsequent day my friends and I made a
dinner of coconut milk and curry with vegetables and
spring rolls with rice paper we found at the local store. It
was fun to hang out and make some food. Mike D was
there to eat one of the meals and it was one of the last
times I saw him. He has since officially tendered his
resignation from Peace Corps Moldova and headed home –
where he is waiting for his girlfriend to get home from
Europe so the two of them can leave for South Korea,
where they will be teaching English during the next school
year.
My family did end arriving on Friday, very late and we
spent the next day walking around Chisinau and attending
the Embassy's fourth of July party. The night was fun and
Michelle and I ended up out very late, talking and burning
the midnight oil.
The next day, we were all too weary to do much and
eventually made our way to my PST host families site for a
dinner. The plan was to eat, have a couple drinks, take
some pills and rest up for our six a.m. flight but, host dad
started pouring the cognac and it turned into a later and
boozier night than we had predicted. We made our flight,

but the first day in Saint Petersburg was all but shot, because we were in recovery.

On Tuesday we didn't accomplish too much either; we realized that the Hermitage was too great a task to accomplish for the day, and the museum we had planned on seeing was closed. I had also managed to get pick-pocketed by a group of Oliver Twist-esque gentleman in the Metro. To top this off, my father stepped on a patch of grass in a park and was almost forced to pay a bribe of $30 to a police officer.

After our first couple days of misfortune, the vacation picked up dramatically.

By Wednesday we were all feeling great and enjoying the beautiful city. We took a boat ride to the palace of Peterhoff, which was amazing. I am told the complex was modeled after the Palace in Versailles, France; but I really can't imagine anything topping it. It's buildings, forests and fountains were amazing and it was even more mind boggling to imagine that one family (with many guests at all times, I assume) would occupy such a tremendous work of architecture. After seeing the sites, we sat outside at a German style pub and had some beers and talked. I have to say sitting in the sun in Russia with my favorite people was one of the high lights of the trip.

The rest of the week was spent doing various other things such as, attending a ballet at the famous Marinskii theater, touring the Hermitage and shopping around for old Soviet heirlooms and stacking dolls.

It was amazing to be able to use the Russian language, in Russia and actually communicate with people. I have a theory that because the Russian here is often mixed with another language, the Russian in Russia is spoken faster and more succinctly. It was also interesting to hear distinct styles of speech and accents among the people I met. I have to admit that the locals in Saint Petersburg were not always the nicest or easiest to get along with but, in general bank attendants and waitresses were willing to take everything in stride with a group of bumbling Americans. Although never a destination in my mind for food, wine and beer, we did end up eating some interesting things. Georgian food reminded me of Indian food in some respects, with different spices and a bit less flavor. One of the most interesting dishes was a loaf of bread, filled with farmer's cheese and baked. After being removed from the oven, an egg was cracked into the hollowed out portion, where it partially cooked in the residual heat. Sushi restaurants were everywhere and I actually ended up eating Japanese four times. The salmon was very fresh, due to the proximity to the Gulf of Finland and, while it definitely isn't authentic Russian food, it was nice for a guy who lives somewhere where he never gets to eat rolls, sashimi or nigiri. Unfortunately, beer was very much the same as it is in Moldova; lacking hops, flavor or variation and, wine didn't do much for any of us either. One goal we did not accomplish was having a caviar and vodka night, like Michelle wanted so badly. After the cognac-filled Sunday however, none of us were in the mood to drink liquor. Given that we were in Russia during "White Nights," the sun never really went down completely. It descended, but the all-encompassing darkness of night never really hit the city. In fact, the first time I actually felt like I was on a normal schedule was when Michelle and I stayed out to get sushi and drinks – well past midnight – and walked home in the twilight. It was hard to get mentally prepared for a night of sleep when night never really came.

The city itself was gorgeous and the canals spread throughout reminded us of Venice – if not much more spread out. The architecture was amazing and even more exciting to see because not 20 years ago, it was almost impossible for an American to travel and see it.
The weather was cool and windy, with a couple days of rain. Keep in mind this was in July – the dead middle of summer. The frightening thought amongst us all was that if the weather was so cool and pleasant in summer, God only knows how cold the winters got. I would love to see the Neva or Moika rivers iced over, but it would be difficult to deal with sunsets at two in the afternoon and arctic winter temperatures. This is also why I assumed outdoor cafes never made much of an appearance in Petersburg; summer is only a couple months and it probably just isn't financially reasonable to waste the time on outdoor seating.

All in all, it was a great vacation, mostly because I got to be with family. I had recently seen them in Phoenix for Michelle's wedding but, hey, give me a break, I guess I just like family.

Now back in Moldova, I am trying to get English sessions going with some of my ninth graders and am possibly going to be introducing baseball to the kids living at our orphanage. The grant I was working has finally come through and, because it is donation-based, all I can do is sit back and wait for the money to come in, before we can start repair work on my classroom (if you are interested in donating, please Email me: samuel.scheurich@gmail.com). There is the potential for another small vacation at the end of the summer but, depending on how things go, I may just be back in Moldova for the extent of the summer. I am ready to start teaching again and getting on with the last leg of service, but for now I have to be patient. With the LSATs looming in September and various other tasks to take care of in the next six or seven weeks, I should be able to keep my mind occupied. Peace.

Life

July 29, 2009

It has been a while since I have written anything, so I'll start off with a quote from the 56th page and fifth sentence from "The Sound and the Fury," by William Faulkner: "I done thought of something."

Again, because it has been a while, I'll try to remember all the incredibly exciting and worthwhile things that have been taking place since my arrival back into Moldova, from Russia.

After getting back to site for a few days, I went back into the city to meet up with some friends. I ended up coercing a couple of them into going down to my site to play baseball with my orphan children. We spent three days playing baseball (or at least trying to teach fundamentals like throwing, catching and hitting) and inspecting various bars in my village. Over the two nights, we made cannelloni and eggplant Parmesan. The cannelloni was interesting because I took a page out of a friends book and made the pasta part out of something that more closely resembled crepes, rolled them and covered them in sauce. It was fun to have some friends down to help me cook food. We also discovered what is probably the coolest bar in my town, only because JT needed to get money out of a bank. It wasn't our usual bank (where the Peace Corps deposits our money), so I had never been to it. Anyway, we went off the main road, to said bank, which was back in a neighborhood and, when we finished business inside, noticed a thatched roof bar on a bluff – overlooking the entirety of the town. It was a pretty cool place and I plan on going back, next time there are Americans around to entertain (I don't do the bar thing alone too well).

After Pat, JT and Brady took off for home, I spent another couple days at site and then went into Ialoveni, where I began the organization of a BBQ held for the new group in the woods. A friend helped out (Mr. McGregor) and it basically consisted of buying large quantities of cabbage, meat, potatoes, peas, mayonnaise, etc. and 10 liters of house wine, of course. It was the first time I have had to organize food preparation for upwards of 50 people and I have to say I enjoyed it – hey, maybe catering is in my blood.
The picnic was a great time and it was pretty fun to see the new group 'loosen up' a bit, if you will.
Other than that, I've just been hanging around, taking the odd LSAT practice test, doing some English club stuff and running. I am more than ready for the new school year to start because, apparently, during the second year, time starts to fly – or as one person put it, you can see the ground move under your feet.

I have been talking to my sister about moving to San Francisco, going to law school and helping out with some sort of secret restaurant. While this is a year off, the first year went by pretty quickly and it is all downhill from here – as they say. So, until then, la revedere (that's some Romanian for you all).

Life II

August 4th

Following suit with summer so far, the last week went by without too much excitement. I tutored for the first time since before the end of the school year – which was grueling because I felt as though I had forgotten all Russian grammar. It was like chipping lacquer off of my brain with a ball-peen hammer.

I went up to Chisinau on Friday night though, by hitch-hike, and the driver of the car – whom I frequently get rides with – told me that my Russian was better than it used to be, which was a good sign.

On Friday, a couple of us went out to eat at a Restaurant called 'Tulip,' which was purportedly Thai food, but it turned out to be ambiguously Asian. The food was good, however and the seating was outside underneath little private huts. I got a chicken dish with peanut sauce (according to the menu) but I think it was actually some sort of curried chicken. I got the feeling they brought you what they felt like bringing...

On Saturday, a couple of us went to Sadova – JT's site – where we made buttermilk fried chicken. JT had purchased about 20 lbs of chicken and we batter-fried it in a domed tractor wheel, over an open flame. All-in-all, I believe we used about 1 liter of oil and 1 gallon of lard to cook the food. My heart was struggling after the meal. In addition to the chicken, I made some horse radish mashed potatoes and Brady brought up some heirloom tomatoes to make a sort of salad with a balsamic/Dijon mustard dressing. JT also had some sweet corn growing in his garden, so we boiled some. I ate a lot.

We played some baseball on Sunday in Cojusna and, while we lost, it was a good time and I caught a fly ball, which was good enough for me.

Now it is back at site for the week, doing some LSAT and Russian studying. My English club seems to have already petered out and I may just hold off on any more school-related activities until first bell on September one. Hai, Poka...

GRANT

2009-08-12

Donate to my grant at:

https://www.peacecorps.gov/index.cfm?shell=resources.donors.contribute.projDetail&projdesc=261-185

(Please)

Never mind the Bollocks

2009-08-17

Summer is coming along nicely at a very steady and calculated pace. Besides meeting with my partner on occasion and studying for the LSAT's, running and visiting friends, not a lot has been happening in the way of excitement. I am ready for the school year to start – as are many of the English and health teachers – because it not only marks the beginning of the last 'stint' of our service, but life tends to get that routine feel back, when one is expected to work the majority of the week.

Recently, I headed to a friend's site, who lives on the Prut, for some swimming and food making. The current was quick and the cleanliness of the river was in question, but it was nice to get in the water and rinse out my greasy hair. Later that night, we made some hot dogs and baked beans, and passed around a few two-liter beers. My friend's host family had made a roasted eggplant and tomato salad, which was pretty good. This same volunteer has a project which involves a grant he wrote to grow heirloom tomatoes in a green house with his partner – vegetables which we used on everything possible. The following day, we made it to the green house, where I picked a few kilos of green, striped, yellow, orange, purple and magenta colored tomatoes. What is great about the heirlooms, is that they all have very distinct and different flavors, not to mention they all vary in size; drastically (I picked some cherry-sized yellow tomatoes and one reddish-purple tomato that must have weighed over a half kilogram). Part of the project is to sell the tomatoes in Chisinau, to embassy folks and to a couple local supermarkets. They are quite a bit more expensive to sell than regular tomatoes, which is why many clients are those who can afford to shop in high-end stores in the capitol and ex-pat, embassy types.

I made a pretty killer tomato sauce when I got back home, par-boiling, skinning and coring them, before chopping them up and reducing them down with wine and tomato paste.

I will be heading into the city again this week for the new group's swearing in ceremony. Last year, our ceremony was held at the ambassador's house, full of news crews, and higher-ups in the political community. This year, the ceremony will take place in a high-school, in the center of Chisinau. All of the mentors will be present and it should be funny to see a new group get 'sworn-in' to volunteer hood.

Later in the week, we have a mandatory language in-service-training, which will take place on over three days; our mid-service language test will take place on the final day.

That's about all the news I have to report, other than I've began (and subsequently almost finished) watching seasons one and two of the British Office... Which is absolutely hilarious, and you don't have to deal with Jim smirking at the camera all the time. On the other hand, you don't get to watch Dwight be the best and funniest human on earth.

Trade-offs.

I also forgot to add that there was an auto-cross in my town yesterday. I didn't get to see any racing, but I ran through the pit/track area, which was in the 'valley' (this is a bit of a stretch, more like a slight depression between hills) in the center of my town. It looked like it might have been time trials on a small dirt track. The cars appeared to be little modified Ladas and such; resembling old rally cars. It was pretty interesting and would have been fun to spend the day at, as there were around ten car trailers and a few beer tents set up. I wasn't able to get any photos, as I was running, and when I went back with my camera later that evening, they had cleaned everything up. Use your imagination!

Almost there...

August 31, 2009

Through the drizzle and windy mayhem that is today's weather, I would like to apologize for my lackadaisical performance as a blog writer. I really have nothing to blame it on, other than the lazy attitude of summer spilling over onto my everyday life.

I guess I should bring any readers up to date on life during the past two weeks.

Our language IST (in-service training) took place the weekend before last, and it was an informative time— and intense, as I studied Russian alone for three days straight. Our organization put us up in a hotel but unfortunately, for budget reasons, they didn't supply us with the usual per diem for food, etc. Most of us blew all of our money in the big city; which is very easy to do. Despite improving on my Russian considerably since our last IST (in February) I was told by my tester that I hadn't moved up a level, something I am very upset about. I can only imagine it has to do with the intricacies and difficulties of Russian grammar and pronunciation. I rarely find myself in situation where I can't explain what I need to, with or without a Romanian speaker around. Never-the-less, instead of feeling well-prepared and refreshed after the three days of language, I felt deflated and let-down that my ranking hadn't gone up. This isn't terribly surprising, given my pessimistic nature but, that's life. During the trainings however, I changed instructors, which was great because we went over vocabulary and word usage that I hadn't covered with my other PC trainer. It would have been nice to study with her from the beginning.

Moving on to the past, the day before the training I stayed at my friend Jeff's new apartment in Calarasi. Jeff, James and I all made some dinner and played a board game called "The Settlers of Catan", which was similar to "Risk", but better. It was a fun and relaxing night and the next morning we decided to get one more round of the game in before we headed to Chisinau for the IST.

I made it home for the week following the IST and did some studying and meeting with my partners at the school. It was a good week even though after taking my 9th or 10th LSAT practice test, I have yet to break a certain score range. Morgan and I are both taking the test on the 26th of

September and we will be very hermit-like for the majority of the month. Unfortunately, we have another IST over the third weekend in September. Regardless, I spent the week doing my thing down at site and then made it back to Chisinau to do a joint birthday party with Pat. John's American family was in town, so after going out to eat, we burned the midnight oil at various pubs around town. The next day we made it to the Nistru river in Vadul Lui Voda where we, again, made our way to various whiskey bars, this time in the presence of the mighty Nistru. I can feel the age creeping up because, even after those two days of celebration (lots of beer) my almost 25-year-old body is certainly catching up with me, not to mention I'm still feeling a bit wrung out on this stormy Monday morning.

As you may have gleaned from my description of today's weather, it is raining and cold; quite a difference from yesterday, when it was sunny and in the high 80's all day. As much griping as I do about the summer-time heat, I am not looking forward to another winter– now that the clouds are starting to roll in... But with the weather is coming the first day of the Moldovan school year (tomorrow) and I am ready to get moving with the second half of my primary assignment. Tomorrow should be a ceremonial day, which is okay by me. We still don't have definite schedules– and won't for a month or so– but this year will be a bit different, because I will be teaching only 10th and 11th grade. I want to really focus on getting more acquainted with people my age at site this school year– I spent a lot of last year spending my free time with American friends off site. One activity I am going to start (an idea I've lifted from Jeff) is going to be adult English classes. This will be an interesting take on teaching– I've been told that it is much more fun and enjoyable than school teaching, for some– and it should be a way to spend time with peers, without heading to the bar to meet people.

In other news, my brother Charlie will be heading over to Turkey soon and he and I are attempting to coordinate our vacation plans. It is almost definite that I will be heading over to Sicily with some friends in December, and may or may not be going to Jordan after that. We'll see where the wind takes me. The one thing that is definite– in my mind– is that Charles will be meeting me here in mid-October for... wine fest! Other than that, it's going to be a slow and steady September, with the climax of the month being the LSAT. October will bring wine fest, November will bring a week-long break and snow and December will bring the cold and muddy winter and a vacation to top it all off. As you can see, the semester is practically over, without even starting.

Finally, as it has been a while since I have written and my writing has been very erratic all summer, I'll keep it up much more now that I have a fixed schedule; I promise. Peace!

1st Week

2009-09-03

The first week has breezed by, leaving me with a fairly simple and straightforward schedule - in theory, of course. I should be teaching only 10th and 11th grade this year, making lesson planning a less than tremendous task and I will be teaching 6 periods solo every week - mostly because the classes are too big for one teacher to handle. In any event, I wrote "in theory" earlier because, for the first month of school, there is no real schedule. Everyday afterschool, teachers go up to the board and look up their lessons for the next day. I don't know why. I would say it is something about the school system here, but all of my fellow volunteers have their schedules for the year already, so it beats me...

I would like to report on some very decent food I have eaten and/or cooked in the past few days:

The night before last, I used some of the tuna that my Mom sent me to make a tuna casserole. I remember from back home, Mrs. Scheurich tended to use canned cream of mushroom (правдо?) soup as the base, but because I looked up the recipe on Michelle's famed epicurious.com, the base was a chicken stock, a roux and mushrooms. It was very good and rich and my host family seemed to like it... Considering Moldova (and Eastern Europe in general) is the comfort food capitol of the world, I would think they'd like it. Last night, my host dad came through with some pretty good stuff; grilled fish and vegetables. My sister came into my room last night and - rather rudely in my opinion - asked me to make salad for dinner. When I went outside, host dad told me not too, that it was taken care of. This was followed by my other sister and host mom asking me if I had made salad. Both times I responded that the sagacious Jorrik had told me not to. It turns out his version of 'salad' was grilled peppers, onions and tomatoes, under a huge pile of grilled fish. It was bony, per usual, but good and had some decent seasoning.

I've been studying for the LSAT for a while now, but have finally hit crunch time. The test is less than a month away, and I'm starting to feel the pressure building up, like a two-liter bottle of beer strapped to the back of a motorbike, going down a crappy village road. That's about all I can really say about the LSAT topic.

While we celebrated a little join birthday last Friday (one reason being that I'm locking myself at site for the month, in an effort to study), a couple friends have made it a goal to come to wonderful Чадыр-Лунга and make some pizza with me. We'll see if it pans out. My site is so far from the capitol, that it is difficult and time-consuming for people to come visit. When volunteers come together, it helps to have a more centrally located site. In any event, I've managed to have a few people conned into making the three hour bus trip. I've definitely made it quite a few times, to meet with friends - most of which explain that it isn't their fault I live so far away. Regardless, when and if I do leave my site for a given weekend, I've got a two and a half hour bus ride, on top of whose ever site I visit... The price I pay to speak Russian...

Peace.

Week Two

2009-09-11

Through some miraculous scheduling error, I was told not to work yesterday (Thursday is my normal off day) but, I went to the school yesterday and looked at the schedule, and I'm not on it for today either... Four day weekend I guess.

The birthday celebrations down south went pretty well last weekend and they consisted of; a factory blessing, bus stop beers, cheese and tomatoes, Craig's house and the pool hall - I'll explain.

On Saturday morning - one of my most productive birthdays ever - I woke up, took an LSAT practice test and took off on a run. At 12:30, I accompanied my family to their new pasta-making space in the center of town and a priest arrived to bless it for them. I'm not sure how that works, money-wise - but it was interesting and we got to eat a whole bunch of food afterwards... The actual blessing was a bit tedious (we had to stand in place for over an hour while he chanted over a bible), but it was worth it for the experience.

I left the factory around three and grabbed a beer at the bus stop, in preparation for my friends to arrive. Craig (my new site mate) showed up around 4:30 and we greeted the friends. We headed back to my house with some 2 liters of beer, cheese and bread and sat around and talked. As the afternoon turned into night, we retired to my bedroom and sat around. Rain started coming down at eight or so, and then the lights went out...

We eventually braved the torrential rain and mud and made it to Craig's place. The plan had been to go eat BBQ at a local bar, but the rain and lack of electricity prevented that. Craig's host Mom supplied us with plenty of food and homemade vodka - thanks Baba.

The night finished with a cab ride to the pool hall, and some very poorly played Russian billiards.

My first week of school went great, and the second went by quickly, if not as well as the first. I am leaning towards moving out into an apartment again, if I can find one. I think I'd be ready to live alone for the remainder of service. I'm a big boy and it may be time to get my own digs. We'll see...

Oh, see how they run.

2009-09-16

While the aforementioned title has absolutely nothing to do with the subsequent blog entry...deal with it.

Today is the 16th of September, and I am officially done with school for the week because there is training on community development and grant writing in the capitol, starting on Friday. It couldn't have come at a worse time - as I am immersing myself, to the neck, in LSAT studying at the moment - but, hey, what can you do? Tomorrow I think I'll take off early and take a practice test in the city. The last two I've taken have left me with very good results - I'm worried though, because tomorrow's practice test will be from a different set of study materials. I am assuming I can reach the level I had. At this point, I'm getting very excited to get the test over with.

Speaking of excitement, I have found a one-room apartment I will probably move into soon, assuming it can be equipped with a washing machine and drying racks. It is in the center of town and I am ready to finally have my own pad... I mentioned it to my host family last night and, not only were they not upset, my host father told me it would be good for me (keep in mind, I tend to forget to take out my trash, I leave the lights on, etc.) because it would be a sort of life lesson. He also said that he was already old and that I was a youth. He had a family - he motioned this by forming an orb with his two hands - and that if I wanted to have friends over, etc., it would be for the better anyway. I told him I had lived on my own in college, but he said that life in America is easier. I went on to explain that I liked them very much and I wanted to come over once-in-a-while and make lasagna...

...speaking of lasagna. I have made (you guessed it) lasagna twice in the past two weeks, mostly for one reason - being that my family has a pasta factory and spaghetti-type pasta starts out as huge discs, is then cut into long, wide strips (lasagna) and then shredded into thin ones. I had my host mom bring back a stack of the wider strips and went from there. I made a sauce from scratch, with tomatoes and peppers from the garden - because the tomatoes cause the sauce to be a bit sour, instead of adding sugar to cut the acidity, I added a homemade champagne-style red wine to the mix. I used the sauce, boiled noodles and a ricotta-ish cheese for layering, and then grated some sharper cheese on top. Pretty damn good stuff.

Hmm... In other news: I thought I'd share another running story, because it's obviously been quite some time since you had some boredom in your lives. Ok, here it goes: I went running at 6 a.m. this morning, and about half way into the run, while I was in the middle of crow park, (Come October, said park turns into a scene from "Birds;" crows (Maybe they are ravens - are ravens bigger?) are everywhere and it is terrifying. They sit on the ground, circle the trees and make a hell of a cacophony.) the sun started to come up over the hills. The park itself was layered (much like lasagna) with mist and the grass was covered in a fine Eastern European dew. That is my story. Oh, it left me feeling whimsical, etc.

Finally...

I found some self-portraits on my computer and, now that I am going to be switching domiciles - probably, at least - I decided to include a picture of myself from about a year ago, and one taken yesterday. See how I've aged?!

And...

Агромный СПАСИБО and THANK YOU to everyone who donated to my grant. The floors are in and the lights will be installed soon. The room looks great and I can tell that my students are smarter, just because of these things!

LSAT HELL

2009-09-23

I taught on Monday. For some reason, I woke up feeling like hell though, precursors to some sort of illness.

I went into school on Tuesday and my partner and director (both of whom know about the LSAT on Saturday) sent me home because they said they didn't want students catching the swine flu from me. I was instructed to take the week off, get better and study - I can't complain about that, but I will anyway. Complaint: "I don't like logic games or reading comprehension. If I am going to be a lawyer, why am I doing poorly on reading comprehension sections?"

The studying is coming to an end on Saturday at 2 p.m., finally, and I am very excited about the prospect. The main paranoia point is that I am where I want to be score-wise, but I am terrified that I will have a horrible test and score far below what I am capable of. In addition, I may or may not get a section of logic games that I am completely familiar with, or I might not. I need to go into the test with a care-free, positive, optimistic and Zen-like mentality and I'm sure I can do fine. I didn't really take the LSAT seriously the first time around and my score reflected it. Now, I am going into the test with a month or two of serious studying under my belt, which makes it that much more nerve-wracking. POSITIVITY!

In any event, feeling unhealthy couldn't have come at a worse time but, there is nothing I can do about this..

The weather is starting to cool down here in Cedir-Lunga and I've taken to wearing sweats instead of shorts and no shirt. The mornings are the chilliest, but it warms up significantly throughout the day.

The apartment search isn't going well. I turned down the first option because it had no washing machine, nowhere to dry my hand-washed clothes and no oven - only a two burner table top stove. Hopefully I can find another place, because I'd like to have an apartment before Charlie comes to visit me.

The visit from my brother has - of course - become a point of difficulty, because he isn't sure he can leave the country without a STUDENT ID, or some nonsense. I was hoping to have a visitor over the PC organized 10k and over the best holiday in the country; wine fest. We'll see if my negative comments and abusive language can persuade him to get his act together.

Speaking of the 5/10k, it will take place on the morning of the 10th of October (if anyone wants to fly out!), right before wine fest. It will be very impromptu, but I'm excited to get some people out to the park for a little run.

Anyway, I should get back to some studying but, keep it American, America.

Sick, again?

2009-10-05

I spoke with my mother yesterday and vaguely remember being in high spirits. Upon waking at 4 a.m. though, I realized that my stomach felt like there was a porcupine crawling around in the walls and my whole body ached. Seeing as it was 'Teachers Day,' I crawled out of bed, moaning, and dressed myself to watch the ceremony. Seeing as I could barely stand-up, my partners sent me home, for the second time in three weeks. Sylvia said that she didn't want me to faint, while teaching.

I called PC medical and was told I had every symptom of food poisoning - cramps, soon to be followed by Montezuma's revenge. The doc told me that my body was trying to get the bacteria out of my system and that I should drink water and lay in bed and not induce moaning - like a small child (those were her words! (just kidding - although I have been moaning all day, literally). It could have been any number of things considering the fact that: Friday, I drank a new batch of house-wine and ate homemade pizza, Saturday, I ate homemade lasagna and Sunday I made more pizza and more lasagna... The family requested the pasta dish when I got home on Sunday. I used the same roux-based cream sauce but, I poured home-milked dairy product into the sauce... It was a bit thicker than normal and my sister explain that it was partially frozen; I don't believe her.

In any event, if anything I write is un-funny or makes absolutely no sense, blame it on whatever food I ate this weekend which is tearing me apart from the inside.

I'll re-cap the last few weekends. The LSAT seemed to go well and I'll get my results in on the 19th of October. Knock on wood. One of the next two diary entries you read will be either ecstatic or, surprisingly bitter (even for me). We spent a bunch of money that night, eating at a nice restaurant and bowling. I have already explained this weekend, so I'll skip it, because my whole body, including my hands hurt.

School has been going well but I've found myself sick a few times already. Two weeks ago, I was un-fit to teach on Tuesday and my partner gave me the week off to study for the LSAT. A week passed of confusing schedule changes (yes, we still do not have a set schedule) and now it is once again Monday, but I am at home.

Charlie Scheurich arrives on Wednesday afternoon and I am going up to the city to meet him. We are planning on spending the night at my old host families house and then making it into Cedir-Lunga the next day. Thursday is my day off, so I'll be showing him the town and then making him watch/participate in my classes... BWahahhahaha.

On Friday afternoon, it is back into Chisinau to get some rest before the 5K and wine fest in the center. The 5K seems to be coming together pretty well. Pat has found a table we can use in the park and we are going to try to set up a registration desk and food/water table for the participants. Chuck is taking off late Sunday, back to Turkey, which is leaving me slightly guilty at missing school today, because I will be forced to miss next Monday as well. Considering though, I am incapable of teaching today, there is nothing I can do about it.

Cross your fingers and hopefully I can get rid of whatever it is floating around in my body by tomorrow. I would hate to miss another day of school.

Here and there

2009-10-14

Charles Russell Scheurich has come and gone from Moldova and, things didn't exactly go to plan. The boy was supposed to land in Chisinau on Wednesday afternoon - giving us time to spend a whole day and night at my site - but he didn't come in until Thursday, late evening. For this reason, we didn't make it far out of the city but, we had a good time none-the-less.

Because his flight was cancelled and it was so late at night, Chuck and I stayed at a friend's house in a near-by village. We spent Friday in the city, drinking coffee and catching up. On Saturday morning we ran the first-annual Peace Corps 5k in the park. I took a decent place and from there, we went on to wine fest. This year, the festival was at Moldexpo, a nice convention center (much like Westworld in Phoenix), instead of in the center park. Charlie enjoyed himself, even though he was accosted by a female volunteer (you'll have to ask him for full disclosure).

Just like that though, he was back on a plane out of Chisinau (which was delayed an hour) to Istanbul. It was great to see my brother and I've already begun counting down the days in my calendar until I get to go see him in Turkey.

A Day in the Life

2009-10-15

As far as it goes (here), today was an interesting day. I woke up around 6:30 and ate breakfast with the family. I ate three slices of bread with goat cheese and jam. It being my day off, I retired to my room to work on entrance essays and applications– Irvine has a particularly different approach, in terms of what one needs to submit for acceptance.

After a couple hours of talking to my sister about the colloquial nature of my one of my essays, I looked at the notes I had taken– from her advice– and decided that I would think more clearly after a run. It is getting colder and windier but, luckily, today was sunny so I donned my shorts and a long sleeve T-shirt to go running.

I got home and made some changes to my essays. While writing, I received a text from the safety and security coordinator which read: "Man with grenade stands in front of the prosecutor's office in Chisinau. No volunteers allowed in downtown until further notice," and then "The man with grenade (in fact, suspicious packet) was apprehended. Please continue with your daily operations. Thank you. " No problem. I hadn't planned on making it into the city for some time anyway. Later on in the morning, I read an article from an Irish newspaper about a grenade exploding and injuring 40 in the center of town. So it goes.

I digress. After my run and edit session, I went to the school for a Russian lesson. It turns out that my grammar is still bad. I realize now ,though, that I need to start working on my word endings and thinking about what I am saying, instead of just talking. I was convinced that if I spoke enough Russian it would become perfect, but it turns out that this is not the case and I actually need to concentrate on speaking correctly. I don't know why it took so long to realize this. I think it is because I communicate rather well but when my former Russian literature teacher/tutor tells me I don't speak well, I don't feel as proficient as usual. It is not that I cannot converse functionally, but it is that I don't do it well.

I found out (it is my day off so luckily I happened to be at school in a Russian lesson) that today was the day that the staff of my school was celebrating all October birthdays. I made it into the cafeteria where the table was set with various meats, кырма (lavosh with cheese and sour cream— sort of like bready lasagna), sliced fruit, wine, homemade cognac, grapes, etc. Even though I used my host families lavosh to make a lunch of egg, corn and tomato in a burrito after my run, I made sure to eat my share. Like a hobbit, I will label this meal 'second lunch.' We toasted the health of our fellow teachers and drank said wines and liquors. The cognac was actually quite good— despite the fact that I think it was 100 proof and went to my head immediately. Someone also brought муст (freshly squeezed grape juice— pre-wine but slightly carbonated) which is always good. The joke with one of my colleagues is that I work for American intelligence so, as I was leaving, I let it slip that I had to go give a message to the CIA. I also toasted (only to him) "За ингтеллигенцияÂ" (to intelligence!).

I arrived home and decided to play some guitar. "Fat Old Sun," by Pink Floyd has a great solo and I've been playing it lately. I had bought a 2 liter bottle of beer on the way home to make pizza dough and share with the family. My host mom was already making food when I got back though, and she explained that she wasn't sure when I'd arrive, so she went ahead and made dinner. Ничего штрашное. While sitting at my computer, I realized that for the second time in my service my neighbors had started the labor-intensive wine-making process. I sat in my room and took photos and then decided that I might as well go out there and shake some hands. I sneaked through the gate and was immediately spotted by the wife. She invited me over and I snapped some photos of this interesting process. It goes like this:

1.Pick grapes.

2.Bring them home in a tractor.

3.Set up a weird crushing machine and insert grapes.

4.Crush the grapes.

5.Take the skins from the crushing machine and put them in a grape-skin press.

6.Press skins for more juice.

7.Take skins and put them out for the ducks/geese/chickens to eat.

8.Take every bit of squeezed juice and pour it into barrels.

9.Let barrels sit for 2 or 4 weeks and....

10.drink wine.

The only dangerous part of the whole ordeal involves carbon dioxide. It turns out that fermenting fruit juice puts off this un-breathable gas. When barrels are left to sit and ferment, sometimes they sit down in cellars (most barrels go down into cellars eventually, to keep and even temperature) immediately. When this happens during fermentation, a whole lot of CO2 is emitted into the air. There have been numerous cases of people going into the cellar and not coming out. In fact, one death has already occurred in Moldova this year. Last year three people died because one went down and died. His brother went down to rescue him and died trying. A third family member went down with the same mindset and died. It is awful but there are two ways to avoid tragedy. Either don't go down into wine cellars during wine-making season or, make sure there are corks in the barrels when you go down. If there are corks, the barrels are done fermenting and there is no CO2 escaping into the atmosphere.

In any event, I snapped some photos of this colorful process and tasted some young white wine with the people working with the grapes. I also got to drink more fresh grape juice. Because the grapes are un-washed, straight from the field, they still have the incredibly sweet taste of fresh grapes, mixed with crushed bees, earth and leaves - which is amazing. My neighbors don't discriminate with their grape selection and it comes out as a sort of light colored red-mix (a rose I believe). I exchanged words with the workers and they were interested in the fact that I only studied Russian in country, but were more interested in the fact that I knew 'wine,' 'cheers,' 'bread,' and 'dog' in Gagauzian. The last word in the next sentence is wine in Turkish.

I am in my chair, the light is fading and I have the feeling of one who has had just the right amount of şarap. In the words of Tom Robbins:

"For her part, on those rare occasions when her customary high spirits showed signs of taking a dive, Gracie, sooner or later, would remind herself of the parting words the Beer Fairy had whispered in her ear.

"We'll meet again someday," the Beer Fairy had prophesied.

"The ordinary world is only the foam on top of the real world, the deeper world— and someday you and I will meet again."

(From "B is For Beer")

I hope you enjoyed my day-in-the-life.

Хай давай!

The dog kicker

October 22, 2009

Not much has occurred recently, short of the usual October gloom. The weather forecast two days ago lied to me and said that it would be sunny for the remainder of the week. The sun did come out yesterday afternoon for about 2 hours, before dark, but I awoke this morning to foggy death-mist; which is cold and wet. Такая Жизнна!

Anyway, the week has gone by, gloomily. I didn't run yesterday for the first time in 6 days because apparently I burned out the motor on the water pump, which provides running water to the house. I might have to help out with the repair cost so... Hook up some spare change, please.

Speaking of running, I went for a jog the other day to get money out of the ATM– knowing all along that the recently ceased rain may just decide to begin, again– and as I got back onto my street (wearing a cotton hoodie sweatshirt and running pants) it opened up on my head. I came back covered in mud and rain water. Now Moldovans are very clean people. They clean everything, from sidewalks to trees (seriously) and when I came home in this state, I don't think anyone really saw the humor in it. I think they were disgusted with me. They don't get the calling though. I'm like a wolf, I need the open air to run around and chase down small animals and children (that is what wolves do, believe me).

I stayed at site all weekend, which is pretty nice to do these days. Last school year, I was very preoccupied with going into the capitol and hitting the night life but, now that I'm in my golden years (year 25 changed me), it is nice to relax at home and drink coffee. Last weekend, I woke up both mornings and belted out application materials– every now and again, weekends in the capitol involve weariness and hangovers, something I tend to avoid at site, in effect making me a much more productive and happy person in the morning.

So, essentially my weekend consisted of going out for a beer with a Moldovan person who wants to learn English, watching a movie or two, sipping some vin de casa and making pizza. The conversations with my Moldovan friend generally just digress into Russian/him teaching me how to swear in Russian, so it is more beneficial to me. The pizza on the other hand, turned out much better than the conversation, although I substituted yeast and water for beer– on the advice of one Kim Dula. The dough came out alright, if not a bit stiff. I made ranch for the family too on this occasion and they enjoyed it. The funny thing was, we had no milk, just mayo so, I used boiled cauliflower, mashed up, to add some texture and take away from the fact that we were eating pure mayonnaise.

That is about it for this entry except for the fact that I will be heading into the city this weekend to help Marion out in her new apartment. Pat and his girlfriend, Jessica, will be coming over and I think I am going to give egg foo young another shot... Should be interesting– last time the patties didn't form well. Marion is purportedly making peanut butter soup, which she claims is of African origin and takes a very long time to make. On Saturday, Pat and I are heading to his old host family's house in Costesti to sample the new wine. Should be good stuff (you may remember photos from last spring, in the cellar).

On a final note: I didn't realize that I was much of an animal-sympathizer-type (I have dreams about killing my neighbors dog by strangulation, because it barks all night). The other morning though, I was walking to school and I saw a group of men standing around, chatting, laughing, etc. One man spotted a puppy (emphasis on puppy) and kicked it, breaking its leg. The dog scrambled around on the ground yelping and screaming and the man walked over and kicked it again, sending it five feet across the dirt. The men in the circle stood, chuckling or staring on indifferently. I will leave you with a thought: It is one thing to kill strays, because they are pests. It is one thing to hit someone in the face out of anger. But it takes a very special person to kick a puppy, break its leg and then– while said tiny animal is flopping around on its broken paw, wailing– kick it again.

Toast

2009-10-23

I went into the kitchen this morning to make my first cup of coffee - the process involves taking my already purified water and boiling it, then adding instant coffee. I stay away from using the tap water, especially lately. A good example of why, is because last night, I made lasagna and boiled the noodles in our tap water. The finished product was a bit gritty and I have a feeling that the water out of the tap is the culprit. My family is now into the idea of mass producing lasagna though, because Barrilla lasagna sells for about 30 lei in Chisinau. There is a whole lot of 'home' pasta in this country, but lasagna is a new concept. Maybe it will be the next big hit and my host family will become multi-millionaires.

I ran yesterday, but the power went out while outside. It was a foggy and very cold day, and when I got home, I was forced to shower, in the tub, using a 5 liter bottle of cold water as my rinser. I felt extremely bad ass, but cold.

Now, the reason I wanted to write something down was because of something that happened while making breakfast. I wanted to make toast (toasted bread) but, our toaster is broken. So, I turned on the oven and inserted said slices of bread. I told my sisters I was gonna make toast. Host dad came in and said, that I wasn't making toast, I was just burning bread. He pointed to our Panini maker (don't ask) and said when you make cheese Paninis - that is proper toast. I said that what I was making was toast in English. He said that I was wrong, even in English, I wasn't making toast. Now, I feel like I have a fairly firm grasp of the English language and yes, maybe the 'toast' I know is a big lie and I don't know what I'm talking about but, for all intents and purposes, toast to me and everyone I know is a piece of bread, inserted into a toaster and made into a jelly carrying receptacle. Yes? If I am ever corrected on my English again, I might have to dip into my brick supply and start throwing them around, indiscriminately. Cheers.

Today

2009-10-27

Not too much to report today. It is nearing the end of yet another month and I am left getting more and more excited about the next part of my life. I know that it is a ways off, but I also know that it will be here before I know it. Throughout service I have checked off months in my day planner (as you may have seen two blogs ago) and it is odd to be checking off number 17. I remember when I was checking off number three, quite well.

This weekend will mark the great holiday of Halloween, although I'm not sure if anything too substantial will be done to celebrate it. There is a possibility of a little shin-dig happening at a friend's apartment but, we shall see. I am, however, going to be playing some music with Martin and Isaac. Isaac plays guitar and Martin plays drums. He managed to collapse a set and bring it over and I think we are going to take our act to the streets of Belti and Chisinau. If the Halloween party happens, we may be making a little appearance there as well...

I have all my applications in for law school, finally, and now I can sit back and wait for the results to come in. I shouldn't hear anything until Jan. at the earliest, so I have some time to sit and stew. Until then, poka.

Den Zdorovia

2009-10-30

День Здоровия!

Today was health day at school. Some of you may remember last year, when I posted photos of students running around the park. Well, this year didn't go quite to plan, mostly because I am an idiot.

After the initial ceremony at school, I sat in on a health class and then was under the impression that the student body would make its way to the park at 11:30. It turns out that they went to the park at 10:30. Meanwhile, I went home to get my own run in for the day. While walking back to the park to take photos, etc., I ran into all my colleagues walking back.

I got to the park to watch the wrap-up of the soccer games that the younger students play and took some photos. I finally realized though what 'health day' is at our school. It is my school's version of field day– to a lesser degree. Instead of high jump, long jump, relays and blah, blah, blah, it is a 30 meter run and soccer games for the younger kids. I realized this because I looked out into the park and all the teenagers were standing around and socializing... Like field day!

Anyway, I talked a bit and then went to the bazaar to redeem my free beer (the Chisinau 'under the cap' game is back), which took a lot of arguing– the little ring had come off the cap and I hadn't bought the beer at that specific store. I also went to the watch repair shop, where I had deposited my watch to get fixed; only to learn that it was beyond repair.

Tonight is Cedir-Lunga's Halloween disco, which I am organizing because my site-mate (Erin, who works with the Integration club at school) is out of town. Should be a good time because you all know how much I like loud techno music and dancing. I'll be sure to get more photos of this wild night!

I'm going to Chisinau tomorrow, where there will be a small Halloween gathering at Marion's apartment, and then taking off to Martin's site to play music for a couple days. I'll be the most diligent photo-journalist I can be, I promise..

Poka!

Crazy Chester and his Dog, Werewolves in London and TDY

November 6, 2009

Crazy Chester and his Dog, Werewolves in London and TDY

Today, I sit in a dark but comfortable apartment in the center of Chisinau. The walls have a paisley pattern of paper and the lighting is ornamental, if not strange. The wooden floors hold the heat well enough and the mattresses are too soft— which is a good thing. Something that stands out about where I am staying is that it is well heated; there is even a radiator by my bed.

I am currently in Peace Corps TDY (a borrowed term from the military meaning 'Temporary Duty') on the last legs of a cold. I came into PC medical two days ago for my mid-service exam and I was told I had to spend a few nights here. As a part of my mid-service exam though, was a visit to the dentist and I was a little concerned that I would infect said dentist with the pig flu but, apparently it was worth the risk. I am happy to say that our dentist here is as professional and his equipment newer and more advanced than that of my own back home. At the end of the brief check-up, my teeth were cleaned with a water jet machine (no more mini buffer that my dentist uses in Phoenix) and I was informed I have the makings of two cavities. I will be visiting him again at the end of November to get this problem taken care of. I'd like to add that every volunteer who visits the dentist leaves telling me that he is a Russian speaker and loves it when people speak Russian to him. I can say that this is true and he was very pleased to hear my Russian. His assistant told me I spoke "clean" Russian which, while untrue, was nice to hear.

Backtracking: On Monday, Isaac, Martin and I went to Belti to play some music in the streets. We began by practicing in Martin's village and then made our way (by hitch-hike and bus) to Belti, the Russian capitol. Martin has a small luggage tote that he drags his set around on and Isaac and I have our guitars. We played a lot of classic rock such as Jessisca, The Weight, Werewolves of London, Sweet Home Alabama, and Layla. It was cold as hell and every time Isaac said, "take a solo," I rolled my eyes and cried, but the people loved it. One guy even told me he was in two metal bands (one of which was named "Phoenix") and he gave me a bass pick he had crafted from a vinyl record. It was a great time and we went out to celebrate that night; a celebration that involved partying with a guy at his birthday party, meeting interesting people in the central park and making it home to sleep it all off. I'd like to add that when I woke up, my body was struggling with the makings of the Flu (or whatever I have). ravaging Ukraine and now Moldova, I was told to sleep in my own room (not share one, as every room has two beds) and to stay out of the volunteer lounge. It has been a boring but restful two days, filled with reading, eating, reading, and partaking in Nyquil induced sleep. There is also a bathtub here and I rested my rapidly aging body in the tub for the first time in about 4 years. The past 17 months, I had never had to stay in TDY but, now I'm wishing I had!

The hotel we stayed at was great, by the way. For about 10 dollars each, we had our own beds and a full breakfast with greasy eggs, sausage, bread, butter, cheese and coffee the next morning.

Moving further back in time, we had a Halloween party on Saturday night in Chisinau and, it went as expected. Very "wet," if you will. Kudos to Meredith and Jessica who brought snacks. I love snacks.

Tonight, Pat and I should be heading out to his host families house in Costesti to make them dinner. I don't feel 100% and while I know I'll be drinking a lot of wine with the Ababis, I think I will survive. Even if I don't (figuratively, of course) I have all of next week to rest because school has been cancelled. You can look up articles online but from what I've gleaned it has to do with the pig flu scare.

That is about it for today. I am going to try to upload a video of us playing "The Weight" in Belti on YouTube and, if I succeed, I will post the link on the blog site… Poka.

Blah, Blah

2009-11-10

Luckily, I was spared going to Pat's host family's house like I had mentioned. I say luckily because still recovering from my illness and I really didn't feel like drinking a bunch of house-wine. Instead, on Friday, we made dinner at Jessica's apartment. I made a sauce using the dried mushrooms Mrs. Scheurich sent me - it was strange. The girls made lettuce wraps which were very good.

Saturday was interesting, in that I witnessed my first Moldovan football game. The teams were FC Zimbur and FC Tiraspol. The two teams clashed and tied on Sunday afternoon and left me wishing I had attended more matches during the summer. In any event, the weather was beautiful and we had a great time, eating peanuts and drinking $1 pints in the stands (a lot cheaper than $10 beers at D-Backs games).

On Saturday night, I headed up to JT's site in Sodova to make some nachos and chili. It was an uneventful night filled with over-eating and sleep. I made it back to my site on Sunday around noon, in time to get a run in and then head to my host sister's beauty pageant. The 'pageant' consisted of the usual Miss America stuff, but also included some other interesting acts including Tsigani (politically correct for "Gypsy") belly dancing and a dance troupe from Cahul. Unfortunately, I forgot to bring my camera to the event. I particularly wanted to photograph the guest models who were wearing this seasons fashion (or something to that effect) because they were ...ahem... less than fully-clothed.

We have another week of work off, due to the swine-flu and I've been spending much of my time in my room, reading and writing. I almost wish we had work this week–

almost. What I need to do is get started on finding funding for the new toilets and plumbing that my school director mentioned to me. Instead I've been writing a short story, playing guitar, running, eating and surfing the internet.

There isn't much else to say. After going through a beautiful week -weather-wise– November is rearing its ugly head and it has been cloudy, cold and misting for two days now. Apparently the sun is supposed to come out later in the week, but we shall see. It makes me miss November in Phoenix, where you can wear a T-shirt all day and night.

Moldovan Relaxation

Sunday, January 15, 2009

Another week of 'break' has come and gone– and what a week. Monday through Wednesday were essentially me sitting around and reading, playing guitar and eating. Restful to say the least. On Wednesday evening, I actually made it out of the house to meet with my two site-mates, our Bulgarian dance teacher friend and a couple who had been living in Japan for the past two years (whom are friends with one of my site mates). We went out and had a couple drinks and then wandered to her apartment to eat their vegetarian enchiladas.

Craig– the other site-mate– had a theory that running in modern running-shoes is hard on the body and it is miraculous that, given the distances and frequency I run, I don't have injuries. He claims that modern shoes were made in an effort to fuel the industry and are not actually good for your joints and bones... Apparently said shoes (which I swear by) are too padded and fool your body into thinking it doesn't have to 'tread lightly,' if you will. He runs in those weird toed-shoes, with little or no padding and they are supposed to teach you how to run and use your body correctly.

A humorous argument he delivered was that man was not created to wear shoes. He claimed "I am a human and we used to hunt and run down animals in our bare-feet" and that humans have been running without shoes longer than with them. This line (I especially appreciated the "I hunt and run down animals") was delivered from the perspective of a guy in a sweater-vest and tie, sitting in a heated apartment. Oh irony.

On Thursday, we have our weekly adult English class. While only two women showed up, it was a fun time. I really enjoy teaching adults because they want to be in class, they pay attention and they are polite. Kids are not. We covered various topics; I had them write a dialog and we read through a National Geographic.

The National Geographic in question helped to solidify my plans for vacation when I complete service, because there was an article on Annapurna and the region around it. I had planned on making it to Nepal to do some trekking and if I can pull it off, I'd like to camp at the base of this fierce mountain. Ideally I will also have time to wander through India but, we'll see (law school may complicate things).

On Friday morning, I got up, ran, read, ate and then hitch-hiked to Taraclia where Aaron— one of the guys from the new group– lives. I hitched with a guy from a near-by village who looked severely hung-over or strung out in some sense. When we got into town, I told him I wanted to find a cafe and read. We found the cafe but then he went inside and bought us both beers and we sat around and talked for a while.

The conversation was very interesting, but he was one of those speakers who used 'as it were' and 'in short' a lot. In Russian, 'karochy' (карочи)) means 'in brief' and 'kak buy' (как бы) means 'as it were' or 'how'd it be.' When people over use these expressions as sentence fillers, it quickly becomes annoying; similar to someone saying 'um' all the time between thoughts.

We covered the economic crisis, cars, jobs and how he thought America was better than Moldova. After a bit, I got up and explained that I'd grab the next round but, as it was sunny and beautiful outside, I really didn't want any more beer, I wanted to sit outside– alone– and read my book. My out– as it were– came when he said "I'll only have one if you do. If I drink and you don't, I will look like an alcoholic..." I explained that I didn't want one and bought myself a water.

I guess the backwardness in all of this was the fact that culturally, one can sit and drink as much as possible, as long as he is in the company of friends. Having a beer alone though, could be seen as a no-no. That being said, the only people I do see drinking alone are old men in beat-up, tweed sport coats. They go to the bar, buy a beer, buy a shot, take the shot, chug the beer and leave. I can't imagine what was going through peoples' minds this summer while

I was studying for the LSAT. Once or twice a week, I would take my practice test to an outdoor bar, have a drink and go over the incorrect answers. They were probably thinking: "Wow! An alcoholic who grades standardized tests while chugging his beer! Where is the shot?"

Anyway, Aaron's host mother fed us wine and food and then we went out to mingle with the locals. I ran into a guy and explained to him that I lived in Cedir-Lunga and I was recently at the beauty pageant. I said that the girl who got 1st place was 'hot' and that she was from Taraclia. As luck would have it, she was not only from Taraclia but she was said gentleman's girlfriend and shortly after this interaction, she made her way to our table. Hm...

Anyway, we met some good people and drank some of that Russian fire water. I would like to add that I think I eat a bit healthier than some volunteers ,meaning my family makes healthier food - карочи! For dinner at Aaron's we ate deep-fried French toast, fried potatoes and fatty, little meat-balls. For breakfast the next morning we ate fried cheese pastries, the same French toast and a bowl of cream-of-wheat (or something along those lines). His Babushka tried to get me to drink a shot of cognac with my breakfast but, I politely refused.

I got home on Saturday in time for a run and to make cookies. The dough turned out well, despite the fact there is no brown sugar in this country but, the oven was turned up to high and the bottoms burned pretty badly. I may have to give it another go today, because– when baked correctly– chocolate chip cookies are the best things on earth. My mother would put these people to shame with her cookies. Despite all the homemade things in this country it is odd that they never make cookies. They pretty much always buy them. My theory is that cookies here are dirt cheap (there is a joke amongst locals that "cookies cost nothing") and they are very good. Some are like short-bread, some are chocolate and peanut covered, some are like Oreo cookies. For lack of a better word, they are awesome.

In any event, that evening I went out for a beer with Craig and we shot the breeze. When it was dark and cold outside, we looked down at our watches and realized that it was only 5:30 p.m.! Damn this 'getting-dark-early' thing!

In the later evening, I watched "All the President's Men" and it gave me pangs, thinking back to when I used to write for the Daily Wildcat. I miss sitting at a desk and making phone calls, interviewing, writing, etc.

Today I am supposed to meet with a young lady from my town to speak English. While outside the beauty pageant last Sunday, I went into a shop to buy a bag of chips and the woman got to talking to me and said she knew me and she had seen me around town. She has a daughter who wants to do a little chatting, so I feel obliged to go sit and talk.

In other random occurrences, a local friend, Alex, told me that he plays music sometimes at the music school. I guess he takes lessons, or something to that effect, and he played a bit of his instructors music that was on his cell phone. I heard the twang of an electric guitar and I am hoping I'll be able to make it in there sometime to rock out.

Speaking of rocking out, there is to be a charity concert here in Cedir-Lunga on December 5 at the house of culture. Our little act is going to play. It will be fun to have amplified equipment (even though this means that I will have to stand in front of a microphone while I play guitar) and maybe I can even get Alex to get his hands on that electric...

Here's to you Deep Throat.

Taking it all in

November 21, 2009

Сегодя I am sitting in the Circelan's kitchen, drinking coffee and trying to think about what to base this blog on. Some rather unfortunate, yet positive things have happened as of late down in Cedir-Lunga, but right now I am very content and happy to be in my favorite house in Moldova. In brief, I had another run-in with host dad. This time he called me insolent (ноглый) and all-around bad (противный). This all began because I made a salad to bring as a gift to a friend (I was going over to this families' apartment to break bread) and I didn't ask if I could make the salad. I had assumed that after 18 months in the country, 15 at the house, and numerous times cooking dinner for the family (the past two week nights, the parents have been working past ten p.m. Both nights, I made dinner and then helped the girls with their home work. Night 1 was beans and salad, night 2 was lasagna. Please don't compare me to Mary Poppins. I guess I could be Marty Poppins, at least that title has proper gender

agreement.) and watching the young daughters while the parents were at work, that I could make a potato salad without asking. Host dad went on to say that:
1. If PC knew how I "was," they would send me home.
2. The whole town thinks I am insolent/impudent.
3. He doesn't, and will never again, take me as a guest because everyone (including him) thinks I am ноглый.
4. Basically, I'm a pretty rotten guy.
The next day, a representative came down from PC to watch me teach on a routine site-visit. Once every school year, someone from Peace Corps comes to view our teaching and meet with school staff. Among points made after the lesson, by my school director and vice-director were:
1. I am beautiful (seriously).
2. When asked if they'd like another volunteer, they responded by saying, "If he is like Sam."
3. He is one of the best volunteers we've had.
4. They wanted me to stay for an extra year.
5. Basically, I'm a pretty rotten guy.
Enough of that though, you don't read my blogs to learn about all the drama (although home life is like an episode of the Real World), you want to hear about what life is like in Moldova and you don't want the grit.

Last night, Victor and I drank wine and talked about the old days of the CCCP. I remember thinking, before I flew over to Moldova in 2008, that the Soviet Union had nothing good to offer people and that former 'Comrades' – if you will – were happy that the union dissolved. Images such as the fall of the Berlin wall and the impenetrable borders of the former Soviet Union solidified these beliefs. Propaganda works both ways. This statement was made even more clear to me as I was doing some research in Cedir-Lunga. I wanted to see pictures of my town, while it was under Soviet control – mostly because we have lots of factories that have gone the way of the dodo; I wanted to see them in full-force. In my mind, there would be groomed trees and grass and people walking around outside with lab coats and clip-boards.

My search began at our local museum, when this turned out to be a fruit-less effort, I walked to the Чадыр-лунгского района библиотека and starting searching for reading material – picture heavy reading material. The closest I got was happening upon a book about Moldova from 1984. It was written in English, Bulgarian, Romanian and Russian (the Romanian was in Cyrillic, just like the Russian and Bulgarian). It was mostly photos of larger towns and Chisinau. Chisinau looked cleaner, there were more Ladas on the streets and the fountains (graffiti-free) were working. I mentioned propaganda before though, and this was a great example of it going in the reverse direction. The book seemed geared towards informing the world about the great progress that Moldova was making. Just like I imagined, there were photos of people in white lab coats, holding trays of recently pasteurized eggs, etc.

Back to our conversation in the garage though. Victor compared the Soviet union to a 'ladder of intelligence' – bear with me here. I was under the impression that the trickle-down economics of the USSR kept those on the top very wealthy, and everyone else was equal. I thought that doctors made what laborers made, etc. This was not the case. Apparently the higher up you went in your education, the more perks life held for you. Victor said that a farm worker would have everything he needed, but a successful doctor would have everything and more. He gave an example of a family friend who had a flat in Chisinau, a house in his home village, a car and a bit higher salary than others. Apparently, this went throughout society. I explained to him that, as a rule, Americans tend to view the Soviet Union as a land filled with terrible corruption and heart-ache. While this may be true in some cases, I have yet to come across an older Moldovan (as in, alive while CCCP was in full-force) who didn't wish the country was still a part of a communist government.

Let's keep in mind that there was undoubtedly top-level corruption. Because, much like a law-firm, all the money was made and put into a 'pot' to be distributed to the masses, there must have been some terrible mistakes – it must have been an accountant's nightmare. There are also still villages out in Siberia without schools, roads and little to no contact with the modern world. Victor said that some of these villagers have never met people from the rest of the world. I am sure these villages didn't benefit much from what the Soviet Union had to offer.

In the United States, it is mandatory to attend school (until the 9th grade, if I'm not mistaken); something Victor didn't know. I informed him of this fact while he was explaining to me that everyone went to school for free back then. The perk was that, the better you did, the higher you went. If you were a good student, you went from high school, to college, to graduate school and on to your doctorate – if you could cut it. For this reason I joked that the only way to move up during Soviet times was to be smart. It was a system based on brains, apparently. Hey, they managed to get a спютник and a man up into space before the us.

In sum, I am now a communist.

In sad news, Donna died recently. Last night Victor and I poured out a little wine (We actually did this, apparently it is a tradition here too. I thought it was only something rappers did for their dead comrades.) for the gigantic, recently departed canine.

In other news: we are going to make enchiladas at Marion's apartment and I am hopefully going to meet up with a Russian devooshka I met at the soccer game last week. I wouldn't mention something like this normally but chatting with her online in Russian has been challenging in itself — something I am quite proud of. I mentioned meeting her to Liuba (my old host mom) and she said "Moladetz!" and then something to the effect of, "its time you starting talking to Russian girls."

Next week is Thanksgiving and we are going to be cooking up a storm. I am on a team with the illustrious Jeff Zundel, among other people; he and I have been planning out our menu, often stealing ideas from Michelle Scheurich. There will be three 'teams' preparing food in three different kitchens for roughly 60 people. Should be a good time.

Ahhhh, finally — I will be, without a doubt, moving out of my host families house and into an apartment. I am kicking myself for not taking the first place I found. I didn't grab it up initially, because I was told it was too expensive, there was no-where to dry clothes and I was being picky. I was under the impression that another place would open up (I even though I'd get a washing machine) and then I gave up looking altogether. I'm upset because it was in a perfect location and a friend – who lives nearby the said apartment – has a washing machine and even offered to do my laundry! Blaaad! I have some more leads and my partner is going to ask around the town today – apparently there are two available in the same complex but, no one is sure whether or not the proprietors want to rent them out. Но, я успею найти квартиру, всё будеть хорошо... Я надеюсь! Удачи вам и всего хорошого. (Translate that one!) Poka.

http://www.youtube.com/watch?v=THfiHQZVSw0

Diary title:

2009-12-01

Just as promised, time really is starting to fly by. Despite the fact that I've had some problems at home, etc., there is no denying the fact that it is already December 1st. I literally have about 3 and ½ weeks until I fly out to Turkey and then I'll be coming back for my 4th and final semester as an English teacher in the Peace Corps.

I remember this time last year vividly and it really doesn't seem that long ago. In fact, last year at this time, there was already snow on the ground and it was far too cold to walk around outside with sweat pants and a jumper. This year, it has barely rained and it is much, much warmer. I am hoping that the warmth will stay up and, before I know it, it will be spring again. False hopes aside, it is unnerving to think that a real winter is probably on its way. There is no way we will make it through December, January and February like this. I can't emphasis enough how warm it is right now. I wear my down jacket to school, but don't really need it.

One difference in the weather that this year has brought us is fog... I'm talking cold, opaque, wall-like fog, that makes running frightening and makes crossing the street a challenge (I might add that a second villager has been killed crossing the street. He was hit by a car last night– I saw him being loaded into an ambulance. The first person was the math teacher at my school. The phrase 'look both ways' has never been more apt.). When I walk home at five with my guitar, it is covered in dew and when I wake up, my shoes are damp from sitting outside. Apparently, if I keep running, I'm going to get sick. It just so happens– this may or may not be what we call an "old wives tale" - that the extreme cold is healthier than the fog.

Thanksgiving went well (I should add that on Thursday - actual Thanksgiving - I went to JT's site, where we baked brined chicken, made horse-radish mashed potatoes and curried onion, tomato and cucumber salad. As usual, this meal was much better than anything else I ate all weekend. When the three of us get together, we tend to make quite a feast.) and I had a great time cooking food with Jeff, Melissa and Alex. I did my best to be a megalomaniac in the kitchen and tried to bark orders at people, even when they weren't necessary. We prepared 8 kilos of mashed and scalloped potatoes, one turkey and five pans of sausage-apple stuffing. I used the Starbucks I was sent by my parents and drank no less than three cups of coffee. Killer.

We used a Peace Corps staff member's house to cook the food (the place was a former country director's house and it is literally gigantic) and I ended up helping translate, when a vet came to pick up the family's dog, to have it spayed. It was the second time I really didn't want to screw anything up, concerning translation... (the first time was in Russia, when I was trying to organize a wire-transfer for Mr. Scheurich)

The eating itself was a bit lackluster. Last year, there were about half as many people and we all seemed to know each other. This year— what with the arrival of the new giant 64-person group— it felt very impersonal. I walked into the 'hall,' as it were, after having finished cooking, to everyone eating away at their tables. After making myself a plate of food and eating, I went to the apartment and took a nap. That night, our safety and security coordinator's band played (he plays the harmonica for a blues/rock band) and I went to watch. Good stuff.

Speaking of music, our little group will be playing at a charity concert at my site on Saturday. Apparently there will be several acts— from music to dancing— and the only admission is a doll or toy to give to local kids. So much for finally getting a paying gig! Poka.

"Ah, Les Braves Hommes" (we volunteers, that is)

2009-12-10

I suppose I have a fair amount to write about. It is a dreary day, suitable for winter, but today there was the slightest trace of snow falling. I think that the mist I referred to in the previous article froze on its way down. In any event it is 8:54pm and the 'snow' has turned back into water.

Last weekend we played a charity concert at my site. It was more of a talent show for kids in the community— spectators (which I am pretty sure were mostly contestants) had to bring a doll or toy, which will be given out over the holidays to the less fortunate. We played a couple songs and I will try to post them on YouTube in a couple weeks— my Internet connection at site can't handle that much information...

In random news surrounding service, my guitar club is doing very well. It is getting to the point where the kids want to meet at school more often than I am willing... I've taken to giving Max, the 'leader' of the group, the key to my classroom. They meet, chat in Russian and noodle around on the guitar. It seems like they enjoy themselves.

I'll be spending a second weekend and third week straight at site, and I think I'll be using my free Saturday to go look at the nearby lake... Apparently we can take one of the town buses to the area of Ceadir-Lunga where townies have their garden plots. Next to these plots is a lake— or so I've been told.

I have just finished reading " A Year in Provence" and to make the outing authentic, I'll have to pack some saucisson and pastis (although, I am still unclear as to what kind of beverage pastis is exactly). I did see a bottle or two of grappa at the local gas station and, while this Italian beverage is supposed to taste and feel like rocket fuel, it may have to substitute.

Speaking of "A Year in Provence", there are startling similarities between Provencal life and Moldovan village life. Although maybe not comparable, both love their wine, both take pride in grapes, both have livestock, etc. (In all honesty, I guess the similarities are only in regards to the realities of village life itself)

The big differences I can see are a lot more emphasis on putting excellence into wine and food– on the French side, that is. There also seems to be something more cultured about French village life– it must have something to do with the proximity of more affluent villages and towns, not to mention Paris, Nice, etc. They have kept their village identity, while still advancing with the modern world.

One thing is a definite though, I love French food and there is no way to get around the fact that I would enjoy life where olive oil is the norm and truffles are sold by the pound. Where I live, people love food– they just love the same 5 dishes (and in all honesty, they don't compare to French and continental cuisine -sorry). On a final note, after having read the book, I've never felt more comfortable with the idea of wine and cheese being a staple in my diet and taking up the habit of smoking fat, yellow cigarettes. As Faustin would say: Normalement!

Something I gleaned while reading though, is that the longer grapes sit out in the sun, the higher their alcohol content. At first this made no sense to me and then I did some thinking and questioned my neighbor about the fine art of grape growing (one thing I'll give to Moldovans, is that they grow their grapes without machinery– all by hand baby). In Moldova, cheaters will add sugar to their wine, to boost the alcohol content– this wine gets you drunk as hell and leaves you with a splitting headache; это не хорошо! I put this fact together with what I read; that a rain can ruin a crop of grapes and they must be picked before the rainy season hits but, not too soon. This is because, when grapes sit out in the sun, the water is evaporated through the skins and basically concentrates the juice inside the grapes themselves. What is left is a product that will turn into a higher alcohol content and stronger, better flavor. When a rain hits, the grapes themselves are diluted as water is absorbed up the grape stems. If I am wrong in any of this, please correct me. I stick by my theory though.

This semester is almost done... As I said, I'll be in the village for a 2nd weekend, to save some money and avoid buses. Now in my 2nd year, I find it equally, if not more, appealing to sit in my room and wander around town on the weekends, as I do seeing friends in Chisinau and other villages. I've turned into more of a hermit than I thought possible. I have one more week of school, a weekend in the city– to celebrate the last week of our semester and Marion's birthday– and then I fly out to Turkey on the 24th.

Productivity is a Relative Term

2009-12-14

Productivity is a Relative Term

I woke up today with a painful cough; my sternum also felt as though someone had hit it with a hammer. My partner told me that if I wasn't feeling well, I should go home. So, I went home and proceeded to watch 5 episodes of ' Lost'... After feeling as though my whole day shouldn't be spent in sweat pants, watching Lost and drinking чай, I put on a different pair of sweat pants and proceeded to finish watching.

The weather is finally turning to winter and it is really, really cold, all the time. It is cloudy most of the time too. What is strange about the weather, is that it hasn't rained for a month, and the time before this rain, was another month in the past– essentially, its rained twice in 2 months (this is with the exception of the strange mist we had a couple weeks back...). Because it is so dry, the ground actually looks cold and feels harder also, any bit of moisture on the ground or on plants has turned into ice. Running is back to being more of an expedition, and I tend to do it with pants, gloves, a fleece beanie, a fleece half-zip and a wind breaker.

Last Friday brought me one of those Peace Corps moments that made me glad I decided to come over here. I was out on a morning run around my town, the sun hadn't quite come up and the darkness of night was hanging on (it never really ended up lifting, as it was a clouded day). As I was appreciating the feeling of running in the pre-dawn darkness and looking at my breath as I sang along to music I realized that I was waving or greeting almost everyone I saw on the streets. Two or three people who knew me in cars honked as I ran buy and I gave the victorious #1 (a reference from the Tour de France, when some Italian kissed his index finger after winning a stage) to my the local furniture repair man— who always picks me up when he sees me. I came home feeling pretty elated. It took a while to feel like everyone knew me (and believe me, not everyone knows me in a town this size).

It also recently became apparent how many people in the community notice me. Almost everyone I meet for the first time tells me that I'm the guy who runs. It is funny being told by total strangers that they see you jogging around their town. At least I'm not the notorious drunk.

Anyway, the weekend was fun and relaxed. I played guitar with my neighbor on Saturday night and drank his house wine. I also introduced him to The Last Waltz and the band as we sipped on champagne. I mention the champagne because as I was leaving, he offered me the bottle as a gift to 'drink with the girls,' as he put it. He ended up coming over to look up Russian songs on line and we drank the bottle. Too bad for whoever these girls might have been.

Ten days till Turkey baby. Boo ya!

Снег Идёт

2009-12-15

It began snowing last night and it has been going strong all day. If I were to hazard a guess, we've got about 6 or 7 inches on the ground. Last year, we had a bit of snow, but this year is a whole different ball game!

I thought I'd put up a blog to show you some photos of the southern snow... If the sun comes out tomorrow, I'll post some more because everyone likes to look at the snow in the sunshine...

SNOW FIGHT!

2009-12-17

Thought I'd write briefly to tell you about the tremendous amount of snow we have gotten in the past couple days. There is literally 4 feet of snow outside, which makes day to day life pretty interesting. I've had a cold for the past few days, which makes shoveling the walk really fun...

I went to get money out of my ATM yesterday, and to buy an electric tea kettle for my room and had to dodge skating cars the whole way! Being the good Samaritan I am, I helped three people out of snow banks.

Wake up Charlie!

2009-12-24

I flew into Ataturk Airport yesterday at about 1:30 p.m. In an attempt to be as thrifty as possible, I was going to take a bus into the center and then a taxi to Charlie's dorm but, I was told that it would even out to about the same price. I ended up spending about 50 lira (or 40 to 45 bucks) on a taxi, which dropped me off to find the illustrious Charles sitting on a brick planter, wearing a grey sweater. What a guy.

Anyway, he took me and showed me around his living area, which is much, much nicer than anything I was used to in college and we proceeded to sip on some cocktails while we discussed the route our vacation would take. After some deliberation, we went to a pub to grab a beer and ate some popcorn. From there, we went to another bar and split a big jug of beer. From there, we went to a very nice Italian restaurant and split a very good mushroom pizza.

After dinner — which was held to see a couple of his friends off — we went out to some bar and hung out for a while, before I took off to his friend's apartment to sleep — I wasn't allowed to stay at the dorm and because I came one day earlier than planned, we didn't have a hotel room booked.

Right now I'm sitting around, thinking about how to get Charlie out of bed. I'd like to go to the spice bazaar today, but we'll see.

2009 Turkey

For the Turkey blog, I will be submitting a blog a day for a couple days. I'll try to correspond photos with the dates I'm writing about. Enjoy?

December 24

I spent the morning sitting around Charlie's dorm room. Eventually, I got him out of bed and we made it over to a kebab place to get some kebab and aryan— which is a salty yogurt drink. Charlie went off to class and I had planned on going back up his dorm room to don my new running shoes and going for a run around the neighborhood.

As luck would have it though, his door man is evil and wouldn't even let me up into the room, without Charlie. I ended up going to his campus and looking for him. It turns out it is a beautiful campus and Charlie is a lucky boy. I digress. I couldn't find Charlie, so I ended up going back to the dorm, arguing some more, going back to the campus and eventually admitting defeat. I ran into Charlie's friend and we wandered around until he was done with class.

After the 'dorm debacle,' the brother and I got a cab to Taksim square and checked into our hotel. It was a very nice place and I finally went out to get a run in, in the square— 20 laps around the central park...

That night, we went out on the street and I had an Iskender kebab, which is shaved meat covered in a sweet red sauce, on top of bread chunks with yogurt.

We got an early night after watching "A Charlie Brown Christmas" and "Out Cold."

December 25

We both slept poorly but, despite our deficit in zzz's, we both felt great and ready to tackle the Grand Bazaar! We woke up, got some food from downstairs and commenced to open our presents. We listened to the Vince Garaldi Trio and snacked on food from our stockings. Thank you to everyone who made it possible to feel like Christmas over here. This was year two being away from home, but the addition of Skype, some gifts, my brother and a nice hotel room made it closer...

After showering and dressing, we headed out to the Starbucks that overlooks Taksim square. It was pretty nice to sip on a cup of Starbucks after all this time in Moldova... As some know, Starbucks has taken on cult status with Charlie and I– we drank a lot of coffee together in college.

After the cup of Joe and a Semit (soft pretzel with sesame seeds), we took the underground to our trolley bus stop and the trolley bus to Sultanahmet– the touristy portion of Istanbul which features the Blue Mosque, the bazaars, etc.

We hit the spice bazaar first and I shopped around for some interesting condiments. From the spice bazaar, we headed to the bazaar of the Grand persuasion and did some more shopping. I got a great pair of leather slippers and some knock-off Ray Bans. Charles and I took lunch in one of the winding corridors and chatted about life.

It was interesting to walk around this part of the city and the Bazaar for the second time. It brought back sensory-based memories, such as the smell of the spices and the way the Turks try to sell, sell, sell. At one point, I talked someone down from 35 lira, to 15. Not bad skills, if I may say so myself.

After bazaaring, we headed back to the Taksim Square area and then went to our hotel group's spa. The hot tub was lined with marble, and the sauna made me sweat out all of those Turkish toxins. There was a small pool and it was fun to hop in for a dip.

After crossing the road on the way out of the spa, I noticed a barber and decided to fulfill my New Year's resolution—haircut time. You see, it was a Christmas miracle that I got this crew-cut and if I hadn't done it on Christmas day, it wouldn't have been the same. In any event, I was very impressed with the hair cut, a talented man, that Turkish barber. I also got a shave with a straight razor, which was frightening, but fun.

For dinner, we went to a fairly nice Turkish place in the Taksim region and split some mixed grill. I have realized that Turkish food is all very similar, no matter how much you pay for it. Lots of grilled meat and vegetables, with pita.

I have also noticed that many of the foods I eat down south are not just Gagauzian, they are Turkish. Merjimik (lentils), Corba (soup), and so forth are all Turkish words. On the Gagauzian note, I chatted with an ex-pat Moldovan on the plane, who explained that Gagauzian is actually only 60% Turkish. She said it was a dirty language and that it is spoken badly. She also said that the one time she was in Ceadir-Lunga, when she was 15, she hated it. She was from Transnistria, and only spoke Russian and Turkish— no Romanian, what so ever.

The 26th and 27th

December 26

I woke up and frantically tried to wake Charles up. I made a realization while in Turkey– Charlie is a college kid and sleeps until noon, on a regular basis. I'm not and I wake up at nine. After showers and a bit of breakfast, we went to our usual haunt, Starbucks, to get some coffee. After fortifying our minds with black gold, Charlie and I left the gear with Kelly and Mike and headed to the rental shop to pick up the Fiat. By the way, the two additions to the Charlie and Sam team are fellow students at Charlie's university. Mike has a perchance for confusion and backgammon, while Kelly was there to attempt to keep Charlie from frowning all the time.

Renting the car was relatively painless and within a half hour we were on the road to Amarsa. The drive up was beautiful and uneventful. It really reminded me of driving up to Boulder one year with Ness. The mountain passes reminded me of the Vail area– Diane and Nick may remember when we ran into them in Steamboat Springs...

In any event, we arrived in Amarsa without incident and walked around to enjoy the sites. We stopped into a tea house to play some backgammon and then went out to eat a fish dinner, which consisted of a big salad, cold beans, grilled blue fish (24 of them) and bread.

It was an early night and we went back to the hotel room to watch the "Bourne Ultimatum."

December 27

I awoke to a beautiful sunrise on my balcony and went downstairs to write in my journal and drink coffee. The weather on the trip so far had been beautiful and it continued on that morning. The sun coming up over the distant sea wall was the perfect sight to be had while writing– no complaints. The coffee was instant but, I've learn to deal with Nescafe in Moldova.

We eventually made our way out of the sanctuary of the hotel cafe to walk around the town a bit and then hop in the car for the ride to Safranbolu. The drive was once again uneventful, but beautiful. The little Fiat had no power, but it was a stick shift and handled great on the windy coastal roads. Mike Scheurich would have appreciated the fun I was having braking into turns and then accelerating out– my passengers weren't however, some even got car sick. I slowed down the driving a bit and we took in the sights of the Turkish country-side...

Upon arrival in Safranbolu we drove down the old cobblestone streets and through numerous one-way roads to the entrance of our hotel. The inn was actually over 600 years old and used to be home to traders. It was a beautiful building and looked its age. The door to the restaurant hall– which was made of solid stone and at some point was heated by a fire– was covered by lamb skin sheets to keep the heat in. The rooms themselves still retained their stone walls and the entrances were small– hobbit-sized if you will.

After dropping off our stuff, we walked around the town and got coffee and played some more backgammon. We then went to grab lunch at a great restaurant. I had some spinach stuffed pastry, Charlie had lamb and the other two had stuffed mushrooms. We stopped in at the local tourism office and were told that there was a cave system about 8 kilometers from the town. We decided to drive up before the light faded and check it out. The hike up was short and fun and we walked through a few hundred meters of a marked off cave. Apparently the cave actually runs for about 6k and the caving club at Charlie's university hiked the whole length of it, seeing the underground lake and river that it has to offer.

We found another very muddy road after the jaunt into the cave and tried to drive up. After deciding that it was stupid and dangerous, we headed back down, coming very close to sliding off the edge of the road, down a hill. Luckily my superior driving skills saved us but didn't save Mike's pants— he was directing me down when the wheel spun out, covering him in mud.

Back in town, we walked around some more and then got rub-downs and skin peels at the local Hamam. After hamaming it, we ate out for dinner at a recommended restaurant which actually turned out to be in a distant part of the town. The food was good, if not great but there was a deep pool in the middle of the dining room— strange.

It was off to a little bar, where a strange Turkish man was singing and speaking a foreign language— often including us, much to our consternation.

Afterwards, we went to room to watch the classic movie "Caddyshack" and then shut out the Ottoman lights for a night of sleep.

Dec. 28th and so on...

December 28th

We woke up and went into the great hall to eat our Turkish breakfasts. After walking around the town for a bit to look at stuff to buy, we got back into the trusty Fiat to make it back to Istanbul. The drive went fairly well and the addition of Charlie's mix tapes made everything better.

We stopped off at McDonalds on the way into the city and then finally into Istanbul. Making our way through traffic in the heart of the city was frustrating, but I was happy to be behind the wheel.

After putting our things back in Charlie's room, drove the car to the gym and got in a 2,000 yard swim. It was one of the best parts of the trip and reminded me of driving to the YMCA back home.

That night, Charlie and I ordered Dominoes Pizza and watched a movie or two.

December 29th

Charlie and I woke up and headed up to Starbucks for a farewell cup of coffee and a bagel. After chatting and crying– not literally; ok, Charlie cried a little– I drove to the airport to drop off the car and get in my plane. It was pretty nice to be able to drive myself to the airport this time, as opposed to spending money on a cab.

When I got back into Moldova, I was lucky enough to have some friends already in town. We stayed at an apartment together and made food for two days. My friend Kim and I bought a set of video game controllers and used them to play Zelda on our computers for about 10 hours on the 30th.....

New Years Eve has come and gone with a flurry of champagne and an odd Santa Clause concert in the center of Chisinau, and now I am waiting in the Peace Corps lounge waiting for the bus which will take me to Braşov and then to Bucharest. My flight to Sicily is on the fourth at five, so I'll have a day to kill in Romania before I make it out there.

2010

The Cannoli that was heard round the world...

The cannoli that was heard round the world...

There is quite a lot to write about since I last published something on this website. The coming of the new year and the realization that I have come down to the final chapter of my service weighs heavily on my mind, but leaves me feeling light in the heart. The first of my good friends in the 22nd group of PC Moldova will be leaving in exactly three months; I'll be leaving in roughly 6 months.

I am happy and it is relatively warm and sunny outside so I can't complain and, I watched "Up" last night, which has given me a whole new faith in humanity.

I arrived home from the last leg of my vacation yesterday and I'll break up the blog into the dates we traveled and what we did:

January 2 and 3

The van came to pick us up a little after 10 in the evening and we began our journey to Braşov, Romania. The ride was bumpy and we managed to pack 11 people into a van (4 on each row), but we made it. I fell asleep during the journey but it was so tight inside the van that the ride was very uncomfortable. I finally spread out over the three other people in the back row of the van and passed out on someone's knee.

When we arrived at seven in the morning, we didn't know where to go, so we got some coffee at McDonald's while the majority of the group tried to figure out where their cabin was.

They were eventually dropped off up at the cabin and Martin, his sister Maggie and I found a nice hotel and checked into a room.

Although we lacked any kind of serious sleep, Martin and I took a taxi up to the ski slope, rented equipment and went boarding for the day. I had to ski in a wind-breaker and jeans (I felt like those people I make fun of at Snowbowl) and we ended the day wet and wind-burned. It snowed the whole time and I froze into a Sam-cicle, but it was fun to get back on a board.

One thing that was different about the slopes here was that there was only a rope tow and 20-person gondolas. I am used to the standard ski lift (and prefer it) and the gondola was a new twist. Unlike ski lifts the gondolas were also really high off the ground...

That evening, we went out to eat at a Romanian restaurant. I wanted to get one of my favorite dishes but, after they brought out Martin's gigantic platter of meats, we decided to share. His meal consisted of cold fried pork skin, pork fat, goat sausage, pickles, onions, cheese and cabbage. It looked good, but wasn't exactly what I had hoped for. The decent Romanian red wine we drank helped it go down a bit easier, though.

Maggie had a dish that was fantastic, however: mamaliga stuffed with cheesed, topped with a fried egg and served with smoked sausage and ham. Delicious.

We got an early night after watching "G.I. Jane".

January 4

I woke up and took a taxi to the train station. At the station, I met a woman who liked to talk, so we killed the hour that the train was late by talking.

Once on the train, I found my little cabin and the woman came in as well. I was tired so, luckily my cabin was full and she had to find hers (I didn't want to talk, ok?), but told me to meet her in the hall after the ride because she wanted to give me a ride to the airport. I don't know how to refuse a free ride– or anything– so I did.

During the ride through the mountains, I couldn't help but wish that I had been put in a place like Romania, where I could wake up in a mountain village and look up at snow covered peaks, instead of brown farmland and mud. I also caught 40 winks and read a bit.

When we arrived my friend held true to her word and told her driver to drop me off at the Baneasa airport. I was 4 hours early, so I lugged my baggage to the nearest mall, bought some pants, ate some Chinese food and then took a taxi back to the airport.

The plane was 2 hours late.

I got into Catania and then grabbed a bus to Siracusa. The one hour ride deposited me in Siracusa at about 10. When I arrived at the hostel, the man working the desk handed me a map and told me how to get to the area where my friends were. I asked him if I could just grab a cab and he said: "No, it's only a ten minute walk." It was decided.

The walk was very pretty as the whole town was lit up for the new year. I made my way over the main bridge to a small off-shoot of Siracusa– technically a small island– and to the Duomo Piazza. I asked around at various restaurants for the Americans and finally found them at a bar.

That night, we grabbed a late night snack consisting of a sandwiched stuffed with grilled chicken, olives, cheese, mayo, artichoke hearts and mushrooms. It was probably my favorite meal of the trip– in its simplicity, it proved to me that there is quality about culture and food that you cannot really describe– I guess it just has to exist.

January 5

I woke up before my comrades and walked around the city a bit.

I love Sicily.

It was sunny and beautiful outside. The streets were filled with mini cars and people jabbering in Italian. As my first coffee in Italy had been instant, at the hostel, I felt I owed it to myself to buy a cappuccino. I made it back but had to wake up my friends. What a bunch of slobs.

After wandering around near the water for a while and eating lunch at a little pizza shop, we got on the bus to Palermo– home of the mafia.

Upon arriving, we checked into the hostel and our hostesses (whom were wonderful women) told us that we would be eating dinner at 8 and to meet them in the office/kitchen.

I went out for a bit to look at the shops and ran into an amazing outdoor market. I love Italian food and good food in general. Here, I found cheeses, meats, liver, bread, canned olives, fresh olives, sardines, peppers and joy.

I bought a bottle of wine and blocks of Mortadella and Asagio cheese and met my friends. After the snack, we met with the hostel owners and they pulled out a jug of house wine and decanted it into a ... well, into a decanter. It was very good and after a glass, they lead us out into the streets, to an outdoor restaurant.

We had meals of grilled food, served with bread and salad. I decided to try veal but the best dish on the table was called quattro formaggi– which was thin steak stuffed with bread, cheese and red sauce.

They took us to an outdoor club which was basically a vendor selling beer and wine to a very diverse crowd. I tried grappa as well, which tasted exactly like the home distilled moonshine you find in Moldova. I didn't enjoy it.

January 6

Rousing 4 people isn't as easy as rousing yourself, especially when you are an early riser. After all milling around and checking the Internet, we got a late start out into the city to see the sites of Palermo.

Among them were a famous cathedral and the Massimo Theater, where the final scene in "Godfather III" was filmed. Wandering through the alleys, we found a restaurant and decided to have a long lunch— the rain was falling and there was no need to get wet.

We sat outside under an awning in the cool air and told the waiter to bring us what was good. He started with a liter of white wine shortly followed by bread and a plate of antipasti: fried eggplant, stuffed tomatoes, bready meat loaf, stuffed mushroom caps, breaded fried calamari and stuffed prosciutto. This was followed by bowls of spaghetti tutti fruti del mare (I may have spelled that incorrectly), which was amazing and laden with tuna, calamari and mussels.

We headed back to the hostel and rested for a bit.

Three of us went out to find some cheeses and whatnot to snack on while we played dominoes but, nothing was open as it was a holiday, so we made do with some crackers. We eventually went out that night to have dinners of pasta and pizza and then came back for an early night.

About dominoes, by the way: I insisted that we buy some and it immediately became a hit with us. We stopped at cafes throughout the trip and played. I have to thank Michelle for introducing me to the game and, in tribute to her, every time I played, I wanted to call her up and ask for the rules.

January 7

On the seventh, we rented a car and headed to Agrigento, where there were some purported Greek ruins. The day began late because something made Brady ill– food poisoning, we assume. He was very upset because, after over two years in Moldova, he had managed to avoid getting food poisoning– a feat. One week in Sicily left him bed-ridden for an entire day and night.

The drive was beautiful and sunny. We had the windows down and the sunglasses on the whole time. When we arrived in the town, we ate some paninis and then drove to the ruins. There was an eight Euro entrance fee, so we just drove around the complex and took some photos.

We drove out to the coast and looked at the water and then got back into the car to drive to a very special village.

I don't remember the name of the village in question but we stopped there in an effort to find some relatives of Mr. Joseph Tamburello (JT). Apparently his great grandparents were born in Sicily– this village specifically.

We stopped at a cafe and asked some local old men and then sat down with coffees and dominoes. It was pretty humorous to hear these old guys talk about us in an attempt to find JT's family. We heard snippets of, "Ingleaza," and "si, si, Tamburello..."

I told JT, "Hey man, think of it this way. We may or may not be sitting and playing dominoes in the village where your family was born..."

After the game, we walked around the town and then headed back to Palermo. For dinner, three of us went out to buy meats, cheeses, bread and olives and this pre-dinner snack turned into dinner— it probably helped that we also played another game of dominoes.

After dinner/dominoes, we went out to drink beers and discuss politics for our final night out in Sicily.

January 8 and 9

We woke and got the car back to the rental shop and then got on the bus to Catania. The ride was pleasant and John pointed out that any form of transportation is nice, as long as it isn't a Moldovan Rutiera. The roads were great the sun was out and I managed to finish a book while looking out at the country-side.

When we got into the center, we only had a couple hours to wander around, so we did just that. Not too much to mention about Catania other than it holds the beauty of all the cities in Western Europe, in its old stone walls and cobblestone streets. I got some gelato, if that is worth mentioning. When we got to the airport, we ate pizza and I had my first cannoli... It was very good and stuffed with sweet ricotta cheese. I don't know why my Dad hates them so much...

The flight was delayed over an hour and we didn't get into Bucharest until two in the morning. The van we hired to take us to Chisinau had been waiting for three hours outside the airport, in the cold, with other passengers. No one was very happy with us, but we weren't too happy either and I didn't hold back in telling them, "Life's a b$%ch," in English, of course.

I don't know what could have been affecting me other than weariness from traveling for 2 weeks but, I managed to be dead to the world for the vast majority of the ride. Even at border checkpoints, I would give my passport to the guard and the fall right back to sleep, only to be woken up when John would give the document back to me. I hadn't had anything to drink and took no sleep aides– I guess I was just exhausted.

All that being said, I arrived in Chisinau feeling somewhat rested. The driver tried to get an additional 50 Euro out of us, which was complete and utter crap, in my opinion. My thoughts were that he had a service he provided for people, if flights get delayed that is a risk he takes in picking people up from the airport. After the fact, we got away with giving him about 20 more Euro than we should have and told him that if his boss had a problem, to call our boss and then resolve it with him...

January 10

I got an early night and woke up at 10, racking in about 11 hours of sleep. As relaxing and worthwhile vacations can be– while you are on vacation, that is– they are exhausting, especially when you factor in travel.

It may only be a two hour jaunt by plane to Sicily, but it took a ten hour bus ride to get to the airport and back– the beauty of trying to travel cheaply. I am starting to realize why people travel first class and avoid ground transportation, if they can afford it.

I am excited to get going on my last semester of school and I have a lot to accomplish. I am not however, very excited to be re-immersed into some of my less-than-favorite things in this country - namely food. I went from Italy and pizza to my house in Ceadir-Lunga where I had rolled oats and pickled tomatoes for dinner. I was so disillusioned by this change in culinary options, that I didn't' even bother to attempt to spice it up with BBQ sauce and Cholula, per usual.

Sunday has left me trying to upload photos and catch up with friends, go for a run and think of what I will make for dinner (I was 'asked' by my host sister if I'd be making the evening meal). It is also leaving me thinking about the grant I have to write and the next six months of my life— a time period which pales in comparison to the time I've already spent here. Until next time, arrivederci.

A work of fiction

2010-01-20

A work of complete fiction

I met Jordan in town on Friday evening, at the bus station— we drank a beer and ate peanuts. We were awaiting the arrival of Jordan's friend Allie and a man named Adrian. I didn't know where the night would take us; I assumed it would be a relaxing night, making food and getting some sleep.

Allie called and said that they were close, in a taxi. When they showed, Allie insisted upon smoking a cigarette– we were going to her school and a smoking female teacher is generally uncouth. I sat in the cab and began speaking Russian with the cabbie– I wasn't going to endure the cold for Allie's cigarette.

From the back seat a gruff five pack-a-day voice spoke up and explained that he was Romanian, to speak Romanian or English. Fine, I said, English it is.

From the bus station we drove to Allie's school– in the local tradition, a handful of teachers stayed behind after the Orthodox New Year's dinner, dancing to local music, drinking local wine and eating local cuisine.

I gleaned what I could from the Romanian man– not much. Apparently he owned hotels and was in town on business. He wasn't much of a dancer and an even worse conversationalist– gruff and abrasive. Toting his own jug of white wine– which he cut with seltzer water– he sat watching, smoking.

After some time, Adrian informed us that we'd be going to a restaurant in town; there, we could eat anything we wanted. The taxi came and we piled in. Here, seven to a sedan is the norm.

Upon arrival it was clearly just another local bar and restaurant. Not bar in the sense that there was a physical 'bar' to sit at and not 'restaurant' in the sense that the food was their main priority. Here every establishment has a small counter-top, preceded by a shelf with cognac and vodka. Sometimes, there is a tap of the national beer on the counter.

We wandered in and Adrian, with his disconcerting confidence, walked us into the back room— a small, private hall. Caught by surprise and confusion, the four of us, Allie, Jordan and Catherine, stared like a kid at a Victoria's Secret catalog. Allie was nonplussed, being rather sedated with local wine, but the rest of us fumbled over awkward greetings in Russian and Romanian. We had stumbled into a private dinner being had by the local mayor, his family and friends.

Quickly enough, we were assimilated into the group. Chairs were pulled up, mulled wine was poured and more bland, local cuisine was offered up. Our acting leader— in his over bearing and uncomfortable way— also kept us supplied with champagne. Chain-smoking and out-spoken, he kept us entertained throughout the course of the evening.

A game of poker came into the mix but, before it could commence, it was decided that Allie and Catherine had to go— the festivities had taken their toll.

So it was Jordan and I— Adrian sitting nearby, lighting cigarette after cigarette after cigarette. Five-card draw is a universal game and so is cheating. I was gullible enough to trust that the well-fed mayor's son was actually pulling straight after straight out of circumstance. It wasn't until his second four-of-a-kind that Jordan started to suspect something and called the son-of-a-politician out on his ethical aptitude. Money in hand, he wrinkled his chin, rolled his eyes and trotted out the door with dad.

I had bet 200 of Jordan's money on a sure thing– two pair. I was in debt and none too happy with my current circumstance. Even after Jordan yelled, "God can see you cheat," at the man, he still decided not to correct the error of his ways.

Adrian said he knew we were being cheated all along. He paid Jordan back for her loss. Not a problem, I'm debt-free. Let the weirdness begin.

After dealing with the return of a distraught and make-up smeared Catherine– who had left her computer at the restaurant ,we again piled into the same taxi to go shoot billiards. Oddly however, the computer remained 'lost' until Catherine had put a call in to our man Adrian.

After losing a game of Russian, I moved onto American pool. After winning a game, I went to sit with the rest. Adrian had toted a now larger jug of wine, which none of us wanted to drink. He just sat there, going through bottle after bottle of seltzer water, cutting his wine and sipping on it. None of us wanted to drink, it being late and we tired.

Finally, Adrian announced that he had called us a cab. It was time to go home! The cab came. And left.

Two more of Adrian's acquaintances were deposited at the pool hall, to our despair– we had hoped that sleep was just on the horizon. After a game of American-style and a second loss for the evening the taxi came back, and this time for us. Throughout the night, it was the same driver, driving the taxi: at the bus station, the school, the restaurant.

A problem arose.

The two girls who had made their exit were unconscious in bed together. Desperate to get home, we pleaded with the taxi driver to find out where he had taken them— he couldn't remember. Adrian began yelling at him, berating him for forgetting, trying to mask his ulterior motives. He offered to take us back to his hotel; 'Oh God,' we thought while images of bathtubs, ice and kidneys flashed through our heads. 'This cannot happen...'

Just then, the taxi stopped. It was in front of a block of two-story apartment complexes. We ran up the stairs... something wasn't right. Back down.

Into entrance number two we ran. The door bell on apartment 27 was rung to no avail and then, suddenly, Jordan discovered the door was open to 28. We went in with undeserved bravado and started using our cell phones as lights. Luckily it was the correct flat and the groggy eyes of Allie and Catherine stared back into the pale blue light that our phones let off.

I ran down stairs to tell the cabbie and his fare off. Sanctuary at last.

The next morning.

Jordan woke to discover she had lost her wallet— what is with these people, I thought as I sat up taking the mornings first cough and stretch. Who else to call but the patron of town, Adrian?

Somehow, the wallet was found. Circumstantially odd, but found: We walked back to the pool hall and I told the neighboring establishment to call my phone if she found a yellow billfold. I was given a nod and I made my way back out. Convinced that all possible had been done— and that it was only a waiting game— we went back to my village.

A phone call later that day told us that the wallet was found. Adrian had informed police and apparently the search came up positive. Oddly though, nothing was missing from the wallet, except some small bills— no credit cards, ID's or passport were gone. A thief stole it from the pool hall, and then dropped it in the street, almost intact, for Adrian to find.

It was too good to be true and our suspicions were confirmed when days later, we all started receiving phone calls. "Sam, its Adrian, you were interested in skiing in Romania yes?"

Jordan was receiving desperate messages, offers of a car coming to pick her up and bring her to Romania, the off-kilter promise of skiing in a foreign country.

I was receiving more phone calls and, hanging up.

Now for some non-fiction

The snow has started up again down south and it is making life beautiful, difficult and really cold— at least colder than Phoenix and colder than last winter. It is supposed to get down into the teens later this week. It is interesting because we didn't have much for snow last year and this year is just the opposite.

Despite my better judgment I decided to don my yak-trak crampons yesterday and go for a run. The following happened while running: I was chased by three sets of dog(s), a car of drunk young men followed me, flipped me off and yelled at me and another man stopped his car, opened his door and asked, "Why are you running?" Because I am fucking crazy, sir.

A few more friends of mine will be leaving early. Maggie, a health teacher, has already left and one more will be soon gone— I feel amiss disclosing its name, because it has yet to inform Peace Corps. Anyway, the lack of enthusiasm from my group (the 23s) is not disconcerting as much as odd to me. I just don't see how this many people can quit, especially this late in the game. If my subtraction is correct, we have the worst turn-over rate in the history of Peace Corps and all of man-kind. I really do like most of the people who have quit but, I can't help but feel indifferent about it— the people whom I keep in touch with will not change - and when we all get on the plane home, for good, it is going to be the same thing. It isn't like we see each other all that often anyway.

I should be presenting a grant to the SPA committee in a couple weeks, in an effort to get some toilets installed in my school. Very shortly, you can all help me with my 3rd grant, by donating money! More on that later though.

I re-read "The Things they Carried," by Tim O'Brien. It's a lot like what I carry to school every day, just listen:

"... P-38 can openers, pocket knives, heat tabs, wristwatches, dog tags, mosquito repellent, chewing gum, candy, cigarettes, salt tablets, packets of Kool-Aid, lighters, matches, sewing kits..."

On second thought, I don't carry any of those things but, if you have any spare Kool-Aid, send it over.

The Coldest day

2010-01-24

This weekend was fairly interesting, as I actually got myself out of the south of Moldova and went to see friends in the big city - or near there. On Friday, I went into the head quarters to drop off some grant information, and then hopped a bus to Calarasi, where Martin, Jeff and I met to make sushi. Jeff has a nice apartment in his raion center and we spent the evening making hand-roll after hand-roll and eating them.

To make the basic sushi roll, we used rice and nori and filled them with green onions, cucumbers, carrots, crab salad (that we made with mayo and fake crab) and cooked shrimp. Luckily for us, we are in a part of the world where they drink a lot of vodka and chase said vodka with various foods. Oddly enough, you'll see mini fake crab bricks out on a counter for humans to eat after they shoot hard liquor. In any event, this simulated crab went into our sushi.

Among odder rolls were something I like to call the 'Moldovan' - mayo, salami, cucumber, bell pepper and onion... As the night wore on, Martin decided to fry an egg and then to fry chicken, to put into the rolls.

On Saturday, we celebrated someone's last weekend at Jessica's apartment and then I went out to meet up with a couple friends from the M22 group. We stayed out late and woke to: "The Coldest Day." I know this, as a fact, because while waiting at the bus station, the water bottle I had purchased not 15 minutes earlier froze. It literally froze while I stood, shaking and waiting for the bus. It was about -5 F, with a wind-chill which, according to weather.com, drops it down to -20 F.

It was so cold last night in my room, that I had to go to sleep under my down sleeping bag and the regular down comforter, in a sweat suit and long underwear bottoms. I did wake up at one in the morning and strip down a bit, but not farther than socks, long underwear and the flannel shirt I was wearing.

The Den

2010-01-28

What is the Den? The den is my room, where I sit and do a whole lot on my computer. I took the week off of running, for my ankle and the cold conditions (my face almost fell off on Sunday), and I've been spending a lot of time in the den. I've gotten quite the workout routine going with pushups, sit ups, arm raises (using a dictionary) and squats.

Back to the computer though; I would die without it. I have been reading a lot more but, I'd die, seriously. Here is why: the other day, the "Octagon," as I like to call it, crashed on me - for the fourth time. I was terrified...

What if I had no movies, no typing, no internet, no games, no Skype, Gmail.... Endless hours of entertainment, gone. As I mentioned, I have been reading a lot but, come on, there is only an hour or two that I can have my face in a book a day.

This led me to my next thought - what was life like in the Peace Corps without a computer! This thought got me thinking again - there was a point when volunteers had no phone access, no internet - letter writing was their medium of communication. Anyway, here's to you, you crazy, crazy 1960's through 1980's volunteers - I'm glad that it isn't up to me to do that voodoo that you do so well.

So, in any event, I did another destructive re-formatting of my computer (it's called this, because it kills all files that were once present on the computer) and now it is back up and running. This is leaving me thinking that this computer will never die and I can use it through law school and on into infinity.

A big goal of mine is to use some of the money I get upon completion of service on an iphone, but upon reading about iphones I've realized that phones in the states actually have something called 'monthly plans,' and you have to pay them– every month! In Moldova, I just buy a phone card when I run out of texts and/or minutes! There is no way I can afford to pay $80 a month just so I can diddle around with an iphone...

Which is leading me to my next point; my computer runs fine, I can't afford bills– of any sort– so I think I'll spend some money on a motorcycle. If I go to Colorado, it will be a dirt bike for the summer and if San Diego (my top choice) a street bike.

Speaking of USD, if any of you readers (if I have any) are religious, please pray for me. I'd really like to go to USD, so pray– I promise I'll use my law degree for the betterment of mankind.

Lastly, I read about the new ipad. It is intriguing. Please leave me your thoughts on the ipad and I will be sure to weigh them in when it comes time to decide whether or not I am going to waste money on something when I get home.

It's still cold out and I'll put up a few photos of the beauty that snow can lend to an otherwise drab town. Poka.

Take this one in stride

February 6, 2010

At the moment, I am sitting in an Andy's Pizza in Cahul, Moldova. The plan for the day was to meet up with a friend and spend the day waiting for more friends, but the friend in question is home sick. This leaves me in quite a predicament, because my last bus to Cahul was at 9:25 this morning and now I have a whole day of nothing to do, until the second set of friends comes by. I am on the second floor of the restaurant– because there are wall plugs– and it is unheated. To top off the temperature, the staff has decided to designate floor two as their balloon blowing-up center and despite the headphones that are blaring music into my ears, my peace is being shattered at regular intervals with the popping of balloons. It's like hearing gun shots while at a rock concert. I feel like Harrison Bergeron - not as talented, equally distracted.

The past couple weeks have gone by quickly. Not a whole lot has happened, although I did win my grant and am now working on paperwork to eventually get the money into my account. It should keep me busy for the next few months.

I happened to be in the neighborhood of an apartment I was considering yesterday and ran into the land lady, whom had already given the apartment to someone else. I asked her if the flat was available, and she said it was...

I am now considering finally taking the plunge and moving into my own place, even if it is only for 5 months or so. Here is why: as of late, I am getting sick of living with a family. I'm sick of my sister coming in and asking me to translate her homework and I'm sick of my unpleasant host father.

To top things off, I now have issues using the bathroom. This may sound like a personal disorder, too weird for print, but is isn't. During the warmer months I tend to go outside, through the door in the hall, to take care of business. When it gets cold though, the door is more difficult to open and it is a big hassle to get outside. The alternative to going outside is walking through the parents and the kids bedrooms, into the old kitchen and then the indoor bathroom. Not many choices.

In any event, I was refraining from fluids at night time and would make it until the morning– let me add that planning your night around whether or not you are going to have to pee is inhibiting. To make matters just fantastic was the addition of a guard dog in the back yard. This three foot tall Cujo of an animal is locked up in the wood shed all day and is let out to roam the yard at night. I was warned by the man of the house, "tell me if you need to go outside to the toilet, the dog will give you a big bite." Jesus Christ. It left me thinking, "what are we guarding, flour?" and "where the hell did this dog (who is easily already five years old) come from?"

Dreams of relaxing and drinking a beer, then getting up to use the toilet, inside, in my own apartment, without host sisters coming in to tell me to warm up dinner because they are busy and no threats of dog bites were going through my head as I went to sleep last night.

In standard fashion, I am questioning whether it is worth it to move out for just five months, but my nerve level seems to be at the breaking point. I, of course, wish that I had moved out four months ago and could then justify the move, but I didn't and now it might be time to just get it over with. Most people wouldn't put up with a host father like mine this long but, I have. I think this has a lot to do with the fact that I love host mom and enjoy the sisters. I go through days where my threshold is met and want to snap at everyone and then days where I enjoy eating dinner with the sisters (though, being teenagers, they have been known to spend whole meals playing with their cell phones, making it like dining alone).

Some of the time though, I sit in my room and realize I am half tensed that someone is going to come in and knock on my door. At least they've stopped stealing my tea kettle. But, on that subject, when I do leave, they always steal it and then put it back the way they found it. "But Sam, how do you know they took it, if they put it back as you left it?" you may ask. It is simple: I use distilled water and they are convinced that when they boil their sulfurous, yellow sludge of water, it has the same effect as distillation so, when I come home after a weekend away, it is where I left it, filled with yellow water.

All these things may be gripes and I could easily make it the remainder of my service without moving. Maybe it is time to finally point out that I don't have to take grief and that maybe I was a bit of a help around the house; a positive and generally good humored addition. After all, I introduced lasagna to Ceadir-Lunga and make it on a regular basis. As I mentioned, I have been called insolent, by he-who-must-not-be-named. I finally realized why: No one stands up to the guy. At dinner, he mentioned that he cleaned my room and left it an 'example.' I asked, "is that how you would like me to leave my room every day?" He responded, "you can live how you want, it's just an example. If you want to live like a pig it is all the same to me." I smiled and replied that I want to live like a pig. Insolence in its purest form.

I would like to add that this entry may not have been extremely positive and I apologize. Overall things are very good and I've had a fantastic service so far, in many different respects. I would like to label this blog a 'rant' of sorts— if Dennis Leary can do it, so can I. I've also made the rather astute observation that the positive volunteers come to a country such as this and seem to be beaten down, whereas the generally pessimistic volunteers come and tend to make the most of everything and learn to become positive. It is a weird thing but I tell you, I am a much more positive person than I used to be and have an easier time dealing with the ups, downs and defeats that one can encounter here. This is my opinion but, for the most part, I have never heard an opinion made by me that isn't observant, poignant and correct.

21 Months

2010-02-14

"'Is that The Mountain?' asked Bilbo in a solemn voice, looking at it with round eyes. He had never seen a thing that looked so big before.

'Of course not!' said Balin. 'That is only the beginning of the Misty Mountains, and we have got to get through, or over, or under those somehow, before we can come into Wilderland beyond. And it is a deal of a way even from the other side of them to the Lonely Mountain in the East where Smaug lies on our treasure.'"

-from The Hobbit

While I am far past the proverbial Misty Mountains, I guess I am right around the base of the Lonely Mountain, of maybe even waiting around the secret door which leads to Smaug's lair. Either way, I am very near the end of the road and, if you don't get the four of five metaphors I just attempted, I really cannot help you.

I woke this morning to the pitter-patter of rain and a grey sky. Shortly after waking, the electricity went out and I was forced out into the cold to boil water on the gas stove— as opposed to the electric tea kettle in my room. The power came back on luckily, giving me the needed current to type this blog (my computer's battery doesn't hold a charge...).

I read something that a friend of mine wrote and it made me reflect on my own service so far and how my role as a volunteer has changed. Like anything else, there seems to be a natural progression. At the beginning, I was a teacher— I partner taught, but the emphasis of my service was teaching in the classroom. While I still work as a teacher, my role has taken a bit of a back seat— correcting grammar and helping where I can. In reality, I'll be gone after this semester and life in the classroom will go on without me. Many of my classes are split up into groups; one partner takes half and I take the other half. Slowly, the groups are being melded back together because again, when I leave, they will be pulled back together into one group. This will make life harder for my partners, but it is a reality.

I view myself now as more of a utility player. I have guitar club, I teach and help out in class when I can, and I work with grants. If I have to miss class for something, it isn't the end of the world; in a way I am an assistant to everyone in the school in any way I can be.

There have also been changes personally. My first year as a volunteer was much more high-paced– every weekend was spent with friends in Chisinau and it was imperative to be doing something. As the second year came around (especially this fall) I found that I started to enjoy being alone, at site and doing nothing. It is relaxing. I have noticed changes in many things though, with the coming of winter and vacation time. It is harder to stay at home all weekend when the weather is cold and terrible. Since our winter break for instance, I find myself trying to get out of site more than during the fall. As the weather begins to clear up in the next month and feel like things will go back to normal. As I said, this transition into the "hermit" way of life is part of the natural progression as a volunteer (for this volunteer at least; I would hate to generalize).

You start to realize that you can literally talk about anything as well. I could spend hours at a bar or on Skype with a select few, talking about people, the oddities of Moldovan culture, complaints about home and work-life... The list could go on for hours. In fact, one of the most enjoyable things to do is make light of every situation. I have realized that my closest friends are the ones with whom I make jokes with. For the most part it is a competition to see who can make the other person laugh. This is how I was before getting on a plane to Moldova and how I will be afterward. The way we cope is very social and life would be very difficult without these methods. I have learned that human contact– even if only verbal– is one of the most important things a person can have. Referencing the 'progression' I mentioned earlier, and how it leads to a more solitary lifestyle, is the perfect way to realize how necessary talking is. Just getting ideas and thoughts out is a big part of life and it takes a few days or a week without it to realize this.

I'm sitting in my partially packed room. The weather is quickly warming up. I was supposed to move into my apartment on Friday but things were delayed. Now, I am waiting until Tuesday, when representatives from Peace Corps can come down to inspect the flat I've chosen. It is odd to live in a packed room— my posters are down and I can barely walk. I am in limbo, waiting for the final chapter in my service— which is marked by the next five months I will spend living alone. I've decided to move and for that reason I don't think I'll be comfortable again until I get into my new place and can settle in for the final part of this incredible journey.

The Final Push

February 17, 2010

I'm in! I am currently sitting in a t-shirt and long underwear in my new apartment. This morning I was naked; it didn't matter, because I live alone. For all you know, I am naked right now. Last night, we made green curry with vegetables, my friends left and then I was alone; I liked the feeling.

The move went pretty smoothly but, as expected, after the PC representative left my house my host father's geniality turned into its usual unfortunate unreasonableness (I'm sure many people love him, but we don't get along). I needed to get money back from him for half the month but he then started making claims about all of the 'damages' I had caused– he explained that he and his wife would figure it all out and get back to me. Fantastic.

I am still very excited to be sitting in my new digs– it is pretty amazing how even the most mundane tasks turn pretty exciting when it is your apartment which is concerned. I was at school today thinking; "what do I need.... soap? shower rack? trash cans? a toilet lid..." After an afternoon run, my dreams of household supply shopping came true and I headed to всё для дома ('Everything for the Home') to buy supplies. Oddly enough, my town has a pretty extensive home supply store. You may be paying more, but they carry everything from Tupperware to toasters; I even spotted an espresso machine.

I made it home, washed my first batch of dishes and installed my new toilet seat. My life is a thrill ride.

Anyway, there isn't much else to say to all of you, other than to say thanks to everyone who cares enough to read about my life. I've got about five months left and I can already tell that they are going to go very quickly.

The Russian speaking volunteers have their first IST this week in Ceadir-Lunga. In an effort to either keep them from drinking too much in the city, or save money on transportation, they are all down here for classes on Thursday and Friday. Peace Corps actually came down a month ago and I am proud to say that I am integrated enough to have provided them with a building to conduct their training– the town library.

The weekend will hold some food making with two friends whom are coming down to see the pad and it was decided– by Kim and I– that Saturday will be filled with drinking beer and playing Zelda on our lap tops (she and I bought universal game controllers in Chisinau and we have a Nintendo 64 emulation program). Chicken chili might be in order as well.

As for tonight, I think I'll use the leftover rice to make flied lice. POKA.

Am I full of it?

February 23, 2010

Today is the national Russian Army Day which, in other words, translates into national men's' day. While we are not in Russia and I am not a Moldovan or Russian citizen I was still given a pair of socks, in honor of this glorious occasion.

The holiday itself though has jogged my memory about a few topics that I'd like to discuss. I think you'll find a cohesive thread, within my rambling words.

I'll start with the celebration we had today, in the library of my school. Everyone had a glass of cognac or wine in hand and a few made toasts to this and that– there are some February birthdays and names were mentioned. One teacher then made a toast involving the army and how great it was (from what I gleaned)– he even mentioned me, talking a bit about the American armed forces. The teacher in question went on to preemptively apologize as he made a statement about how, when he was in the Russian army, they were on their way to defend Cuba against America, when some sort of peace agreement was made. I am not sure if I gleaned everything from his speech correctly. He was the staunch type of Russian man who would probably never be caught drinking out of moderation but, who likes his cognac, does everything by the book and smokes the odd cigarette. Undoubtedly one who may have misgivings about an American in their midst. Loyal to the core.

I'd like to digress for a moment, and talk about last night– now keep in mind the local mind set of the 'man's man,' who can't cook, hangs out with men in silence and plays backgammon, etc. Last night, a few female co-workers came over for dinner– I had cooked a lot of food for the weekend and had some left over. They brought cookies and wine (as is custom) and we drank a bit, overate and then drank tea. I sat back for the majority of the dinner (especially as the wine took its slight effect on my friends) and listened to the three women gossip about what boy is dating what girl, which kid is slow, which kid is smart and why the administration is odd/evil/strange, etc.

To this effect, when I mentioned that I had heard the administration was going to give us socks for today's holiday, they all commented that the higher-ups at our school were crazy; you only give socks and other undergarments to family members. So, all in all, it was a funny night and they all seemed to love me– I knew this, but me making a couple traditional dishes (a man cooking!) and inviting them into my apartment really sealed the deal. Throughout the evening though, I couldn't help but feel strange– I cannot imagine any male I've met at site entertaining three older women and cooking for them. The cultural and language gap is one way I rationalize the disparity between gender here though; I am very different than the locals and I do what I can to integrate myself. This particular instance also got me thinking about how much closer I may have been to people like my colleagues (who all live in the building across the street) if I had moved out sooner.

I've gotten far off topic but, the difference between me and the rest of Moldova is one of the main points I'd like to stress as I go on with my story.

Think back to the severe Russian teacher, his hand tattoos, soviet-era eyeglasses, and traditional views, and now think of a easier, more amicable history teacher. The latter is a friend of mine at school and an extremely nice guy; always willing to chat about our respective countries and always open to the fact that life is life and holds no grudges against me for being from the USA. This was made clear to me on one occasion in particular, the Olympiad. As we sat out front of the school, waiting to grade students' papers (the "Olympiad" is a kind of essay writing contest held yearly, for all students, throughout the country) we discussed different topics. One that came up was the Vietnam war. Ivan Ivanovnich compared our conflict in Vietnam to the conflict the Russian army had with Afghanistan. I got to thinking about the two conflicts and realized that Ivan and I should be mortal enemies! We fought a war in Vietnam, against a Soviet-backed North Vietnam. In the same respect, Ivan's friends died fighting a CIA funded Afghanistan. In every respect, both were products of the Cold War. It is absurd to think that we would stay enemies and I know this. I was not actually thinking, "hmm... this guy should hate me!" but, under the right circumstances, it would be very easy to hate each other; the circumstances being that our governments made us do something that affected each others' lives in some way.

It made me realize some of the futility in armed conflict in the first place. You can be friends with anyone or— at the very least— live around other people and not have any intention of killing them. War is just the opposite. It made me realize that, in reality, there are no enemies, just politics. Maybe this is one good thing I am doing here; I don't care if anyone loves their neighbor but I think a good world-wide mind set would be to look at your neighbor (the guy you hate with the stupid cat and wife) and say, "Meh, I'm not gonna kill him today."

These are lesson I already knew and I guess that it took some Noam Chomsky and boredom to get them down onto paper. My brother once said that what I'm doing is perpetuating the silent hand of American imperialism. I'm sure he is right in many respects. Tony Hawks, in his book "Playing the Moldovans at Tennis," even touched on this subject upon meeting a volunteer in Chisinau. He said it was either America's way of planting a McDonald's in every country on earth or volunteers are crazy for putting themselves in these conditions. I wouldn't say it stung, reading this, but I did find it particularly ironic, coming from a Brit (whose own government has been pretty keen on colonization throughout history).

The point is, is that while we (PC volunteers) all may be paving the way for America's control of the universe, none of us joined to promote this ideal. Both my brother and Mr. Hawks have valid points but they don't consider all of the people who agree to spend two years the Peace Corps— how could they all be that interested in such a greedy ideal?

In this respect, maybe it is our government taking advantage of some altruistic people— giving them the opportunity to help out in the world and promoting their own agenda at the same time. Either way, whether for adventure or philanthropy, we (volunteers) all had the best intentions when that first group went to Africa quite some time ago. It leaves me wondering, just what was JFK thinking?

Spring Break #1 2010

2010-03-06

I decided to spend my second to last school break in country, traveling around and taking in all of this little country. Needless to say, the week generally involved lots of food and drinking - as any good vacation should - and Saturday is leaving me ready for the routine of the work week and a break from our decadent consumption(s). I forgot my camera at site, but here is a recount of the week so far without photos:

Last Friday, I had a couple friends down to my site and we made some curry with rice. It was an interesting dish because I used ground pork and beef in the curry.

Naturally, most curries would not be made with the sacred cow, but I'm not Hindu and it was delicious.

On Saturday I headed into the city for a night out at the bars in Chisinau. It was the usual Opa (a Greek restaurant) Bier Platz (a bar with giant beers) and Autobus (a bar with giant pitchers of beer with spigots). After this wild night out (it really wasn't too wild) I headed to John McGregor's site. Although we wanted a much more tame night, we were forced into some wine drinking because it was a start of spring holiday. I made it out pretty light even though the 14-year-old brothers came into John's room and insisted we drink more wine. They were certainly consuming quite a bit. Finally, John's host father came into the room and started drinking and conversing with us. He eventually left to the families part of the house, where they undoubtedly kept the 'party going.' Let's keep in mind that when the two young brothers came in to peddle their vin de casa, I was sitting in bed, playing World of Warcraft and just didn't really feel like drinking wine. I did consume quite a large amount of white bread however - and wine.

On Monday, I headed up to Drochia to meet with Kim Dula and her boyfriend. We had a relaxed night of lasagna (her site is large and has a few fairly decent restaurants) and iced, blended coffee, of all things. I saw the movie "There Will be Blood" and fell asleep to the sound of dogs barking. Ah Moldova.

On Tuesday, I ventured farther north to the village of Cotova, where Justin Allen lives. Justin, Vince and I hung out at Justin's house for a while and then went to a masa at his friends house. The meal consisted of fried fish, mamaliga, fried pork fat, grated brinza, fried dumplings stuffed with cabbage, fried eggs and bread. We brought some beers but the host insisted that we take 2 shots of his notoriously strong raciu (moonshine or 'white lightning' arguably upwards of 80% alcohol). We were feeling like our arteries might explode and our hearts might fail us as we trudged through the cold back home.

On Wednesday, we went to Vince's site and made an effort to find a goose to kill... We found no geese (We asked his boss– the mayor - to look around and he called various homes to asked if they had spare geese. Quite humorous, when you factor in that he did the phone calling from behind his desk in the Mayor's office.) He did however tell us he had rabbits and he would be happy to kill and clean one for us for the sum of $13 American. He dropped off a skinless and headless animal in a plastic bag later that day. With said rabbit I made a fairly interesting dish. I began by cutting up the animal with a knife– hammering away at the joints and backbone to break them– and then letting it simmer for over an hour. After the simmering, I fried the parts in a skillet and then tossed them with some sautéed onions and carrots. We ate the rabbit with a crab and corn curry salad and a grated carrot, cabbage and tomato salad. Later on in the night a friend of his partner's came over to shave my head. This was also quite funny, because Vince and I had gone to his partner's house earlier in the day, to ask about hair clippers, and she told us that she'd send someone over later in the night to start shaving. Vince's apartment is heated by a wood oven, a throwback to the old Soviet days. He has a stone bust of Lenin on top of the wood-burning stove as well... It is a nice little place, but like all apartments in Moldova, it is located in a truly terrifying apartment building.

On Thursday, I came into Chisinau to meet with friends. Kim's brother flew in and we ate at a pretty decent little restaurant and then came home to get some sleep. Chris (her brother) is actually on his way home, as he just completed service in Thailand. He showed us some pictures and told some stories– leaving me wondering why I chose Eastern Europe as my post. On the other hand he informed us that there are 4 forms of Dengue Fever and his friend– a volunteer– got three of them while posted in Thailand. Apparently you build an immunity to each strain as you get them but, most people don't survive all four. The Thai people call it 'the bone-breaking disease' because it leaves you immobilized in bed for 2 weeks while you feel as though every bone in your body is being crushed.

Friday was a great day. I felt good and I laid around and played Warcraft and slept. I got a run in around the park and then we essentially repeated last Saturday night, so I'll spare you the gory details. I did eat a jar of pickles and a block of cheese when I got home.

Today, I am left feeling the effects of last night and staring out into the ...ahem... SNOW. That's right; last weekend we celebrated the coming of spring and it freaking snowed last night. It was a lucky break for Chris though, who has been living on the equator eating fried cockroaches for 2 years. I am also left realizing that I have 10 more weeks of school and one more spring break before I leave this country. I may have to quit a few weeks early because I'd like to spend time with my brothers and travel America before I go head-long into graduate school.

In any event, the excesses of this week (who knows what tonight will hold) leave me ready to get back into the teaching routine and take a break from the late nights. One thing said late nights have given me though is the knowledge that I have introduced dominoes to the volunteer community in Moldova. After learning the game from my sister, I decided to buy a set in Sicily and then a newer, better set here. JT, John and I tend to play every time we get together in the city or at each others' sites. A truly great game with some good friends.

On the school hunt note, I've now been accepted to Oregon to add to the list of tier one schools. As of now though, I'll still be attending Denver. POKA!

Sunshine

March 17, 2010

Spring is coming upon us fast and it has been very nice getting back into the groove of school and life after our first spring break. Life alone in my apartment is better than it ever was living with a host family and it also gives me a few more tasks to keep me busy (for example, I have to decide what to eat every night and there are clothes soaking in the tub right now that I will have to hang up to dry later tonight).

Besides these mildly boring observations, there isn't much else to say about life over here lately. I am getting more and more antsy as my time comes to go home— I have resolutely decided to go home a bit early in order to spend time with the family and will be getting on a plane in about three and a half months. It is odd how little time I have left and sad, especially now that I live alone. I have come to realize that if I had lived alone for the extent of my service, I would have gotten to know people in the community much more. For instance, I hung out with a friend last night, at the apartment, three weeks ago, I entertained some teacher friends, at the apartment, and I'll be doing the same the day after tomorrow, at the apartment. It's not a bad gig either as Moldovans— almost as a rule— bring me wine and conserved vegetables, the latter which I can use throughout the week to substitute the lack of vegetables in my diet (they are almost too expensive to eat during the fall and winter months).

I went to Raion Anneni Noi last weekend to watch some Peace Corps friends of mine play basketball against the Raion's team. The officiating seemed biased, to put it politely, and the American boys ended up with 2nd place (I thought it might make them feel better to say 'second place' as opposed to, 'they lost'). No matter, they were still given medals and we were hosted at a masa where the wine and food flowed and sat on the table, respectively. We were even subjected to an exhibition, as an old man there had a few gymnastic and judo tricks to show us. I'm pretty sure he was an alcoholic but, none-the-less, he was a well-rounded alcoholic who undoubtedly took pride in the callisthenic work he probably put in while serving in the Soviet Army.

Finally, I would like to add that I am fairly proud of the guitar club I have with my kids. While I am little more than a guy who noodles around on guitar and hands out advice

when I can, and the club is little more than students who
come to learn what they can and hang-out, I feel that I
have certainly popularized the guitar at my site. Some kids
played prior, but the excitement over getting to come
together and meet two or three times a week has caused
others to go out and find guitars in an effort to hop on the
bandwagon. In this case, the band wagon is a good thing. I
am even giving one girl my old classical guitar because she
was my first club member and one of the most enthusiastic
(when I say enthusiastic, I don't necessarily mean motivated
to play, as much as she thinks playing the guitar is just
swell). The only apparent misfortune is that she was rather
upset when I cut my hair– apparently I "looked just like
that Nirvana guy... (I guess all angst-filled teens are
obsessed with Kurt Cobain and his mopey ways, regardless
of generation.)"

I have added some photos of the game and some other
random stuff. POKA!

March 25, 2010

Oh, what an effect the weather can have on my well-being.
I sit in my apartment with the sun streaming in through the
window, sipping my "Indian" style tea and think about the
winter– long, brutal and cold. The heater is off, I have
clothes drying on pieces of pink twine in the kitchen– the
kitchen window open with a mild breeze coming in– and I
just finished a cookie.

As Ignatius Reilly would say, Fortuna's wheel is spinning in
my direction. Please do not associate me with Mr. Reilly,

however. As you may have guess, I have just finished reading "A Confederacy of Dunces," leaving me glad that I don't have a 'valve' and that I seemingly have a firmer grasp on reality than the tragically funny main character. Whoa!

Living alone has been better than every lately, especially now that we have been having full and sunny days. I have been reading and running more, not to mention getting some color back in my pasty skin. Cooking for myself has been very repetitive in that I cook rice and sautéed vegetables for the most part— sometimes I don't want to spend the money, so I sauté conserved vegetables from a jar that my partner gave me. I have some good curry powder from Turkey that I eat daily and a jar of panang curry which is stronger and more sporadically used in my simple dishes. I have turned into something of a vegetarian— mostly because I don't feel like purchasing meat products. I try to get my protein from peanut butter, brinza and milk. I've taken to drinking quite a lot of tea and milk.

I have finally gotten all of my forms in for the second grant I am working on and by the time I get back from France, I should have the money in my account and we can start putting some toilets in at my school. By the time this is done, the school year will be coming to a close and with it, my service will be coming to a close.

I don't have much to write about as of late, other than to tell you all that I'm happier than ever and am really (really, really, really) enjoying the weather. Winter was very difficult and painfully cold at times. Let's not forget that I was only able to travel by unheated bus and every building (sans the

Peace Corps building in Chisinau) is poorly heated. Not to worry though, spring is here and life is good. Soon, the baseball games will be starting up again, something I am looking forward to. Until later, poka.

(I have run out of space for any photos on this blog (cheapskates) so to see more of me and my life, please take a look at my Facebook page.)

France I

For something different and potentially embarrassing, I am going to write a few excerpts from my journal, which I've recorded so far. At the end of this little trip, I'm sure I'll write up a day-by-day account but, in the meantime: 18:57;

April 1
"The plane took off an hour late because the engine lights were coming on. Great. I actually thought we were going to have an on time departure, leaving the terminal.
It turns out I like Bucharest quite a bit, it is a pretty city, especially the fountain in the center. I watched Alice in Wonderland. It is a pretty amazing movie and I enjoyed it. Apparently we will be landing around 8:40 pm. I hope the shuttle into Paris waits on us. This will, in any event, leave me eating snack food all day, with the prospect of a pre-prepared sandwich in the future (at the airport).

April 2, 2010
I am sitting in Café La Briche Doree waiting to head up to the Dali museum. I was in this area 7 years ago with my

sister and it will be interesting to visit the museum again. Apparently, the first stop will be the Sacre-Coeur on the top of the hill.

Last night, I got in at 11 pm, finally, had a glass of wine with Kieran (the girl I'm staying with) and slept solidly. For the record, the wine I had last night was much better than the famed Purcari (a wine sold in Moldova). I am not sure why I raved about the stuff so much. Lack of options I guess.

14:23
I went into a pub across from the Notre Dame to get out of the rain. So far, I've seen the Scare-Coeur and went through the Dali museum. I bought a hat and it's actually turning out to be a good decision because it's raining fucking cats and dogs.
**

Note to self: Sun 4 F1 Malaise, Gran Prix at 10 pm.
I decidedly do not like the rain. If I can pull it off I would wander from café to café drinking coffee. No part of me wants to deal with the rain and it doesn't help that the umbrella Kieran lent me is essentially non-working.
I just spotted a woman with Starbucks — that is my new mission.

April 3, 2010
I sit at a Café O'Joules and watch the rain fall outside. Earlier, I saw a group of runners go by. To my amusement, a pair stopped, one man hopped on another's back and started doing squats. I don't think there is anything goofier than two Frenchman doing power squats on each other. As I said, it is raining; a distinct contrast from the France I

remember with Michelle. Then, it was hot and muggy, at times, and it was easy to stay out later at outdoor cafes. Luckily, Paris still has many enclosed patio sections which are heated. Upon completion of Dali yesterday and after my pint, I went to the Louvre and walked down the Champs D'alleys(I couldn't figure out how to spell this). The rain had subsided and I distinctly remember walking down the road towards the Arc de Triomphe last time I was here.

My system is beginning to regret the 6 Gauloises cigarettes I smoked yesterday, but they were very enjoyable. There is something in good wine, good food and cigarettes (in France); like eggs and bacon. Plus I was feeling nostalgic, because Michelle and I smoked Gauloises when we were here last. I will, however, leave them at home today. Last night, I had Cassoulet au confit de Canard and Ginot D'agneau with Vin rouge. (I ate alone at a café and had wanted to try a 'formula' menu, but couldn't. I ordered far too much, but wanted to have at least one full-on French meal.)

So; as it stands, (and it will stand) I am heading to Nice tonight at 22:00 and will arrive in the morning. Seeing as the weather will be too cold for swimming, I may try to go straight up to Avignon. We will see.

Coming from a village, I realize that cities give you a constant backdrop of activity – a semblance or façade which makes one think there is more going on than there is. If you take a body and deposit it in Ceadir-Lunga, for example, life is slow: wake, wash clothes, work, eat, sleep. A body here though: wake, café for coffee, Metro to work, elevator to desk, coffee from shop, work-out at gym, Metro home, dinner, etc. Walking to my school and sitting on the Metro are essentially the same things. The latter, however, leaves a person folded into the belly and heart of the city, literally. It seems that there is so much more to life, when in reality, we are just people living in different settings. I know we are destroying the earth by covering it with concrete and polluting it, but I think it's magnificent. I look outside and realize that there is probably 1/10,000 the amount of cement in Ceadir-Lunga but it is amazing and wonderful in Paris (and many major cities). Humans have truly tunneled and stacked and spread (concrete) to make a masterpiece. City life may not be my life of choice, but it is quite a way to live.

Spring-ish

April 13, 2010

I'm back in Moldova and enjoying the spring weather. The cherry trees are blossoming and I can see their white petals out of my third story apartment window.

The rest of my vacation in France went very well and I eventually made it back to Moldova– despite getting robbed (essentially) by a taxi driver in Bucharest. On Saturday night, we all stayed up until 6 am and said goodbye to Brady and JT who have now finished service. I'm next!

Here is a few more excerpts from the journal:

*If I refer to 'we,' it is not the royal 'we,' but a group of people I met in Nice or one person from that group whom I happened to be wandering around with at the time.

4/4   8:19 am

As far as I can tell, we are about 10 minutes out of Nice the coast here is beautiful and rocky, much like Turkey and Sicily.

I slept a good 6 to 7 hours on the train and feel relatively rested.

The man next to me and I made shrugging motions at each other (we don't speak the same language) when deciding on seating and then I went to the food car to buy a beer and a bag of Pringles. He produced a beer, 2 baguette sandwiches and finally, a demi-bottle of Burgundy. He came prepared and I plan on copying him on the return journey.

For the record, first class seems to be little more than a newer compartment with more legroom. The train is double-decker, however, which is swell. When this train stops in Nice, I will need to find a bakery, a cup of coffee and a camera shop.

Ah, it seems we have one more stop, as we have just passed through Cannes.

4/5

I am sitting in the hostel in Nice and it is 8:40 am. Yesterday, I wandered around and saw the coast and a big open air market. I saw some very odd looking heirloom tomatoes and green and white speckled bean pods... While ordering a sandwich, I ran into three Canadians and started wandering around the city with them. We made it up to the highest point in Nice and the cemetery at the top. Funds are low, but life is good.

4/6

I'll be leaving for Paris at 15:30 because there is a train strike.

Yesterday, we wandered around Monaco, saw about 15 Ferraris and checked out the Monte-Carlo Casino. We ate a chevre, mushroom, olive and mozzarella pizza by the harbor. Notably, the giant yacht in the harbor is allegedly the king of Saudi Arabia's. (Kaddafi?)

4/8

Ah Paris. After arriving late, I sneaked into Kieran's apartment and went to bed.

The train ride was fun: we met a French woman and played cards with her and I helped a Russian family (or I helped the cashier who was trying to help them, rather) who didn't understand why their bank card wasn't working.

Yesterday, we ate breakfast and then I went for a run. We headed through Rue Mouffetard and took a beer at a pub near the Eiffel Tower and sat for about an hour. The bar gave out free peanuts, which I think should be mandatory.

We headed to the Champs D'Elleys (spelling again) next and walked from under the Louvre to the Arc de Triomphe.

I sat outside of Cafe O'Joules (the cafe near Kieran's apartment where I tended to get coffee and breakfast in Paris) waiting for Erin Erickson, (my old site-mate who was coming to Paris on vacation) drinking a glass of wine. When she arrived, we went to the supermarket and then finally dinner at a Thai restaurant, around 11 pm. All I had eaten was bread, butter, a croissant an apple and some peanuts all day and was starving. I had 'Thai Chicken' (kinda like curry) and white rice. Slept like a rock.

11:16

"To the Demon within" (inscribed on Jim Morrison's headstone, which I saw on my last day in Paris. I also ran into Oscar Wilde's and Edith Piaf's graves. Wilde's is covered in lipstick.

To the airport:

Take #7 to Chalet (towards La Cournevre 8 Mai 1945) switch to # 1 line towards La Defense to Port Maillot...

21:20 (Romania time)

I'm in the plane after leaving the Paris Beavois airport. I am in quite a dilemma, considering that I don't have a secured ride back to Moldova. I guess I'll find a warm spot of concrete at the Gara de Nord and wait until the 6 am train to Iasi. That or beg a ride.

My vacation was pretty much fantastic. I met people, ate great food and did things on my own terms. Success. I guess I can attribute this to my old fall-back saying; "kto ne reeskooyet, tot ne pyot shampanskoe."

(Forgive my ignorance on this next passage)

I have to say, that in talking to Canadians, they are much more independent than previously perceived. I had (in my own selfish and self-righteous way) equated them with people who lived above us, in the shadow of our country.

There was nothing specific which changed my mind to this— as far as customs go— but, it was their perception of USA which made me realize how different we are.

Regardless, I stand by the opinion that there are no such things as consciously created enemies. To hate someone in the nationalistic sense can only be done by force. Bria's (a person I met traveling and with whom I discussed the Canada/America dilemma) perception of "Americans" was instilled. There is no real reason to dislike Russians, Canadians, Americans, or Armenians as a people— there can only be reason to dislike specific people. This is why it was interesting to hear why Bria did not see me as a 'typical' American. Whether I am 'typical' or not shouldn't matter. The only thing that matters is how you get to know people on a personal level. I would have some pre-conceived notions, but I think they would actually be less than that of those from the rest of the world: "I'm [insert nationality]." "No, you are you, act like it." (however you see fit, for that matter.)

I was also told that most Americans don't have passports, in an effort to perpetuate the argument that we are close-minded. I countered this with the idea that maybe it is because most Americans don't have the means to facilitate inter-continental travel... being in the EU and located in Western Europe has its perks.

That being said, in Paris I did notice that from lawyers to businessmen, to construction workers and grocery store security guards, there was a high perceived level of interest, intelligence and culture. I am specifically referring the grocery store worker who helped me with wine, and the painter who was reading the paper in a cafe and drinking a macchiato.

Maybe it is that there is simply more elegance in an espresso and a cafe than a 16 oz. Dunkin Donuts coffee and a drive through. Maybe it is forced culture and the augmented level of intelligence is perceived rather than real.

Открой род!

April 22, 2010

As I walked into the x-ray room, I noticed that it was old, wooden-floored and furnished in a similar manner to my apartment. The x-ray apparatus was soviet-era— a large machine with a yellow, cylindrical tube attached, where I assumed the x-ray visioning takes place. Out of the cylinder, black, corroding cables sprouted out of each end. While we waited on the bench— which was covered with a stained bed sheet— the technician mopped the floor.

I was called up, and before asking, the technician told me to press my face against a board and he put the yellow monster to the back of my skull. He walked away, I heard whirring and a clink, and the process was finished. It was only later that I informed him it was just my teeth and the surrounding nasal passages which needed imaging, not my whole skull.

You may be wondering why I was in a Moldovan hospital, getting images taken of head. It turns out that I had a bit of an infection going on in and around my seventh molar. What I thought was my wisdom tooth pushing its way into my mouth, was actually a great deal more complicated.

Last Wednesday I began having pain on the left, upper part of my jaw and called PC medical. They wanted me to come up, but I had the intention of finishing the school week. The pain got worse though, and I came up.

My first visit was with our dentist in Chisinau. As antiquated as the x-ray scene sounds, the dentist we see on a regular basis has an office and equipment far more modern than mine at home. He also took an x-ray of my teeth, but a stronger picture was needed to determine whether my infection had spread to my nasal passages. It hadn't.

So, after my initial visit to the dentist, I went to have said x-rays done, and then to a local oral surgeon, who insisted that he drain the abscess which was perched on the roof of my mouth. Due to PC regulations though, it is required to get an American staff doctor's okay before proceeding with surgical procedures. So, I spent a restless and painful night in bed and headed to medical to get my second injection of antibiotics, before heading back to the hospital. Luckily by this time, the docs back in Washington had said 'yes.'

Ahhhh... They not only said yes to the surgical procedure, they insisted that I get a root canal of the molar in question before-hand. So, today was spent with drills, scalpels and needles in my mouth— let's not also forget the needles in my butt, to deliver the antibiotics.

I will get a temporary filling in my molar (which is now wide-open to allow drainage) on Monday so, in the meantime, I will be in TDY (the apartment PC provides for ill volunteers (stands for: Temporary Duty, which is a term stolen from the military (borrowed, I guess, since we are both government organizations)). Even after the filling though, I will be here waiting until everything clears up.

I feel guilty, in some ways, that I am missing school right at the end of service, but it is better to have teeth in my head and let's keep in mind that I did want to stay at site until Friday... To add to my already staggering hubris, after insisting that I teach all week, the PC doctor told me that she didn't understand why we teachers insist on putting off medical problems, in order not to miss school— God I am courageous. In all seriousness though, it was nice to be told I had to lay around and watch The Sopranos all-day.

Finally, I'd like to add that when the monotony of life becomes just that (monotonous, that is) I enjoy change. Maybe I'm weird, but I really didn't mind all the medical procedures, because it was a break from the norm. In some ways, coming up was exciting— a change of pace.

I felt the same way when the government building in the Capitol was set on fire– I hoped no one was hurt but, at the same time, it was a bit of a thrill to be (however distantly) involved in something potentially catastrophic. While this is different than being sequester here awaiting dental work, it is a similar feeling.

If I were to describe why I was almost happy to be brought up here on this occasion, I guess it is essentially like staying home from school. You have no guilt at be lazy and sitting on the couch. While I can find ways to do this if I want, during my normal routine, I always have that nagging feeling that I should be doing something productive. At the moment, this feeling is non-existent.

I'd like to add, that the Peace Corps staff has been very helpful. Violetta, the doctor on staff, has been with me at all times. It is like having a mom come to the doctor with you– except in this case, she is helping with the medical terms in Russian, which I don't always understand. There is nothing more frightening that having a doctor bring a needle towards your face and say, "don't breath," in Russian, when you don't understand him (not that my Russian isn't perfect in every sense, but it can be hard to understand things with a mouth full of Novocain and trepidation at the potential pain it is about to undergo).

Also, I am privileged, because PC provides us and the staff with cars and drivers, when needed. Nikolai is someone I've ridden with on numerous occasions and he is always fun, and funny, to be around. A Russian proverb he told us was, "The weather is just like a woman. They are both always going back and forth in their moods."

May 4

LET'S START CALLING IT THE WAR JOURNAL

It has been a while since I wrote anything down on this blog and this may have to do with the simple fact that it's hard to top travel writing, coming down from the high of actual travel. More precisely, there isn't much I can report that I haven't covered at some point in the last two years and– short of boring you with my musings– I felt there was no need to post.

In the last week or so however, things have started to happen. The first major event was the annual teachers concert at my house of culture. Colleagues from all over my region came to my site to perform, as a sort of teachers talent show, showing off the skills that the school has to offer. I was a part of a few songs– all of which were in Russian and one of which was a Russian war ballad (another was titled "My Homeland," obviously in reference to Phoenix, AZ). It was hilarious and fun. I can't sing worth a damn, but I was told that I had the strongest voice and they could hear me in the back of the auditorium. They said I had a great voice, and I think they meant it! While I know that I cannot hold a key, I think it may have something to do with the way you sing Russian ballads– just imagine a guy like General Patton walking around his troops, swinging his arm back-and-forth across his chest and singing in a deep and manly voice.

I am back in the Capitol as we speak, because I had to have more dental work done. It turns out that the decaying tooth which needed the root canal wasn't the only decaying tooth. Another filling was made and now I am sitting in TDY because I have to be in the city tomorrow for my group's COS conference. COS stands for 'Completion of Service' and the conference will consist of three days' worth of discussion about service, life after, etc. There will be mucho "we had it so rough guys," and "you all did such a great job," followed by dart playing, eating and drinking beer. As sarcastic as that may have sounded, I'm pretty excited. My time in the Peace Corps has gone so quickly that I can't really explain the feeling. I sit here with two months and one day to go before I go back home. I'm leaving at 25 years and arrived at 23. My brothers are 23 now! What the fuck! My sister is married! Sweet baby Jesus!

I'll tell you what though. As wild as all these things are, I am the most surprised at how happy I am to be going home to fluoridated drinking water. If I ever have to (I will in one month, so this is a ludicrous wish) have another needle or drill stuck in my mouth, I'm just gonna lose it. I'll go stir crazy. You'll have to hold my tongue.

POKA!

Bike-Tripping

May 21, 2010

The weather has been in a process of crumbling into chilly rain, a surprise as it has been sunny and warm as of late. You know what they say though: â€œ May showers are the result of April fool's day (I know they don't say this.). □

Despite, the weather is nice enough to go around town in a hoody or a T-shirt and the sun is supposed to be back very soon...

A few things have happened since I last wrote anything on the blog. For one, we completed our COS conference (completion of service) and it was nice to relax out in the woods at a resort " I may have mentioned this though.

The work on the indoor toilets at my school is almost complete and I am rife with anticipation to get the receipts so I can begin closing the grant out with US Aid and Peace Corps. To my pleasant surprise, the toilets they've installed are normal sit-down type, as opposed to the hole-in-the-ground squatters I was expecting. Fantastic.

I don't work on Thursdays so, yesterday I rode my bike to Taraclia, which is about 30 K from my town. When I got to Aaron's baba's house (he is the volunteer in Taraclia), we drank some vodka tonics and ate curry. The following morning, we went to the market to buy pork to make sausage. His host Baba makes some pretty killer, spicy sausage " akin to chorizo. The process entailed grinding up meat with a hand-cranked grinder and then adding bebir, chili powder, salt, black pepper and sliced, dried chilis " in very copious amounts. I was unaware but, all it has to do is sit in the salt for a day, refrigerated, and then it is put in skins and hung outside to dry and cure. No cooking or smoking needed (I hope).

I made the trip back on my bike. It is much more interesting to ride from town to town, as opposed to being stuck in a cramped and stinking rutiera. Outside, you can smell the air and flowers and feel the wind. You also are allowed a much less constricted view of your surroundings. Moldova is a beautiful place in the spring time and the recent cloud-cover makes for some interesting lighting.

About the bike: I purchased it from my neighbor after nearly destroying it. It is a full-suspension mountain bike-type and one day I borrowed it to go on a ride out in the hills. On the way back (shirtless) I tapped the front brake a bit too hard and literally flew over the handlebars and somersaulted onto my back. I slid down the hill for a while, losing some skin, the whole time thinking 'how bad is this gonna be on my body?' It wasn't terrible, but the shower back home was... After the spill, I sat up in the dirt, rubbed some out of my eyes and started laughing. It was a pretty humorous situation; me on a hill, shirtless and bleeding, in the middle of Moldova with goat-herders looking on quizzically.

So, after this fateful day, the decision was clear that I needed a bike. This was made easier because I have not been able to run much lately because my shin splints hurt too much. The general idea is 'Sam-going-stir-crazy-prevention' through my outlet of exercise.

Tomorrow at 1 a.m. I am leaving with my students and partner, Tatiana, to see the castle in Sorocca. It is a 6-hour ride and I guess we'll catch some shut-eye on the bus... We will be back in Ceadir-Lunga on Saturday evening.

As I mentioned before, I cannot put up anymore photos on this site, but you can sign up with Facebook and check out my photos there. www.facebook.com.

Yo soy Sam

May 25, 2010

The days are flying by as are the birds?

Last weekend I took a class field trip up to Soroca and monasteries in the area. We left by bus from Ceadir-Lunga at one in the morning on Saturday and came back at one in the morning on Sunday. It was a six hour, over-night ride up to the north and then we spent the day ping-ponging between points of interest. Needless to say, I was exhausted at the end of the weekend, even thought I passed out on the bus every time we got back in to move from site to site. You may also have discovered that I found a solution to the photo issue, so I will inundate you pictures from the trip. Boo ya.

My grant is about done and I have to head up to the capitol on Friday to deal with paperwork to close it out. When I head back down to site, we have our 'last bell' celebration on the following Monday and then a BBQ down at my site with fellow volunteers on the first of June ," Will and Charlies' birthdays! Bwa bwa.

I have run out of money and my water distiller has broken. Rather than get a new one though, I've been buying bottled... I may actually be saving enough money on my electric bill to make up for this. Regardless, it is near the end of the month and I have been literally out of money for a week. I have been reduced to buying cheap goods at the market on credit (they know me pretty well and know where I live) and cooking rice with canned corn and garlic for dinner. Lunch is, ahem... non-existent.

Not much else to say at the moment other than the weather is still fantastic. I'll see some of you soon, right around the start of July. Poka.

June 6

2010-05-30 to 2010-06-06

To all three of my devoted readers:

The weeks are still flying by and as of yesterday, I have one month in country left to go. Last weekend, we slaughtered the lamb and cooked it up over some coals. The camping aspect was canceled, due to rain, but I managed to squeeze about 14 people into my apartment. The night went without a hitch, except for two instances. One being, the neighbors were not pleased about the noise and two being a Polish fellow who lives in Comrat. He stood next to my map of Arizona and began to tear it, slowly. I asked him to stop and he would not. Things got heated. I yelled at him. He responded by telling me that it was just a paper map and could be replaced. I kicked him out.

Really though, the gall of the guy. Ripping someone's map under the pretense it is only paper? I told him the map was twenty years old and my father had given it to me as a gift. What a bozo.

The grant is completely closed out now and I literally have nothing pressing on the agenda. I'll be going up to Martin's site tomorrow to help with his sports camp and then I'll be heading to Val Lui Voda for our two year in country celebration. On Saturday, we play softball against the embassy folks and then will all retire to the center of town to watch the USA/England World Cup game. Let's beat those Brits!

Finally, I'm left with a very odd feeling, considering how much time I've spent here and how little I have yet to go. It is hard to stay motivated to do pretty much anything and unfortunately, as a teacher, there is precious little to keep myself occupied with. It is very easy to mark off the weeks when you have a job to go to for 5 of the days, but almost daunting when you look at the time like a big void. A large, month-long void. That being said, it is nice out in Moldova these days and the vegetation is green. Just like last summer, there are generally a few three or four day stretches in-between the next leg of travel and activity and, at the moment, I'm using said time to clean my apartment and try to get some laundry done.

Opa!

2010-06-28

The end of my service is coming to a close. In fact, it is charging towards me at an incredible rate of speed. There is nothing I can do, except pretend to know what is going on as I scramble to get things done before I get on a plane at the Chisinau airport for the last time.

The past few weeks have been a speedy blur of dinners and activity, including softball games and camps and paperwork. There is the DOS, the SHR, the close of service medical, the COS interview, the COS check list and the ET agreement " let's not forget the EFT forms and SPA closure agreements. Acronyms are great and I refuse to explain any of them to you.

I spent last weekend with my PST host family in Ialoveni and will spend one more night with them before I leave. They are truly one of the greatest things I got out of service. Victor has become like a brother to me and I always feel welcome at their home. I guess it is a combination of whatever traits they found endearing in me and luck that allowed me to find a family in Moldova. The morning after Victor and I cooked shashlik and drank wine, Luba " host mother " sat me down and told me how much she enjoyed getting to know me over these two years, and how I was important to them. I left the house with an eerie feeling " it is something very special to form such a bond, especially on the other side of the world with a foreign family.

I am leaving soon though and I should mention that the Circhelans are a family I grew to know over two years here, but I am going home in 8 days to my real family, who are, by far, the most important people in my life. I have been making devious plans with the twins on a weekly basis. So far, I've even managed to convince one brother to help move me into my apartment in Denver and go to a wedding with me.

In the next few days, I have to get paper work completed, pay for some missing text books (I think our school librarian is a crook...) and say goodbye to a few people down south. On Wednesday the Peace Corps car is coming to pick me and my belongings up and then I will head to Chisinau where I have more people to see, bank accounts to close and paperwork to complete. On Wednesday evening, I'll spend one more night with my old host family and then say goodbye to them forever. Peace Corps is moving me into a hotel on Thursday and I will sleep there for the remainder of my days in country. Saturday will bring the annual US Embassy Independence Day party and then I leave at four in the morning on Monday the fifth.

At the moment, I really can't describe the feeling I have, knowing that I leave so soon. It has been tiring (For instance, I was up until three in the morning last night, celebrating 12th grade graduation with teachers and students at a restaurant Ceadir-Lunga. The ceremony was too long, but the food and wine was plentiful and I learned how to dance two different forms of the 'Hora,' so all is well. It is custom for students to stay up to greet the sun, but I was too tired and went home 'early.') as of late and I almost feel as though I was more excited planning and thinking about this time than I actually am. Life has its ups and downs and I'm somewhere in the middle right now.

As of late, what with all the celebration, traveling and so forth, I feel like it is feast week. In fact, Moldovan dinners tend to resemble Medieval feasts, with plates of food and jugs of wine stacked all over the table. As you can imagine I am tired of eating for four hours straight and need a few days to rest and get everything in order before I leave. I regret not spending time with some people who live around me in Ceadir-Lunga but, I have come to the point where none of this is reversible and I need to get packed, get the bills paid and leave Moldova in a good mood.

I'm ready to get home though, that is for sure. Poka!

POST MOLDOVA

I left the country of Moldova on the 6th of July very early in the morning. After a long 3-leg journey, I made it back to my home of Phoenix, AZ. Now August 2, it has been a while since I wrote anything and a lot has happened since the close of my Peace Corps service.

Shortly after arriving home in Phoenix, my family and I took off on a week-and-a-half road-trip to Yellowstone National Park, Wyoming to visit our aunt and uncle and see the sights.

Essentially, a trip through the park is a lot of driving and seeing natural land formations but, lucky for us, our uncle is the deputy chief ranger of the park. Because of this, we hiked in eight miles to a ranger station at Heart Lake and slept in the ranger cabin. The lake was full of fish and another perk of being ranger kin is that you get to take canoes out on the lake - something that civilians are not allowed to do. My brother and I took one out on the last morning and caught six fish, three of which we hiked back out. It is illegal to keep some fish but the three keepers were Lake Trout - an introduced species of fish which one is required to kill upon catching. They taste good and because all three of the fish caught were 20 inches in length, we had plenty to eat.

The expedition into the back-country was the height of the trip for me. The following six days were mostly day trips into the park to see things like Old Faithful and the Yellowstone Falls. On the second to last day though, my uncle took me up for a flight in his Cessna 172 and I got a great view of Grand Prismatic and Upper and Lower Tower Falls.

The trip came and went, which left me back in Phoenix, whiling away my time until I leave for Durango, CO for a friend's wedding and then on to Denver to begin law school.

Being back in USA is a strange feeling, because it is so normal. I was gone for two years and it seems as though nothing has changed. It is hard to grasp all that I encountered while abroad - it is as though it was a blip on the radar - some kind of speed bump in my life. Looking back on it is like reflecting back upon a dream (as trite as that may sound).

The first week I was back, I was excited to drive around in a car and run errands, get Starbucks and eat out. I still enjoy these things but they have lost their initial cache.

Anyway, I'm back and 10th Avenue looks the same. It is good to be back though and it is hard to imagine that I was sitting in my apartment in Ceadir-Lunga a little over a month ago, watching downloaded copies of "The Wire" and drinking Балтика.

Unfortunately, photographs are not included in this journal because the quality of the photos on the blog site did not reproduce well.

ABOUT THE AUTHOR

Sam Scheurich is a lawyer recently graduated from Denver University, Sturm College of Law. He has spent most of his life in Arizona and has a degree in journalism from University of Arizona. He spent two years in the Peace Corps which is the subject of this journal. He currently lives in Denver, Colorado.

Made in the USA
Middletown, DE
11 December 2016